FAIL U.

FAIL U.

THE FALSE PROMISE
OF HIGHER EDUCATION

Charles J. Sykes

ST. MARTIN'S PRESS ✿ NEW YORK

www.stmartins.com

Designed by Richard Oriolo

Library of Congress Cataloging-in-Publication Data

Names: Sykes, Charles J.
Title: Fail U. : the false promise of higher education / Charles J. Sykes.
Description: New York : St. Martin's Press, 2016.
Identifiers: LCCN 2016003175 | ISBN 9781250071590 (hardcover) |
    ISBN 9781250091765 (e-book)
Subjects: LCSH: Education, Higher—Aims and objectives—United States. |
    Education, Higher—Social aspects—United States. | College costs—
    United States. | Educational change—United States. | BISAC:
    EDUCATION / Higher.
Classification: LCC LA227.4 .S95 2016 | DDC 378/.010973—dc23
LC record available at http://lccn.loc.gov/2016003175

Our books may be purchased in bulk for promotional, educational, or business use. Please contact your local bookseller or the Macmillan Corporate and Premium Sales Department at 1-800-221-7945, extension 5442, or by e-mail at MacmillanSpecial Markets@macmillan.com.

First Edition: August 2016

10   9   8   7   6   5   4   3   2   1

To my father, Professor Jay G. Sykes,
who got it all started

CONTENTS

Acknowledgments   ix

PART I

I TOLD YOU SO   1

Introduction: Scenes from a Graduation   3

1. Bursting the College Bubble   7
2. Déjà Vu: *ProfScam* Twenty-eight Years Later   21

PART II

THE COLLEGE BUBBLE   35

3. The (Escalating) Flight from Teaching   37
4. The Reality of Academic Research   57
5. What Do Students Learn (and Does Anybody Care)?   65
6. The College for All Delusion   81

PART III

BLOAT   93

7. Our Bloated Colleges   95
8. Academia's Edifice Bloat   105

PART IV

JUNK SCHOLARSHIP, HOAXES, AND SCANDALS   117

9. Does the Emperor Have Any Clothes?   119
10. A Scandal Reconsidered   129

PART V

VICTIM U. (TRIGGER WARNING)   151

11. Grievance U.   153
12. Rape U.   189

PART VI

IS THIS TIME DIFFERENT?   215

13. Time for a Bailout?   217
14. Netflix U.   223
15. Smaller, Fewer, Less   243

Notes   253
Index   273

ACKNOWLEDGMENTS

I owe a considerable debt to those who have gone before me as well as to the many individuals, inside and outside of academe, who once again offered me their counsel and insights—as they did twenty-eight years ago when I first published *ProfScam*.

In particular, Richard Vedder, the director of the Center for College Affordability and Productivity, was kind enough to review an early version of this manuscript and gave me valuable feedback and encouragement. I have also relied on the excellent work done by the American Council of Trustees and Alumni, Glenn Reynolds, who

chronicled the higher education bubble while it was inflating, and
Heather Mac Donald who reported on the rise of "microaggressions"
before the deluge. I am also indebted to the scholarship of Richard
Arum and Josipa Roksa, James Rosenbaum, Andrew Hacker, Claudia
Dreifus, Charles Murray, Mark Bauerlein, Emily Yoffe, and Nathan
Harden, as well as the many whistleblowers of the academy.

Once again, this book would not be possible without the efforts of
my agent Glen Hartley and the vision of my longtime editor George
Witte, who saw potential in my return to the scene of academia.

PART I

I TOLD YOU SO

INTRODUCTION: SCENES FROM A GRADUATION

ON A BEAUTIFUL LATE spring day in Washington, DC, at a graduation ceremony at one of the nation's better universities, a middle-aged couple sits in folding chairs on the lawn and watches the ceremony. The scene on campus is idyllic (especially if one avoids student housing), and more than one onlooker has the wistful feeling that all of this is perhaps wasted on the young.

The father turns to his wife (or significant other) and says, "We did good." It is a sentiment repeated hundreds, perhaps thousands of times at similar ceremonies around the country, capturing our attitude toward college, or at least the attitude of parents. Getting a child through college is one of the sacraments of parenthood, a milestone of achievement and success at least as important to parents as to the holder of the degree. And indeed, that degree for many has offered entrée into the respectable middle class, exemption from work that involves getting dirty, and access to attractive members of the opposite sex.

Books on higher education, such as this one, often assume that colleges are primarily or even largely about academics, but the reality is far more complex. The four-year or longer sojourn in the groves of academe is a kaleidoscopic experience of classrooms, frats, lectures, keg parties, all-nighters, political correctness, hookups, alcohol, athletic spectacle, and the occasional intellectual insight.

At some point in their college experience, students are thankful that their parents have only the vaguest idea what they have been paying for on campus—not just the extracurricular bacchanals but also the bizarre cultural intolerances, the obsessive rituals of conformity, the absentee faculty, teaching assistants unable to speak English, the hair-trigger racial, cultural, gender, and political sensitivities, and the junk courses with their effort-free As. Even some of the professors—elaborately begowned for the commencement ceremony—recognize that much of what happens on campus is silly and that their pretensions are a target-rich environment for satire and ridicule. Perhaps that explains the higher education complex's chronically thin skin and its shrill defensiveness in the face of occasional criticism.

But the degree has covered a multitude of sins.

"We did good," and the financial burden behind those words, had little to do with their child's curriculum or the quality of the interaction with faculty; it didn't matter whether the proud graduate had ever read Shakespeare or even whether he or she could pass a test in basic critical thinking. "I have never heard a single parent speculate about what value might be added by those four undergraduate years," novelist Tom Wolfe wrote, "other than the bachelor's degree itself, which is an essential punch on the ticket for starting off in any upscale career."[1]

"We did good" was simply the essential, required rite of passage: obtaining the degree. What that degree actually signified beyond the validation of social and economic standing was almost an afterthought. At least until recently.

THE BUBBLE BEGINS TO BURST

In March 2015, Virginia's Sweet Briar College announced that, despite having an $84 million endowment, it was closing its doors after the spring semester. The liberal arts all-women's school, with one of the most idyllic campuses in the country, was basically out of money. It was closing, officials said, because it faced "insurmountable financial challenges," including a steadily declining enrollment. However, after an alumni revolt, Sweet Briar was able to win a reprieve that allowed it to keep its doors open—at least temporarily.[2]

But Sweet Briar was not alone. Moody's Investors Service has been downgrading the financial outlook of dozens of schools in recent years, and the number of private four-year institutions that have shut down or been acquired doubled from 2010 to 2013. "What we're concerned about is the death spiral—this continuing downward momentum for some institutions," Moody's Susan Fitzgerald told Bloomberg in the wake of Sweet Briar's closing. "We will see more closures than in the past."[3]

Allowing for its unique circumstances, Sweet Briar's story was a familiar one among colleges. Like other schools, it had spent generously on amenities to attract students. It boasted the country's largest indoor equestrian arena, "which included an enclosed lunging ring, seven teaching fields, and miles of trails."[4] For tuition and fees of $47,095 a year, Sweet Briar also provided its students with a bistro, four libraries, and a Fitness and Athletic Center that included a three-lane elevated track, a newly remodeled gym, and squash and racquetball courts. The college's Prothro Natatorium featured a six-lane competitive pool, deck space for home swim meets, and a balcony overlooking the pool for spectators.

The school also offered what a sympathetic account in the *Atlantic* called a "prolific academic program." Despite having only 532 students, Sweet Briar offered no fewer than forty-six majors, minors, and certificate programs. Its administration remained fully staffed and it retained a faculty of 110, including 80 full-time professors. Classes were small, some with only a single student.[5]

"Needless to say," the *Atlantic* deadpanned, "these features are very expensive to maintain."

CHAPTER 1

BURSTING THE COLLEGE BUBBLE

HAVE WE SEEN THIS before? Rapidly escalating costs, irrational exuberance, and massive debt confronted by collapsing values? Political posturing, easy money, extravagant spending, and exaggerated claims of future benefits?

With striking parallels to the housing bubble of the last decade, the cost of a college degree has soared by 1,125 percent since 1978[1]—four times the rate of inflation—even as the value of that degree is increasingly questionable. A generation of graduates is emerging from higher education carrying a crushing debt burden, but without the skills or job prospects that once had been taken for granted.

Despite a lagging economy, colleges have bloated their budgets, raised tuition, ignored students, and indulged in a culture of bread and circuses—because they can. One former president explains that higher tuition often worked like higher-priced vodka or watches—nothing was different, since they tasted the same and told the same time, but consumers were willing to pay more for the brand.[2]

Where did the money go? Spending on instruction remains flat, even as spending on administration, buildings, promotions, athletics, and noninstructional student services has exploded. Campuses vied with one another to add amenities, including Taj Mahal–like facilities, while multiplying the number of administrators. Recent decades have seen the proliferation of vice-presidents of student success, directors of active and collaborative engagement, dietetic internship directors, and sustainability directors, along with vast arrays of administrators devoted to "diversity" and "inclusion." Even as professors became increasingly scarce in the classroom, the number of administrators metastasized. Between 1975 and 2005, the number of full-time faculty in higher education rose by 51 percent—but the ranks of bureaucrats rose by 85 percent, and the number of "other professionals" by 240 percent.[3]

All of this was floated on an ocean of expanding student debt—*$1.3 trillion and rising.*

Ironically, at the very moment that the value of high education is being questioned, campuses across the country found themselves besieged by the Snowflake Rebellion—the emotional and often melodramatic uprising of hypersensitive activists (the "snowflakes") who demanded that colleges create "safe spaces" by silencing viewpoints that made them uncomfortable. Rapidly spreading from campus to campus, the protests saw the rise of what Roger Kimball called the "cry-bully, who has weaponized his coveted status as a victim."[4] Even benign emails suggesting respect for intellectual diversity could trigger new rounds of confrontations and protests that, ironically, made college campuses decidedly unsafe places for students, faculty, or administrations with differing viewpoints. Even liberal faculty members

complained about the climate of fear on campuses and the use of Kafkaesque tribunals that can jeopardize academic careers. [see chap-
ter 11: Grievance U.]

The irony was not lost on many observers: "tolerance," has taken
on a new meaning on many campuses. As the Snowflake Rebellion
spread—from Yale and the University of Missouri to dozens of colleges across the country—it was followed by the now-familiar pattern
of appeasement and capitulation by administrators, who often agreed
to demands to increase funding and staffing for their already bloated
diversity programs. While the complaints and behavior of the activists were often met with skepticism and derision outside of the academy, American higher education has largely responded by redoubling
its efforts to multiply programs that institutionalize and reinforce the
demands for ideological conformity and to search out microaggressions. A growing number of schools have published lists of words and
phrases to avoid, including the seemingly benign phrase, "America is
the land of opportunity." At one school, even the term "political correctness" has been deemed to be a microaggression."[5]

On the surface, this wave of disruption seemed baffling, because
as one Yale student wrote, "there are few institutions in American life
that are so utterly beholden to the left and its principal tenets."[6] But
the campus disruptions exposed how utterly the intellectual climate
on American universities campuses has been transformed in recent
decades. The upheaval has also reinforced doubts about the wisdom
and value of what passes for the higher learning at perhaps the worst
possible moment for the higher education complex.

STICKER SHOCK

For some families, sending a child to a private university now is like
buying a BMW every year—and driving it off a cliff. If the education
is financed through student loans, paying for college is like buying a

Lamborghini on credit. By 2012, the total cost of a four-year education at a private college had exploded to $267,308; the cost of public college had risen to $122,638. The price tag for attending Duke University is now more than $60,000 a year, but that is less than the price tags of at least forty-eight other schools including Bard College ($63,626), Dartmouth College ($62,337), Wesleyan University ($61,498), Boston College ($61,096), and Southern Methodist University ($60,586).

Since 2004, student debt has more than quintupled; 66 percent of students now borrow to pay for their education—up from just 45 percent as recently as 1993. Between 2004 and 2014, the number of student borrowers grew by 92 percent and the average student loan grew 74 percent. The average student now graduates with around $30,000 in student loans, while the portion of students with $100,000 or more has doubled.[7] Millions of students carry debt burdens without getting any degree at all. Student loan debt now exceeds both the nation's total credit card and auto loan debt. The delinquency rate on student loans is higher than the delinquency rate on credit cards, auto loans, and home mortgages.[8]*

The problem will haunt not only Generation Debt, but the overall economy for decades to come.

Until very recently, higher education's model of "ever bigger, ever more" worked because consumers were willing to pay inflated prices for the coveted credentials it conferred. For most students, parents, and trustees, higher education was still living up to its end of the bargain. Universities required little of students, and in turn, students asked little

---

*How does that compare to mortgage debt before the housing bubble burst? According to one analysis: "From the first quarter of 1999 to when housing-related debt peaked in the third quarter of 2008, the sum increased from $3.28 trillion to $9.98 trillion. Over this period, housing-related debt increased threefold. Meanwhile . . . the balance of student loans grew by more than 6x. *The growth of student loans has been twice as steep* [emphasis added]." ("Chart of the Day: Student Loans Have Grown 511% Since 1999," *Atlantic,* August 18, 2011)

of universities. The fact that the degree could be acquired with minimal effort or stress was not seen as a particularly vexing problem for students who were able to glide through four or five years with few demands being placed on either their abilities or their work ethic. As long as they acquired the desirable credential, as long as it got them into good-paying jobs and ensured entry into the middle class, they were more than satisfied. Despite all of the problems associated with higher education, that credential still worked as it was designed. Whether it actually signified any skill or body of knowledge, it conferred legitimacy and prestige, and was still accepted by society and employers as a sign of accomplishment. Its absence still carried a stigma and considerable economic penalty.

But what happens when the ticket punch no longer works?

While the average student debt load rose 24 percent in the last decade, average wages for graduates aged twenty-five to thirty-four fell by 15 percent. In 2011, 53 percent of college graduates under twenty-five were unemployed or underemployed. Many of those who found jobs discovered that their career choices were dictated by their mortgage-like monthly loan payments; others found that starting life with six-figure obligations made them unmarriageable.

Those doubts are spreading. A survey of 30,000 alumni by the Gallup-Purdue Index found that only 38 percent of recent college graduates "strongly agree" that their degree was worth the cost. Only a third of graduates with student debt, thought their education was worth the price tag.[9] Their skepticism is understandable.

A study by the Federal Reserve Bank of New York found that in 2012 roughly 44 percent of recent college graduates were working in jobs that did not require degrees—the majority of them in low-wage jobs.[10] One study by Richard Vedder and Christopher Denhart found that there are more college graduates who are working in retail jobs than there are soldiers in the US Army "and more janitors with bachelor's degrees than chemists. In 1970, less than 1% of taxi drivers had college degrees. Four decades later, more than 15% do."[11]

WOULD YOU LIKE MOCHA?

Students are of course welcome to pursue their bliss or work toward degrees in esoteric fields from pricey colleges, but they should not be under the misapprehension that they are necessarily making a sound investment. Some of them—or their parents—will pay $270,000 for a degree only to find themselves in a job that requires them to ask "Would you like to try our pumpkin spice latte today?" Specifically, the New York Fed study found that a majority of recent college graduates with degrees in liberal arts (52 percent), communications (54 percent), technologies (55 percent), agriculture and natural resources (57 percent), and leisure and hospitality (63 percent) were working in jobs that did not require a bachelor's degree.[12]

Degrees with highly unlikely paybacks include screenwriting and production from a school that charges $61,731 a year (Drexel); feminist, gender, and sexuality studies from a school that costs $61,498 a year (Wesleyan); theater from a school costing $61,940 a year (Scripps College); or fine arts from a school charging $62,031 a year (the University of Southern California).

And these are the students who actually graduate, sheepskin in hand. The picture for those who do not finish is even grimmer. Even as government aid and loan programs have encouraged the largest possible number of students to attend institutions of higher education, it has simultaneously guaranteed that many of those students will receive at best a mediocre education. For higher education and many would-be students, federal largess has proven to be a classic Faustian bargain. Only 34 percent of students entering four-year institutions earn a bachelor's degree in four years, and barely two-thirds—64 percent—finish within six years.[13] Rather than benefiting from a wage premium, many of the dropouts, especially those who end up with a load of debt and no degree, find themselves actually worse off than if they had not enrolled at all.*

* An analysis by Moody's concluded:

CHEAP MONEY

Like other bubbles inflated by cheap credit, the college bubble was floated on the belief that the value of the degree would continue to appreciate in value. But now, default and delinquency rates have reached the level where alarm bells are being sounded by the ratings agencies. By late 2014, 7.1 million borrowers with $103 billion in debt were in default on their student loans—a default rate of 19.8 percent, a staggeringly high number.

"This all makes sense," Jason Delisle, the director of the Federal Education Budget Project at the New America Foundation, wrote in the *Wall Street Journal*, "when you realize that the student-loan program has been designed to achieve two political goals: Loans should be available to any student, at any school, pursuing any credential; and student debt is bad and burdensome, so it should be easy for borrowers not to repay."[14]

Even at the height of the housing bubble, mortgages were models of fiscal prudence in comparison with student loans. Student borrowers do not have to provide any evidence that they have the ability to pay back the loan. There is no collateral. And loans are as available for the study of flower arranging as for engineering.

Moody's Investors Service warns that worsening performance of student loans "reflects the fact that student loan origination standards

---

The long-run outlook for student lending and borrowers remains worrisome. Unlike other segments of the consumer credit economy, student loans have not demonstrated much improvement in performance despite some improvement in the broader economy. . . . there is increasing concern that many students may be getting their loans for the wrong reasons, or that borrowers—and lenders—have unrealistic expectations of borrowers' future earnings. Unless students limit their debt burdens, choose fields of study that are in demand, and successfully complete their degrees on time, they will find themselves in worse financial positions and unable to earn the projected income that justified taking out their loans in the first place. (Cristian Deritis, "Student Lending's Failing Grade," *Moody's Analytics*, July 2011)

were not tightened as they were for other types of consumer loans."[15] One reason for this is that the federal government pumped money into the loans and provided lenders with guarantees. "With no supply constraints and a federal guarantee taking losses in the event of a default," Moody's noted, "lenders had little need to curtail their lending and every incentive to expand it." With echoes of the government's push for the issuance of more subprime loans, the government policy "permitted borrowing to remain robust at the cost of poorer performance." In some ways the explosion of student debt was even more reckless than other forms of lending, including the so-called NINJA mortgages ("no income, no job, and no assets"), which played a notorious role in the housing bubble. The Moody's report noted:

> While other forms of consumer lending depend highly on the borrower's current income streams and prior credit history in determining creditworthiness, student lending is a more speculative. Borrowers and lenders alike hope that the higher income resulting from the human capital investment justifies the cost of the loan. This has not been the case for recent graduates thus far.

This is how bubbles work: We all think tulips are valuable until we don't. Buying stock in the South Sea Company or the dot-coms is a sure thing—until it isn't anymore. We think housing prices will continue rising forever until we realize that they won't. Bubbles burst when buyers realize that the value of the asset is not worth the inflated price.

The education bubble bursts when puffery is confronted by reality. Increasingly, the economic model of higher education no longer works for many students, who realize belatedly that they have placed themselves in a financial stranglehold for unmarketable degrees. Charles Murray notes that the bachelor's degree still confers a wage premium on its average recipient. But, he says, "there is no good reason that it should."[16] In other words, we have decided that the degrees are valuable when there is no objective reason to do so, and there will come a moment when the market catches up. That moment appears to be now.

"This is just the beginning of the college implosion," tweeted businessman Mark Cuban after Sweet Briar was threatening to close its doors. "At some point," said Cuban, the owner of the Dallas Mavericks, "it's going to pop."[17]*

Entrepreneur Peter Thiel is convinced we are seeing a "classic bubble."

> It's basically extremely overpriced. People are not getting their
> money's worth, objectively, when you do the math. And at
> the same time it is something that is incredibly intensively
> believed; there's this sort of psycho-social component to people
> taking on these enormous debts when they go to college
> simply because that's what everybody's doing.

---

*Cuban has been warning about the bubble for years, posting on his blog on May 13, 2012:

> The formula for the housing boom and bust was simple. A lot of easy money being lent to buyers who couldn't afford the money they were borrowing. . . . Who cares if you couldn't afford the loan? As long as prices kept on going up, everyone was happy. And prices kept on going up. And as long as pricing kept on going up, real estate agents kept on selling homes and finding money for buyers. . . .
>
> It's just a matter of time until we see the same meltdown in traditional college education. Like the real estate industry, prices will rise until the market revolts. Then it will be too late. Students will stop taking out the loans traditional universities expect them to. And when they do, tuition will come down. And when prices come down, universities will have to cut costs beyond what they are able to. They will have so many legacy costs, from tenured professors to construction projects to research, they will be saddled with legacy costs and debt in much the same way the newspaper industry was. Which will all lead to a de-levering and a destabilization of the university system as we know it.
>
> And it can't happen fast enough.

In some ways, Thiel says, the current education bubble may actually be worse than the housing bubble. Student loans are harder to get out of than mortgages, because they cannot be discharged in bankruptcy. "If you borrowed money and went to a college where the education didn't create any value," he says, "that is potentially a really big mistake."[18]

The education bubble is not an "asset bubble," notes economic analyst and *Forbes* contributor Jesse Colombo on the website TheBubble -bubble.com, but it is definitely "a *bubble-like phenomenon* with very similar risks and implications as asset bubbles." All of the major elements of bubbles are there: "a highly convincing and partially legitimate boom story, soaring prices and profits, decreasing affordability, a highly overpriced/overvalued product, blatant profiteering, a 'gold rush' mentality, extrapolation of the boom's growth far into the future and debt-fueled overinvestment/overexpansion."

In the end, when this bubble bursts, he says, "the higher education industry will have no other choice but to drastically downsize until it is much smaller than its current size. Expect to see mass higher education job layoffs, slashed salaries and benefits, colleges merging or consolidating, while many colleges will simply be forced to close their doors."[19]

A QUESTION OF VALUE

But is this just a phenomenon of the weak economy, or does it suggest a deeper problem in higher education? There is in fact mounting evidence that the intrinsic value of that degree does not always measure up to the ever-increasing price tag. Author Kevin Carey went to the website of one of the nation's most expensive colleges (with a sticker price of $60,000 a year) "to look for some kind of data or study indicating how much students at George Washington were actually learning. There was none." This should not, however, have been surprising. "Colleges and universities rarely, if ever, gather and publish information about how much undergraduates learn during their academic careers."[20]

There is a reason for this. In their book *Academically Adrift*, Richard Arum and Josipa Roksa concluded that nearly half of college students "did not demonstrate any significant improvement in learning" during their first two years of college, while more than a third "did not demonstrate any significant improvement in learning over four years of college."[21] That depressing finding was consistent with other studies, including the Collegiate Learning Assessment Plus, a test of 32,000 students administered by the Council for Aid to Education, which found:

> Four in 10 U.S. college students graduate without the complex reasoning skills to manage white-collar work. . . .
>
> The test, which was administered at 169 colleges and universities in 2013 and 2014 . . . reveals broad variation in the intellectual development of the nation's students depending on the type and even location of the school they attend.
>
> On average, students make strides in their ability to reason, but because so many start at such a deficit, many still graduate *without the ability to read a scatterplot* [a mathematical diagram showing the relationship between two sets of data], *construct a cohesive argument or identify a logical fallacy* [emphasis added].[22]

After this story was published, a friend emailed me: "They might not graduate with marketable skills, but at least they'll know they are special snowflakes." This was unkind but not untrue. The education establishment has not embraced the mantras of self-esteem and participation trophies for all without effect. For years, academia—much like elementary and secondary education—has effectively masked this decline by lowering academic standards, both for admission and graduation, and by inflating grades.

As the scope of the problem has become apparent, the reaction has often been to blame politically unpopular scapegoats, such as the for-profit schools, including the notorious Corinthian Colleges.[23] The problems at the for-profit schools are quite real—graduation rates are poor and defaults on student loans often twice as high as at other institutions—but the focus on the for-profits is a distraction from the rest of academia. Once again, critics draw parallels with the mortgage crisis: like the worst subprime lenders, the for-profit schools represent some of the most dramatic abuses. But they are hardly alone. Barmak Nassirian, associate executive director of the American Association of Collegiate Registrars and Admissions Officers, put the problem in perspective when he told the *New York Times*:

> Mainstream higher ed can really self-righteously look at the big problem out there and say, "The problem lies with the other guy." . . . If you are looking at highway robbery and raping and pillaging, that is true. But there are all kinds of unfortunate practices in traditional higher education that are equally as problematic that are reaching the crisis point.[24]

Indeed, the current crisis can be seen as a product of the academic culture that has dominated higher education for decades now. Reflecting the upside-down priorities of higher education, the flight from teaching continues apace. At some schools that charge $50,000 a year or more for tuition, students will find senior professors to be merely a rumor. As it has done for more than half a century, the professoriate and its academic enablers justify abandonment of the undergraduate classroom and the beclowning of the curriculum in the name of research, however that term might be defined in the halls of the modern academy. The result is a tidal wave of unread, unreadable junk scholarship that fills library shelves but adds little to the sum of human knowledge.

All of this suggests that academia faces not just a crisis of cost, but one of value.

FREE MONEY

Remarkably, the instinct of the political class seems to be to double down on many of the same policies that created the current bubble. Even though much of this bloat has been fueled by easy government money—the more aid, the higher tuition costs have gone—politicians seem intent on spending even more. Many on the left have responded to the declining value and escalating cost of higher education with a variety of ideas: debt forgiveness, loan deferrals, income-based repayment plans, increased aid, and even two years of free community college. All those proposals reflect the desire to transform at least some of the cheap money of student loan debt into "free money."

Taken together, the proposed "solutions" will only further inflate the bubble while doing nothing about the question of underlying value. Dealing with this current crisis requires addressing both value and cost. Focusing solely on making student loans cheaper addresses neither. If history is any guide—and it is—cheaper money and more federal aid will merely worsen the problem, leading to higher tuition, more debt, and less accountability.

Here is the reality of the higher education complex today:

- **Too many colleges and universities have abandoned their commitment to actually teaching undergraduate students.**

- **Too many institutions of higher education waste too much money on things other than education.**

- **The continued flight from teaching has inflated the cost of a college education while sapping its value.**

- **Colleges and universities alike have abdicated their responsibility to offer students a coherent curriculum.**

- **Rather than teaching students how to think critically, too many campuses demand a stultifying ideological conformity.**

- **As a result, the bachelor's degree signifies pretty much nothing other than the student's successful survival of four years of a dubious college experience.**

And here is the reality for students:

- **Despite the cant about "college for all," the reality is that too many students are already going to college.**

- **Too many students spent too much time there.**

- **Too many spend too much money there.**

- **Too many go to the wrong college to study the wrong things.**

- **Too many are graduating with costly but worthless degrees.**

- **Too many drop out without ever getting a degree.**

- **The result is that far too many pay too much for too little.**

The truth is that none of this is really new; the current bubble has been a long time coming. For decades, academia has ignored warnings and sloughed off critics who questioned its priorities. I know, because I was one of them.

CHAPTER 2

DÉJÀ VU: *PROFSCAM* TWENTY-EIGHT YEARS LATER

IF ALL OF THIS seems familiar, it is. Especially for me.

I wrote about it twenty-eight years ago.

In 1988, I published *ProfScam,* an admittedly harsh indictment of American colleges and universities and the professors who occasionally taught at them.[1] The book grew out of an article that my father, a tenured professor, wrote for a magazine that I edited at the time. Both his article and my subsequent book excoriated higher education's abandonment of undergraduate teaching—"professors would rather have root canal work than spend time with any undergraduates"—and the bizarre obscurantism of what passed for academic "research."

The result is a modern university distinguished by costs that are zooming out of control, curriculums that look like they were designed by a game show host; nonexistent advising programs; lectures of droning, mind-numbing dullness often to 1,000 or more semi-anonymous undergraduates . . . teaching assistants who can't speak understandable English; and the product of this all, a generation of expensively credentialed college students who might not be able to locate England on a map.[2]

I laid all of this at the feet of the professoriate. This was, in retrospect, somewhat unfair. There were many parties responsible for this fiasco, and none of them should be left off the hook: the mediocre K-12 education that feeds unprepared students into college; administrators, trustees, alumni, legislatures, the federal government, and parents themselves. There was more than enough blame to go around.*

* *ProfScam's* indictment was, admittedly, sweeping:

For students, it has meant watered-down courses; unqualified instructors; a bachelor's degree of dubious value; and an outrageous bill for spending four or five years in a ghetto of appalling intellectual squalor and mediocrity.

For parents who pay college costs (especially those who chose a school because they thought their children would actually study at the feet of its highly touted faculty), it has meant one of the biggest cons in history.

For American business, it has meant hiring a generation of college graduates who are often unable to write a coherent sentence, analyze even simple problems, or understand why their elders keep talking about a Second World War (was there a First)?

And for American society—which has picked up the tab for hundreds of thousands of literary scholars, social workers, sociologists, economists, political scientists, psychologists, anthropologists, and educationists—it has meant the realization that we are not discernibly more literate, more competent, more economically secure, safer, wiser, or saner than we were before spending untold billions on this embarrassment of academic riches. (*ProfScam*, 8)

The result was a bachelor's degree whose value—even in 1988— was increasingly questionable:

> In the last several decades . . . the bachelor's degree has been so completely stripped of meaning that employers cannot even be sure if its holder has minimum skills that were once taken for granted among college graduates. Somewhere in the professoriate's endless curricular shell game, the universities lost track of the need to teach critical thinking, writing skills, or even basic knowledge about the world.[3]

Having set out my critique and brief and hopeful suggestions, I ended the book with one of the most embarrassing and naïve sentences I have ever written (and there have been quite a few): I appealed to "true scholars—and their students" to "keep the tiny flame of learning alive on campuses. . . . They will inevitably form the core of a reborn higher learning. In the meantime, they should keep the candle in the window lighted."[4]

"Help is on the way," I wrote.

But it really wasn't.

Not only did nothing change, but almost everything I described in the book got worse, leading us to the current crisis. So this book is likely to be equal parts déjà vu and "I told you so."* It will also try to explore why so little has changed for the better and what that bodes for the future.

THE ORPHANS OF HIGHER EDUCATION

There is a paradox at the heart of higher education. As a class, undergraduates have proven immensely lucrative to these mostly nonprofit

---

*The "dammit" is implied.

institutions. Without millions of new students, teachers colleges could not have turned themselves into universities, and universities could not have mutated into multiversities. In effect, students are hostages held by the universities to ensure society's continued goodwill, so it is important to publicly insist on a commitment to their education.

But if the new students are important as a class, their status as individuals is quite different. Because the new students are not really paying their way, they can be safely ignored, while the faculty pursues increasingly lucrative research opportunities. By 1988, it was becoming obvious that higher education had become an elaborate shell game. "A chasm had opened between academia's purported goals and its actual practices," I wrote then. "In fact, while professors were still expected to teach, they were now increasingly judged only by their research activities. Those professors so naïve as to believe that their teaching duties were important discovered their error when they were denied tenure by their peers."[5]

When faculty did deign to show up in class, I noted that the courses taught were often hyperspecialized to align with the professor's own exquisitely narrow specialty. Often, the courses were simply "guts," courses notorious for their undemanding standards and easy As.

At the University of Illinois, students could work toward their BA by taking Pocket Billiards or The Anthropology of Play, which was described as "the study of play with emphasis on origin, diffusion, spontaneity, emergence, and diversity." Auburn University offered a course in Recreation Interpretive Services, which was described as "principles and techniques used to communicate natural, historical, and cultural features of outdoor recreation to park visitors." Occasionally, students stumbled upon the mother lode, such as those lucky few who enrolled in Applied Social Theory and Qualitative Research Methodology at the University of North Carolina at Greensboro. Known affectionately as "Deadhead 101," its course materials consisted of Grateful Dead cassettes and reviews of past shows. Students were required to attend

Grateful Dead concerts to "observe the subculture that surrounds the band."[6]

ProfScam* also mocked the obsession with arcane, irrelevant, time-wasting research that was cloaked in the impenetrable jargon I called "profspeak."[†]

> Probably only American higher education could have pro-
> duced something like one professor's study of the phenom-
> enon of high school cheerleading. The researcher concluded
> that cheerleaders are not only an "erotic icon" but were engag-
> ing in an "institutionalized-biological ritual," which can be
> compared to religious symbols described in a passage cited by
> the researcher as "polysemous, affective, and prescriptive
> signs, deriving their power from their multireferential or
> multivocal nature and their ability to encode a special model
> of reality."[7][‡]

* "The research culture is founded on an almost religious faith in the search for new knowledge, and professors have a marked tendency to drift toward pietistic unctuousness in describing the importance of their work. To hear academia's boosters tell it, the scholarship that is produced by the professoriate is the glory of the academic enterprise and, indeed, something of a national treasure." (*ProfScam*, 103)

† Profspeak is the direct product of the academic culture's triple imperative of obfuscation. The use of obscure jargon, convoluted syntax, and the symbols and trappings of mathematics are essential for any academic because:

1. It can make even the most trivial subject sound impressive and the most commonplace observation immeasurably profound, even if the subject is utterly insignificant.
2. It makes it much easier to avoid having to say anything directly or even anything at all.
3. And, most important, It is easier than real thought or originality.

‡ "The dominant theme is careerism, and it colors every aspect of the enterprise. Unread and unreadable, the product of the professoriate is seldom intended to expand the horizons of human knowledge as much as to keep the academic machine running smoothly, the journals filled, the libraries well-stocked, the resumes bulging, and the grants awarded. Volume rather than insight is what counts, and conformity rather than originality is what is rewarded." (*ProfScam*, 109)

Personally, I was never able to look at cheerleaders again in quite the same way, though I doubted the article added much to the store of human knowledge on the subject. But that wasn't really the point, was it? The point was to get published and tenured, while making even the most trivial observations sound profound and "scholarly."

This was in 1988. Academia, predictably, reacted with howls of wounded outrage.

Despite their tenured status, the professoriate is notably thin-skinned. Faculty were annoyed at the criticism of their research and defensive about having the value of their obscure publications questioned, but it was their shrinking teaching loads that touched the most sensitive nerve. Confronted with evidence that many professors had settled into a seven-and-a-half-hour workweek, the professoriate responded with indignant denials and protested that its members were in fact victims of an academic sweatshop. Some insisted that they put in sixty- to seventy-hour workweeks, but they protested too much. The reality was that my father's estimate of a seven-and-a-half-hour weekly load was generous even for that time. Nonetheless, they loathed us for pointing it out.

Fueling the academic anger was the fact that *ProfScam* was favorably reviewed by the *New York Times,* the *Washington Post,* and the *Wall Street Journal,* and that it was leading to awkward questions from outsiders who paid the bills.

As a result, my visits to university campuses and the occasional debates with academics were interesting but occasionally awkward affairs. Flat-out denial that anything was amiss was a frequent response, and it was often accepted by credulous trustees, parents, alumni, and boosters. Universities do not spend massive amounts of money on public relations for nothing. Sometimes those efforts led to interesting confrontations.

One of my harshest critiques of university education circa 1988 was aimed at academia's reliance in the classroom on teaching assistants who could not speak understandable English: "The selection of TAs is symbolic of the status of teaching in the university. Many of the teaching assistants are drawn from the ranks of foreign graduate students whether or not they can speak understandable English."[8]

This was not a nativist complaint. Especially in the sciences, engineering, and math, many (if not most) of the graduate students were foreign students. Their presence was a tribute to the respect the world had for American higher education, and they were often diligent students, harder working and often better prepared than their American counterparts. To a large extent, the presence of foreign students helped maintain or raise academic standards in fields that might otherwise have been dumbed down. But there was a problem.

Many of those students, while proficient or advanced in their fields, had a limited mastery of spoken English. Many of them had difficulties making themselves understood, while others lacked an understanding of American pedagogical methods, such as they are. Wherever I went, this was among the top complaints of undergraduates: Not only were the actual professors mere blurs in the parking lots, but students had been foisted off on TAs they could not understand.

The replacement of professors with TAs was both a symbol of the university's low regard for classroom teaching and a classic example of academia's bait and switch. Many academics had the grace to admit the problem, although they were reluctant to do anything about it. Some universities simply chose to ignore it.

At one lively forum at the University of Wisconsin–Madison, one indignant faculty member rose to challenge me directly for saying that there were TAs who did not speak comprehensible English. It was, he declared, simply not true—an insufferable slander—for critics to suggest that such a thing happened. I confess that I was momentarily taken aback, given how obvious and widespread the problem was at universities like Wisconsin. Rather than get into a tedious "is/is not" back-and-forth with the professor, I simply asked the rather large crowd of UW students to give me a show of hands: How many of them had been taught by TAs who didn't speak understandable English?

The show of hands was overwhelming. The professor sat down (undoubtedly resolving to prepare a sharply worded complaint about offensive campus speakers).

Others took the book quite personally.

My father had taught in the Department of Mass Communication at the University of Wisconsin–Milwaukee and for a time was chairman of the department. After his death, I taught some of his classes on a part-time basis. After the publication of *ProfScam,* one reporter, writing about higher education, tried to contact me by calling the department's office. When the department secretary told the reporter that I no longer taught in the department, someone in the background declaimed in a loud voice, "And never will again!" (Indeed, I did not.)

An article in the *New York Times* mentioned the controversy stirred up by *ProfScam* and noted that I had also taught journalism classes at Marquette University.[9] Shortly afterward, the dean of the school—a protégé of my father—called me to politely ask that I never ever under any circumstances allow my name to be associated with that institution. Of course I agreed.

This is not to say that all of the academic critics were closed-minded or in denial. I spent a good deal of time on university campuses and found many faculty members and administrators who sympathized, or who were at least trying to size up the enemy. One of my favorite academic reviews described *ProfScam* as "an angry, vitriolic, and outrageous diatribe against the American higher education establishment in general, and professors in particular." The critic noted that it was easy for academics to dismiss the book on "the grounds of being strident, exaggerated, and to some extent, misdirected." But then he concluded sadly: "It is, therefore, most unfortunate for academia that Mr. Sykes is fundamentally correct in much of what he says."[10]

Stephen Joel Trachtenberg, then president of George Washington University, also offered extensive and thoughtful criticisms and tried to induce his colleagues to take some of the problems more seriously. Trachtenberg agreed with many of his fellow academics that *ProfScam* was "exaggerated" and said that it was "understandable that many faculty members and administrators reviled or simply ignored *ProfScam* even while its author was garnering applause and approval from members of the American middle class and upper-middle classes." He warned that while the book had been dismissed by academic elites, *ProfScam* had (for a time) become required reading "not only for state and federal legislators who deal with higher education but also among the broad American public." Trachtenberg worried that "Sykes and his ever-growing number of sympathizers and imitators could represent" what he warned could be "the thin edge of full-blown Margaret Thatcherism where higher education is concerned."[11]*

Others also suggested that academics make an effort to pay attention to the critics. In his 2006 book, *Our Underachieving Colleges,* former Harvard president Derek Bok noted that "many people [presumably his fellow academics] were surprised that books about undergraduate education, such as *ProfScam* and *The Closing of the American Mind,* could sell so many copies." Bok attempted to explain: Half of young Americans went to college; a quarter of them got diplomas. "Virtually every aspiring lawyer, doctor, minister, scientist, and schoolteacher must earn a college diploma, and almost all future corporate executives, legislators, and high public officials will do the same." So the stakes were high. "If colleges miseducate their students, the nation will eventually suffer the consequences. . . . Small wonder, then, that critics care

---

* Trachtenberg took a much more favorable view of my follow-up book, *The Hollow Men: Politics and Corruption in Higher Education,* writing that "it carefully avoids every one of *ProfScam*'s overenthusiastic and sensationalistic faults." Trachtenberg admitted that the book offered: "(1) an accurate rather than exaggerated indictment of the type of 'core' curriculum that increasingly prevails at many universities—including the major 'pioneer' of such curricula, Stanford University—and (2) a broader indictment of increasingly common academic practices in this country—one that is judiciously written, in eloquent but controlled and even academic language." His reference to my use of "even academic language" may explain why *The Hollow Men* went relatively unread. (Stephen Joel Trachtenberg, "Academia Under Indictment," *AGB Reports,* Association of Governing Boards, January–Februry 1991)

enough to write with such passion and that large numbers of people want to read what they have to say."[12]

This was all very flattering, but the reality is that nothing ever came of it. *ProfScam* was a buzzing gnat, brushed off by the academic bull. Some critics suggested that it was easy to ignore *ProfScam* because I was an outsider. This was of course true, but how then to explain academia's ability to brush off similar critiques from so many academic insiders, including those from the loftiest pinnacles of the ivory tower—Derek Bok, Ernest Boyer, Stephen Trachtenberg? Dozens of monographs, articles, and books documented the crisis of higher education—the escalation of costs, the flight from teaching, the trashing of the curriculum, the various forms of academic bloat, and the increasingly questionable value of the bachelor's degree. By and large they were shrugged off by an academic cartel that was determined to pursue its own priorities, the consequences be damned.

Obviously, it's not enough to simply say "I told you so." We have to try to figure out what has made higher education so impervious to reform. Why did nothing change? Why in fact did it get worse?

And is there any reason to expect that attempts at reform will be any more effective this time around? The answer with numerous caveats is a qualified maybe.

The reason is the bubble.

An analysis by Bain & Company concluded that higher education in the United States "is at a tipping point." Too often, the report said, leaders of higher education think their problems are temporary and will go away when the economy improves. "But those who see things this way probably haven't been exposed to the data [that] show convincingly that this time is different."[13]

The current crisis is different, because it does not appeal to higher education's conscience—it aims at its wallet. As Bain noted:

If you are the president of a college or university that is not among the elites and does not have an endowment in the

billions, chances are cash is becoming increasingly scarce—
unless you're among the most innovative. The reason is
simple: Approximately one-third of all colleges and universities
have financial statements that are significantly weaker than
they were several years ago.

Colleges and universities find themselves with more debt, higher
debt service payments, and rising costs "without the revenue or
the cash reserves to back them up." In the past, this was a more man-
ageable problem, because colleges could simply pass the additional
costs onto students or state and federal taxpayers. "Because those parties had the ability and the willingness to pay," the Bain report noted,
"they did." That has changed.

But the recession has left families with stagnant incomes,
substantially reduced home equity, smaller nest eggs and
anxiety about job security. Regardless of whether or not
families are willing to pay, they are no longer able to foot the
ever-increasing bill, and state and federal sources can no longer
make up the difference.

Higher education also faces another challenge—obsolescence. Our
universities are rotary dial phones in the age of the app. Perhaps nothing will prove as disruptive to the status quo as the rise of new free
open online courses, which threaten not only to transform traditional
classroom teaching, but pose a direct existential threat to the higher
education complex.

Futurist Nathan Harden sees the massive open online courses
(MOOCs) as a mighty and irresistible model of creative destruction:
"Big changes are coming," he wrote, "and old attitudes and business
models are set to collapse as new ones rise. Few who will be affected
by the changes ahead are aware of what's coming."

His vision was apocalyptic:

In fifty years, if not much sooner, half of the roughly 4,500 colleges and universities now operating in the United States will have ceased to exist. The technology driving this change is already at work, and nothing can stop it. The future looks like this: Access to college-level education will be free for everyone; the residential college campus will become largely obsolete; tens of thousands of professors will lose their jobs; the bachelor's degree will become increasingly irrelevant; and ten years from now Harvard will enroll ten million students.[14]

The bottom line is that students will be unwilling to pay tens of thousands of dollars for something that they can get for free—something that is perhaps even more prestigious than the more expensive credential. He envisions "a merciless shakeout of those institutions that adapt and prosper from those that stall and die." But for students, he envisions a new era of empowerment:

Meanwhile, students themselves are in for a golden age, characterized by near-universal access to the highest quality teaching and scholarship at a minimal cost. The changes ahead will ultimately bring about the most beneficial, most efficient and most equitable access to education that the world has ever seen.

So far this has not happened. But will the threat be enough to shake the higher education complex out of its institutional inertia? Will it be enough to break the carapace of denial and arrogance of the academy? Will it be enough to get colleges to actually address their responsibility to provide value to their students? With their finances squeezed in a fiscal vise, will their hearts and minds follow? The questions are worth exploring.

And that brings me to this book.

In the chapters that follow I examine the continued flight from teaching, the inflated and absurd claims made for academic research, the bloated spending of colleges and universities, the failure of learning in academia, and the new stifling ideological orthodoxies of political correctness—from "trigger warnings" and the campaign against "microaggressions" to the Orwellian approaches to sexual assault on campus. In addition, I survey academic myths, scandals, and hoaxes that illuminate the pretensions and hypocrisies of the higher education complex, and the delusion that we should continue to encourage everyone to attend college. I will also address the various proposals to bail out higher education—proposals that are as misguided and costly as they are ineffective.

Finally, I offer some modest suggestions for what the new university might look like.

PART II

THE
COLLEGE
BUBBLE

CHAPTER 3

THE (ESCALATING) FLIGHT FROM TEACHING

"IF ITS OBJECT WERE scientific and philosophical discovery, I do not see why a University should have students," John Henry Newman wrote in the Preface to *The Idea of a University*. His successors in academia, while not so candid, have clearly wondered the same thing. Their solution? To spend as little time and effort with students as possible.

Back in 1988 I wrote in *ProfScam:*

The University of Wisconsin campus is dominated by
Bascom Hill, which in turn is dominated by a massive statue

of Abraham Lincoln seated in a state of contemplative repose. Generations of students have heard the legend surrounding it: Abe will stand up whenever a virgin walks past. The story has undergone a slight revision. Lincoln now stands whenever a virgin or a senior professor who teaches more than two undergraduate courses a semester passes by.[1]

In the mid-eighties, the University of Wisconsin administration acknowledged that the average professor taught only six hours a week. But even that was questionable. Auditors for the State of Wisconsin found that the six-hour average included only the fall semester, where teaching loads tended to be higher. Worse yet, the audit of teaching loads covered only the 1,318 UW professors who were actually teaching at all, which represented fewer than two-thirds of the profs on the payroll at the time. The rest were off doing something else—administration, sabbaticals, research.

By the late eighties, the flight of the professoriate from teaching had affected nearly every aspect of life on UW's Madison campus: Class sizes were often huge and students often could not get the courses they needed to graduate. Typically, the UW administrators of the time took out their wrath not on the faculty but instead on students and the taxpayers: Tuition was raised, the number of students was cut back, and programs for undergraduates were slashed.

Fast-forward to today. By almost every measure, the situation has gotten worse. The average professor at a major university rarely teaches more than two courses a semester. Since the average class hour is fifty minutes, that translates into about five hours of actual teaching a week. Evidence suggests that the flight from teaching is accelerating as even liberal arts colleges and second- and third-tier universities emphasize research over classroom teaching.

UNCORKING A FINE WHINE

Back in 1987 a Wisconsin legislator had the temerity to propose legislation mandating a teaching load of fifteen hours per week—and the university predictably exploded in indignant outrage. Critics waxed eloquent, predicting that requiring professors to teach more would "make research impossible"; UW degrees would be worthless; and the only faculty who would stay at Madison "would be those who are duds." Needless to say, the doomsday bill never got to the floor of either house of the legislature.

Something similar happened in 2015, when Wisconsin's governor Scott Walker suggested that "maybe it's time for faculty and staff to start thinking about teaching more classes and doing more work."

Although many professors had minimal teaching loads, Walker's suggestion has been met with "incredulity" on campus. UW president Ray Cross led the chorus of indignation, saying that he was "frustrated" by the talk of having professors teach more. "I think it's a shame that people don't understand what faculty really do."[2] One of the most voluble critics was Professor Jo Ellen Fair from UW–Madison's School of Journalism and Mass Communication. Fair doesn't simply insist that professors work hard, she says they work *extremely hard*. "Most faculty members I know are working 60, 70 hours a week. I'm not sure what else they can do," she told a reporter. She went on to list a litany of things that take up professors' time: "Preparing for and teaching classes, working with students during and outside of office hours, writing letters of recommendation for students applying for jobs and further education, advising students and grading assignments and exams."[3]

But for Professor Fair herself, the list of duties did not include actually teaching classes—at least not during the semester in which she was complaining about the onerous professorial workload. Fair, who makes more than $120,000 a year, had *no classes* on her schedule during the spring 2015 semester. Instead, she is assigned to "administrative duties." Despite her catalog of academic duties, Fair did not have to prepare for or teach a single class.[4] She assigned no readings, graded no assignments or tests.

This is not a criticism of Professor Fair. She was undoubtedly an accomplished researcher and a very busy woman. Her resume says that her "research is international, humanistic, and interdisciplinary. Thematically, it links journalism, media studies, visual cultures, popular culture, and social theory." She also spends a good deal of her time on academic committees, including "the University Committee, the University Academic Planning Committee, the Commission on Faculty Compensation and Benefits, and the steering committee of the Humanities Center."[5]

So the question is not whether Fair works hard enough, *it is whether she is actually available to students.* But like so many of her colleagues, she had something else to do—something apparently more important than teaching classes to undergraduates. For Professor Fair is a sought-after teacher: she "has conducted journalism-training workshops in Nigeria, Ghana, Benin, Senegal, Zambia, South Africa, and Namibia." But in Madison, Wisconsin, where students are paying tuition to study with professors like Fair, she taught nothing during the semester in question.

Interestingly, Fair defended the light teaching loads by saying such a spare schedule was all for the benefit of students.

"Students come to UW–Madison because they get to work with some of the finest scholars, researchers and teachers in the world," Fair said. "If it's not the best place for students, we're going to have students leaving the state."[6]

This statement was unintentionally ironic coming from a professor whose committee work, research, and administrative duties left her no time that semester for teaching any of those students. But she was hardly alone.

An independent journalism group looked at seven of the UW faculty members who were quoted in the media criticizing the idea that professors ought to spend more time with students. The analysis found that of the seven professors:

- Only three taught any classes at all in the spring semester of 2015.

- The three professors who did actually teach averaged just 1.66 classes per week, with an average of 3.97 hours per week in the classroom.

The critics included a political science professor who made $140,199 a year and had a teaching load of zero in the spring semester and a professor of food science who opined that the idea "shows a total lack of understanding of how a university functions," and illustrated as much by having no classes at all, despite an annual salary of nearly $118,000 a year. Another political science professor insisted that "If you increase the teaching requirements, faculty who can get jobs at schools with lower teaching requirements will move." That professor made nearly $125,000 a year and did not have a single course on his schedule.[7]

How unusual is this? Another media analysis found that UW–Madison's highest paid professor made $306,030 a year, but did not teach a single course during either the fall or the spring of 2014–2015 semesters, spending his time instead "overseeing graduate students as they write their theses." The analysis found that the ten highest paid professors in the UW system "earned an average salary of $269,253 but are only teaching a total of 15 different courses. Four of those ten professors are only teaching one course, and only one is teaching three."[8]

The high salaries and low teaching loads need to be seen in juxtaposition to the fact that in 2012, nearly half of UW graduates graduated with student loan debt—on average $24,700.

THE RATCHET

So, why do faculty members want to avoid teaching undergraduates? In recent decades, avoiding students has become not just a status symbol, but a perk.

Perhaps inadvertently, UW–Madison's chancellor Rebecca Blank exposed a central fact of life in the modern university in an interview with the *Wall Street Journal*. Defending the status quo at her campus, she described how she went about bidding for professors—and how time in the classroom was one of the first things to be dropped:

> She said that 15% of her professors last year received outside job offers, and as chancellor, *she bids against those offers in part by cutting the course loads of researchers so they will stay* [emphasis added].
>
> "I am an economist," she said. "I live in a market."[9]

And indeed, this is the academic market. In their book *Higher Education? How Colleges Are Wasting Our Money and Failing Our Kids—and What We Can Do About It,* authors Andrew Hacker and Claudia Dreifus recount a job interview for an assistant professorship at CUNY's Queens College, a job that ostensibly entailed teaching basic classes in American government.[10]

As the authors tell it, the candidate's very first question to his interviewers was "What's the teaching load here?" When the department chair responded that it would be three courses a semester, the candidate quickly shot back: "That won't work." He explained that he had research work to do and "it's important." His previous school had expected professors to teach only two classes a semester. Then he asked about sabbaticals, in which he would be paid his full salary for doing no teaching at all. The chair explained that he would get a year off after six years of teaching.

This was also received as appalling news. "I couldn't consider that," he insisted, noting that at more enlightened schools, he could get a full year off after teaching just three years.

The good news, such as it is, is that the applicant didn't get the job. But Hacker and Dreifus note, "Despite the downturn in the economy, the academic culture that produced the young man hasn't changed." In the "alternate universe" of the professoriate, they note there was nothing at all odd about a would-be academic asking "How little can I do?" This culture has been nurtured, protected, and jealously guarded by higher academics for generations. In academia, everyone knows the rules. Rewards and prestige flow to those who emphasize research; in fact too much attention to classroom teaching can be the professional kiss of death.

Of course, like so much else described here, this is not new.

As far back as 1968 (and actually even earlier), academic critics noted the reward system of higher education. In their book *The Academic Revolution,* scholars Christopher Jencks and David Riesman wrote that "in terms of professional standing and personal advancement it makes more sense to throw this [their time and effort] into research than teaching."[11]

In retrospect, it is clear that 1945 is the great divide in the history of higher education. Swollen by the ranks of veterans returning from the war, American universities found themselves flush with cash, prestige, and power. Imbued with a postwar confidence bordering on arrogance, the modern university developed the taste for sheer mass and weight that typified postwar America and that would shape the nation's military, corporate, and cultural thinking. Often the lines between various enterprises would blur as universities became research extensions of the federal government and began to think of themselves as "knowledge factories," in the University of California president Clark Kerr's unfortunate, if memorable, phrase. The newly flush universities quickly adopted the rhetoric of entrepreneurship but inherited the grammar of bureaucracy. During the student rebellion of the 1960s, the universities would be bitterly attacked for their impersonality and interlocking relationships with government and business. Many criticisms struck home because the universities had become so tied into the infrastructure of the modern world that they had assumed a shape that would have been virtually unrecognizable to a prewar academic. Those were higher education's go-go years in which colleges redoubled their efforts to become universities, while universities mutated into vast impersonal research-dominated multiversities. Teaching loads dwindled, class sizes skyrocketed, and curricula were increasingly tailored to accommodate the new priorities.

Clark Kerr acknowledged the decline of undergraduate education, going so far as to say that "there seems to be a 'point of no return' after which research, consulting, and graduate instruction become so absorbing that faculty can no longer be concentrated on undergraduate education as they once were. This process has been going on for a long time; federal research funds have intensified it. As a consequence, undergraduate education in the large university is more likely to be acceptable than outstanding."[12]

As the pressure to bring in grants mounted, graduate students as well as undergraduates began to feel the shifting priorities. Michael Zimmerman, a biology professor at Oberlin College, recounts a conversation he overheard when he was a graduate student at one of the new multiversities. A student complained that a faculty member did not spend enough time with him. "The professor explained that her research time was more valuable to the university than was her teaching time," Zimmerman recalled. "Faculty members, she said, bring in four times as much money in grant overhead as students pay in tuition. . . . In many places the old slogan 'Publish or Perish' seems to have been retired and replaced with the more lucrative, if less alliterative, 'Find Federal Funding or Perish.' "[13]

The new culture of federal dependency inevitably also affected graduate education. One study by Edward Hackett, a professor at Rensselaer Polytechnic Institute, found that "the pressure to produce federal grants—and research results to get the grants—tended to result in principal investigators' being less willing to invest time in teaching and supervising the postdoctoral and graduate students working in their labs." Moreover, students received fewer opportunities to pursue independent research and were more likely to develop strictly technical skills rather than learn how to solve problems.[14]

But the effect of federal largess was not limited to the elite research universities. The shift to research changed academic culture as a whole and has exerted a tremendous attraction for schools in the grip of status envy. Often schools saw the prestige and riches and wanted to share in the glory. So they had their faculty turn out a dozen articles and declared it a knowledge explosion. They cut their teaching loads, called themselves research universities, and waited for the day when they would wake up as Johns Hopkins. It never happened. What did happen was that many of them eviscerated their undergraduate programs, turning themselves into second-rank schools with third-rate research. Professional accreditation agencies, moreover, began insisting that even the most modest state schools adopt the trappings of their elder siblings. Inevitably, the greatest impact fell on those faculty members who considered themselves "teachers."

At Northwestern University, for example, one survey in 1989 found that only one professor in ten thought that undergraduate teaching was rewarded "quite a bit" or "a good deal." Nearly four times as many said that teaching was rewarded "basically not at all."[15] The lesson is not lost on young professors. Many told me that to emphasize teaching or to be known primarily as a teacher was to commit professional suicide. As a result, even professors who wanted to be teachers or who enjoy teaching closed their doors, cut office hours, eliminated papers in their classes, gave multiple choice exams instead of essay exams, and published to save their lives. Given the rewards, their decisions were a perfectly rational response.

In *ProfScam* I wrote:

The academic culture is not merely indifferent to teaching, it is actively hostile to it. In the modern university, no act of good teaching goes unpunished. . . . * It had become obvious that the

---

* After *ProfScam* was published, some critics singled out this line as an overgeneralization. Which of course it was. At a meeting in 1989, Bryn Mawr's president,

higher one rose in academia, the less one had to teach. Big teaching loads were a sign of small rank: avoidance of teaching a perquisite of eminence.[16]

But twenty-eight years later, this active contempt for teaching still comes as a rude awakening. A 2005 article in the *Journal of Higher Education* found that "college professors actually get paid less the more time they spend in a classroom." Researcher James Fairweather noted that "for the vast majority of faculty irrespective of institutional type, teaching an additional hour [was] a negative factor in pay," while "publishing an extra article [was] a positive factor in pay."[17] Lest this be dismissed as merely anecdotal or an outlier, the teaching penalty was confirmed by a comprehensive 2012 study titled, appropriately enough, "The Teaching Penalty in Higher Education: Evidence from a Public Research University."[18] The authors concluded that "devoting more time to teaching results in a significant wage penalty, even when research productivity is carefully controlled."

The word quickly spread among the wannabe profs. In a 2011 article titled "10 Tips for Junior Faculty," Daniel S. Hamermesh bluntly advised: "Unless you are at a liberal arts college that stresses teaching, don't over-prepare your classes. . . . most institutions do not take teaching into account unless you fall below some standard."[19] Mark Bauerlein described the process similarly: "As graduate students trudge toward filing their dissertations, as adjunct teachers struggle to win a permanent position, and as assistant professors march toward that glorious or catastrophic tenure decision, one thing stands perpetually in their way: undergraduates."[20] In other words, as Gordon Winston once

Mary Patterson McPherson, cited the controversy over the status of teaching in academia stirred up by *Profscam* and specifically this quote. "However, the Bryn Mawr president made a distinction between small liberal arts colleges, where teaching has always been the primary mission, and universities where research is important to the economy and to society. She said that in these universities, the teaching is too often left to graduate students or adjuncts." (Joseph Berger, "Teach College Teachers to, Yes, Teach, Panel Says," *New York Times,* April 19, 1989)

wrote, "undergraduate teaching . . . can be viewed as something to be avoided like the plague by any modestly ambitious and savvy young scholar."[21]

Not surprisingly then, ambitious academics negotiate for as little class time as they can manage. The result is the "academic ratchet," by which teaching loads are competitively dropped lower and lower. Former Harvard president Derek Bok explained how it works: "When we go to recruit a star professor, the bargaining chip is always a reduced teaching load—never a reduced research load."[22]*

The process works in the academic marketplace that Rebecca Blank cited because institutions compete with one another by offering minimal contact with students. As more institutions scramble for prestige and higher ratings, the pressure to drop teaching loads has intensified.

So UW's Chancellor Blank was not revealing anything that is not well known and well established inside academia. But her willingness to it say publicly—in the hearing of parents, students, and policymakers—was nonetheless revealing. It also helps explain why the flight from teaching has been accelerating throughout higher education.

THE ABSENT PROFESSOR

Hacker and Dreifus documented what the flight from teaching looks like at the top of the academic pyramid. In the 2010–2011 academic year, twenty of the forty-two (47 percent) professors in Harvard's history

---

*As higher education researchers William F. Massy and Robert Zemsky explain, "It is the department's insistence that all members be treated not just fairly but nearly identically that drives the academic ratchet. . . . A reduction in teaching load won by one member of the department because of an outside offer, a research grant, or another external opportunity becomes the new norm against which all members of the department measure their own required commitments." (William F. Massy and Robert Zemsky, "Faculty Discretionary Time: Departments and the 'Academic Ratchet,'" *Journal of Higher Education* vol. 65, no. 1, January–February 1994, 21)

department "were off doing research, leaving many students to be taught by adjuncts and visitors." At Williams College—an elite liberal arts college—they found that four of seven of the faculty in the religion department were "also away on leave."[23]

But these examples fail to capture the scope and breadth of the flight from teaching, not just among elite institutions, but throughout higher education.

A recent study by the Higher Education Research Institute (HERI) based at the University of California not only found "a significant decline in time spent teaching," but also that "students are increasingly taught by part-time faculty in institutions, particularly in introductory courses." The proportion of faculty reporting that they spent nine hours or more per week teaching (roughly a quarter of their time) is currently 43.6 percent, which is a considerable decline from a high of 63.4 percent two decades ago and from 56.5 percent just ten years ago.[24]

The number of faculty who reported minimal teaching loads of just one to four hours a week (or one scheduled class a week) had doubled in the decade from 2001–2002 to 2010–2012. The study also found a sharp drop in time that professors spent in class preparation: "A considerable drop—from 65.6% to 59.1%—in the last three years in the amount of time spent in preparation for teaching (more than nine hours per week) also mirrors the decline in scheduled teaching hours."

The abdication of teaching to TAs and the "academic underclass" of part-timers was a major theme of *ProfScam,* but that trend has also escalated. Indeed, the HERI report found that "contingent faculty, defined as educators appointed to academic positions off the tenure track, now represent the majority of individuals holding academic appointments at colleges and universities."[25]

THE RISE OF THE ACADEMIC UNDERCLASS

"Contingent faculty" encompasses part-timers, itinerants, lecturers, adjuncts, graduate students, and non-tenure-track faculty. Together they comprise the academic underclass, a group of underpaid and generally unappreciated instructors who increasingly are being entrusted with the teaching duties that have been abandoned by their tenured betters. Most of the adjuncts make only a fraction of the salaries of tenured professors, often teaching courses for only a few thousand dollars apiece.

But over the course of decades they have become the backbone of American higher education; even as tuition skyrocketed, more or more of the teaching was turned over to nonprofessors.

Consider this: In 1975, fully 43 percent of the faculty was made up of "contingent faculty." By 1993, the proportion of contingents rose to 57 percent of faculty employment. By 2011, according to the American Association of University Professors, that number had risen to 70.2 percent of total faculty employment.[26]

The picture in the classroom was actually even worse than that. Perhaps nothing illustrates the flight from teaching more than the following numbers of instructional staff employment (which also included grad students).

In 1975, there were roughly 783,000 college instructors in the United States. Of those, 227,381 were full-time tenured faculty, while another 126,300 were full-time tenure-track faculty. Even then, they constituted a minority (45.1 percent) of the actual instructional staff. In 1975, there were 80,833 full-time non-tenure-track faculty, 180,000 part-timers, and nearly 107,000 graduate student employees.

So, in 1975, after decades of the flight from teaching, the academic underclass already comprised nearly 55 percent of the total instructional staff in American higher education. What followed, however, was an explosion in the number of part-timers and other contingents.

Between 1975 and 1993, the number of part-time instructors more than doubled from 180,000 to 369,758. By 1993, the academic underclass, including grad students working as teaching assistants, made up 65 percent of the college/university instructors. By 2011, the number of part-time faculty members had risen to nearly 762,000; the number of graduate students employed in the classroom rose to 355,916; and the number of full-time, but never-to-be-tenured faculty rose to

284,303—up from just 80,833 in 1975. By 2011, fully 41.3 percent of all instructional staff were part-timers.

The result was that by 2011, the academic underclass made up *76 percent of the instructional staff of American higher education.*[27]*

Seventy-six percent.

The exploitation of this underclass to cover for the absent professoriate has in fact become so widespread that it has generated significant blowback for universities, including growing efforts to unionize the "contingent" faculty. "Universities are being shamed," said Walter Benn Michaels, a tenured professor at the University of Illinois at Chicago. "People are paying good money to send their kids to [these schools], and they expect a faculty with a certain level of expertise."[28]

The irony is striking. A central tenet of the academic orthodoxy is the insistence that research is critical for the quality of teaching. But the universities have in fact turned over much of the teaching of undergraduates to teachers who have no such requirement. The status of the part-time/temporary faculty reveals the circularity of the argument about research. The academic establishment insists that only professors who do research can be good teachers, so they need to spend most of their time outside of the classroom; and because they are off researching (to become better teachers, remember), they are replaced by part-timers or temporaries who may do little or no research at all.

HOW HARD DO PROFESSORS WORK?

For some critics, all of this raises obvious questions about the professorial workload. In 2012, one longtime academic, David C. Levy, a for-

---

* "Students taught primarily by part-timers—who often don't have private offices, regular office hours or adequate time to prepare for class—have lower retention and graduation rates than those with full-time teachers, according to Adrianna Kezar, co-director of the Pullias Center for Higher Education at the University of Southern California." (Douglas Belkin and Melissa Korn, "Colleges' Use of Adjuncts Comes Under Pressure," *Wall Street Journal*, February 16, 2015)

mer chancellor of the New School University took to the pages of the *Washington Post* to note that even with the most generous assumptions of the time they spent in the classroom and preparation, "their workload is still only 36 to 45 percent of that of non-academic professionals." (Levy noted that most professors work only a thirty-week year, which left "almost 22 weeks for vacation or additional employment.")

"The cost for such sinecures is particularly galling," wrote Levy, "when it is passed on to the rest of the middle class and to taxpayers in states that are struggling to support higher education. Since faculty salaries make up the largest single cost in virtually all college and university budgets . . . think what it would mean if the public got full value for these dollars."[29]

This is an awkward issue for academics, who often respond by insisting that they are tireless in their pursuit of higher learning. Inevitably they will cite their voluminous research, as well as their committee work and their community service. It is not unusual to see faculty members and their administrative enablers claiming that faculty put in sixty- or even seventy-hour weeks (see below).

This seems unlikely. Levy may actually have exaggerated the workload of the professoriate. As Richard Arum and Josipa Roksa note in *Academically Adrift,* evidence suggests that professors "spend only limited time on preparing instructions, teaching classes, and advising students."

> On average, faculty spend approximately 11 hours per week on advisement and instructional preparation and delivery. The time use data also indicates that faculty report directly engaging in research activities from two hours per week in liberal arts colleges to five hours per week at research universities.[30]

The rest of the time is spent on things such as committee work, answering emails, reviewing manuscripts, even consulting. As Arum and Roksa note, "many of these additional activities likely advance faculty careers, but are largely unrelated to undergraduate instruction."

But the real issue here is not whether the faculty is lazy; *it is whether they are available to students.* And here they are on much shakier ground. In addition to the leisure time it affords the tenured faculty, the light teaching loads mean that undergraduates are treated like the orphans of higher education.

TEACHING BADLY

Inevitably, there are consequences to the flight from teaching. One of the most obvious is the difficulty students have in getting the classes they need to graduate. While there are certainly a number of other factors at work here, the lack of professors in the classroom is a contributing cause to the spread of the five-year, even six-year bachelor's degree. In the University of Wisconsin system, for instance, only 31.4 percent of freshman students who began in the fall of 2009 semester received their diplomas by the spring of 2013.[31]

While some schools continue to encourage close contact between faculty and students, increasingly students are a distraction. The 2008 National Survey of Student Engagement found that 38 percent of freshmen "never" discuss ideas from readings with their instructors outside of class, while 39 percent said they did "sometimes." This disconnect also extended to upperclassmen. At the University of Texas and the University of Wisconsin, 54 percent of seniors said they had not written a paper of twenty pages or more during their senior year.[32]

Not surprisingly, on the occasions that professors do deign to instruct, they often do it badly. In *ProfScam,* I outlined the "Five Ways of Teaching Badly." Professors who wish to expend the least amount of effort in the classroom can:

1. Merely regurgitate the textbook.

2. Rely on notes prepared when they were younger, more ambitious, and without tenure.

3. Dwell on their own specialties without bothering to translate the material from the arcane jargon.

4. Turn their classes into rap sessions, a tactic that has the advantage of being both entertaining and educationally progressive.

5. Fail to prepare at all and treat their classes to an off-the-top-of-the-head ramble, leaping from topic to topic in what they think are dazzling intellectual trapeze acts, but which usually are confusing, frustrating muddles for the students.[33]

Tales of each are abundant.*

Another inevitable result of the flight from teaching has been the spread and growth of mass classes. Not surprisingly, universities have been particularly zealous in attempting to conceal the extent of the shift. Occasionally, schools will claim that a vast majority of classes are taught by faculty and that most courses are small. That reflects only the perspective of the faculty, many of whom teach small seminars on subjects carefully crafted to match their own specialties. The student's point of view is radically different. At the University of Texas, for example, a school notorious for mass classes and impersonal

---

*The indifference to teaching had even seeped into the sciences. In *ProfScam*, I wrote:

> In the sciences, we can find the purest expression not merely of the academic culture, but of that culture's virulent contempt for an indifference to teaching. The teaching loads of professors in leading science departments make the five-hour-a-week loads of their counterparts in the softer sciences seem enormous. . . . It is not surprising then that over the years academic science has been turned into a forbidding no-man's-land for undergraduates or that Harvard's professors of the natural sciences would be described as able to "bore the buzzards off a shit-wagon." . . .
>
> The result is the increasingly rapid spiral of decline: shrinking numbers of American students who are in turn replaced by foreign students who become TAs, who in turn manage to frustrate and discourage even more undergraduates from pursuing a career in the sciences. (*ProfScam*, 227)

bureaucracy, the administration claimed in the early 1990s that it had a student-faculty ratio of roughly 22 to 1. But Interpersonal Communication Theory had 570 students, Introduction to Psychology had 392. When the school's president boasted of the 22-to-1 ratio, one student leader complained: "To say his use of the number was misleading would be an understatement. By not explaining what the ratio actually represented, he left people with the impression that it has some relation to classroom conditions. It doesn't."[34]

FUDGING THE NUMBERS

All of this is potentially embarrassing and difficult to explain to legislators and taxpayers. In response, some institutions have devoted considerable effort not to fixing the problem, but to fudging the numbers.

In 2008, for instance, the University of Nebraska claimed that of its 1,081 faculty members, only 11 were not full-time. But this was sleight of hand: Nebraska was reporting only tenure or tenure-track faculty. As Naomi Riley notes, "Given the fact that most colleges reported that more than 80 percent of their faculty were full-time, it seems likely that other schools were also engaged in some creative accounting."[35]

At the University of North Carolina, administrators put out numbers claiming that the average professor in the system taught 3.37 courses a semester. "This estimate seemed to be extremely high," deadpanned the John William Pope Center for Higher Education Policy, which undertook its own analysis. Unsurprisingly, the center's study found that even using generous assumptions, "we would not likely come anywhere near the average of 3.37" classes—even at the state system schools that supposedly focused on undergraduate education. Instead, eliminating faculty who may have supervised a single doctoral or independent study student, the Pope study found that the average UNC system professor generally taught only about two courses a semester.

For example, the 49 faculty members in the English lit department at UNC Chapel Hill taught 107 courses, but 28 of those courses enrolled fewer than 3 students. Pope estimates that the average professor in the department taught 1.61 courses a semester. Even this was slightly misleading; the study found that six professors in Chapel Hill's English department taught only a single lecture class. The total teaching load for another five professors was supervising a single dissertation. The numbers suggest, as one analyst put it, that the university was "hardly an academic sweatshop." As the Pope analysis concluded: "Such low teaching loads in the humanities are an extravagant luxury."

But not a rare one. The Pope analysis found that having professors teach, on average, "*just one more course every two years* [emphasis added]—a 10 percent increase in productivity—could save North Carolina taxpayers close to $100 million annually."[36]

This echoed another study of the University of Texas by the Center for College Affordability and Productivity that found that if "the 80 percent of the faculty with the lowest teaching loads" were to "teach just half as much as the 20 percent with the highest loads," tuition and fees at UT could be cut *in half.*[37]

The Texas study is revealing because it documents the huge imbalance in the allocation of teaching duties. The Center for College Affordability and Productivity found that a fifth of the faculty at the University of Texas's flagship campus in Austin taught a majority (57 percent) of all of the student credit hours. But this fifth also generated 18 percent of the campus's research funding. "This suggests," the study noted, "that these faculty are not jeopardizing their status as researchers by assuming such a high level of teaching responsibility. In other words, there are hundreds of UT faculty who appear to teach large numbers of students while maintaining an active sponsored research program."

The flip side of the small number of professors who carried the bulk of the teaching load were the "least productive 20 percent of faculty" who collectively taught only 2 percent of all student credit hours.

Interestingly enough, this group generated "a disproportionately smaller percentage of external research funding than do other faculty segments."

As it turned out, only a small segment of the faculty was actually generating the bulk of the school's research funds. "Research grant funds go almost entirely (99.8 percent) to a small minority (20 percent) of the faculty; only 2 percent of the faculty conduct 57 percent of funded research."

But most striking of all was the cost impact of the light-teaching majority of the faculty. Even though 80 percent of the professors taught only a minority (43 percent) of the student credit hours, the group "accounts for 72 percent of all faculty costs to the Austin campus. Per-student costs associated with these 3,360 faculty members are $2,142 per student per year, more than three times the level of cost per student for the 20 percent of the faculty who carry the largest teaching loads."[38]

Even adding a *single class* to the teaching loads of professors could have a dramatic impact on the university's revenue. More teaching means that the universities would be able to offer more classes, teach more students, and theoretically take in more tuition revenue.

Michael Poliakoff, a vice-president of policy at the American Council of Trustees and Alumni, noted: "Even a marginal 10% increase in teacher productivity means an enormous boost for student access, it means more courses are available, and it straightens out a lot of bottlenecks."[39]

Unfortunately, given the institutional aversion to teaching that has become pervasive throughout higher education, this is unlikely to happen any time soon.

CHAPTER 4

THE REALITY OF
ACADEMIC RESEARCH

THE USUAL EXCUSE FOR the flight from teaching and the dis-
mantling of the curriculum is the necessity for professors to pursue
knowledge through research. But pitting teaching against research
begs the question, because it presupposes that the professors really do
as much research as they claim and that their research has some value.
Chester E. Finn, Jr., a former assistant secretary of education, once
estimated that only one in ten professors makes any genuine intellectual contribution at all.[1]

I suspect that he was being charitable.

Some studies have found that 40 percent of faculty members publish "little or nothing."[2] Lawrence B. Martin, a professor of anthropology at State University of New York at Stony Brook, has developed algorithms to quantify and demystify the question of faculty productivity, measuring publication rates and balancing them with teaching loads. Martin estimates that colleges and universities waste somewhere between $1 billion and $2 billion on salaries of professors who have low teaching loads but who seldom publish anything. "If the least scholarly and productive 20 percent of faculty, who are effectively producing little or no scholarship are receiving reduced teaching loads," he said, "then the cost of that is staggering."[3]

In *ProfScam* I argued that it was not necessary to insist that no worthwhile or valuable research is being done at the universities "to recognize that much of what passes for knowledge creation makes only the most piddling contribution to the pool of human wisdom. Much of it is merely humbug."

At the time, I noticed how defensive academics were about their "research" and suggested that there was a reason for their touchiness:

> Indeed, all parents forced to take out a second mortgage on
> their homes to pay college tuition can take heart, knowing that
> their efforts have made it possible for America to maintain its
> edge by supporting one professor's research into the "Evolution
> of the Potholder: From Technology to Popular Art," complete
> with a chart tracing the "Distribution of Potholders, and Hot
> Mat Design Motifs by Decade" (including the frequency of
> "fruits and nuts, animals, birds, insects, fish," and mottoes).[4]

And who could forget the scholar who explored (at some length) the question "Are pigeons and children different?" (Which she answered, in part, by concluding: "The answer to this question must wait until the science develops innovative methodological procedures.")

Or the paper on the features of Mickey Mouse that concluded that "Roundness is the essence of the neotenous configuration."[5] In academia, none dared call it time-wasting drivel.

Whenever any of this enterprise is questioned, university administrators and their armies of public relations bureaucrats rush to point out the cutting-edge medical or scientific research that not only is bringing in big dollars but also is curing cancer/heart disease/glaucoma/etc. But for every breakthrough on the mysteries of the atom, there are dozens of articles dealing with issues like "Intimacy in Conversational Styles as a Function of the Degree of Closeness Between Members of a Dyad," in the *Journal of Personality and Social Psychology*, which found, after ten pages of mathematics and complex formulas, that "acquaintances were generally more similar to strangers than they were to friends." For every scientist featured in the alumni magazine, there were hundreds of articles on the order of "The Influence of Contextual Variables on Interpersonal Spacing," in which the author writes that "room size and shape influenced interpersonal distance," but that "interaction indicated that room size affected distance only in rectangular rooms."[6]

No matter how trivial the research or inconsequential the conclusions, however, the academic writing is invariably cloaked in jargon-laden "profspeak." Consider the professor who later wrote this bit of what Russell Jacoby called "academic gibberish."[7]

> The politics of difference lives on to rethink the minority not
> as an identity but as a process of affiliation . . . that eschews
> sovereignty and sees its own selfhood and interests as partial
> and incipient in relation to the other's presence.

Of such stuff are academic careers minted. At the time this bit of prattle was penned, the author of it was the Anne F. Rothenberg Professor of English and American Literature and Language and was the director of the Humanities Center at Harvard University. All across academia, professors still strive to match that level of obscurantism in their own works.

THE PUBLICATION RACKET

Research, however, is not enough. It must—somehow, someplace—be published, but not in anything resembling a popular or widely read magazine or journal. Instead, the research has to be published in one of the thousands of academic journals unread by the masses, for obscurity is vital. Collectively, the professoriate—in search of tenure, promotion, invitations to academic conferences—produces hundreds of thousands of these new nuggets of created knowledge. I wrote in *ProfScam:* "These publications represent the heart of the academic enterprise. They were the justification for society's support and indulgence, and the reasons that teaching loads are so small, classes so huge, and undergraduate teaching the orphan of higher education."

If anything, the situation has also gotten worse since then.

When I wrote *ProfScam,* the rush to research appeared to be in full flood, but the reality was that it was only gathering momentum. Since the 1980s, the pressure on faculty to publish has spread from research universities to second- and even third-tier institutions. In the endless search for higher rankings and prestige, schools that aspire to be the Harvard of Wherever have decided that they must ape the practices and priorities of the elite schools if they hope to rise.

The doctoral dissertation was the perfect vehicle for the shaping of this new breed of professor. Instead of insisting that would-be professors extend the range and breadth of their learning, the academy insists that the PhD candidate choose a subject of exquisite narrowness and produce a hundred to two hundred pages of detailed research. No matter how tiny or insignificant the subject might be, the dissertation was the essential admission ticket. And here, again, nothing has changed. A quick survey of recent titles finds:

Affect in Epistemology: Relationality and Feminist Agency in Critical Discourse, Neuroscience, and Novels by Bambara, Morrison, and Silko.

Disgust and "Normal" Corporeality: How Cultural Ideologies About Gender, Race, and Class Are Inscribed on the Body

If I Were He: Tracing a Female Butch Lineage in American Literature

The Military-Masculinity Complex: Hegemonic Masculinity and the United States Armed Forces, 1940–1963 *(Master's Thesis)*

Contesting Sphere Boundaries Online: Private/Technical/Public Discourses in PCOS Discussion Groups

An Investigation of Interpersonal Disruptions and Secondary Traumatic Stress Among Mental Health Therapists

"I Don't Kiss on the First Date": Symbolic Convergence Through Women's Ritualistic Watching of Reality-Dating Television

Don't Tell Me Who to Blame: Persuasive Effects of Implicit Arguments in Obesity Messages on Attributions of Responsibility and Policy Support

Examining Individual and Joint Sense-Making in Stressful Relational Narratives

Trauma and the Rhetoric of Horror Films: The Rise of Torture Porn in a Post Nine-Eleven World

Library shelves across the country groan under similar effusions, but on such productions are academic careers launched and kept afloat. Meanwhile, academia continues to turn out articles for the "journals." One recent estimate put the number of scientific articles published every year at around 1.8 million.[8]

What was never clear, however, was whether anyone read them. In *ProfScam,* I cited what was known as the "1 percent Rule": Among scientists, half of all technical reading is done in less than 1 percent of the scientific journals. Less than 1 percent of all journal articles have anything more than the tiniest readership, while any given article is probably read by less than 1 percent of the journal's readers. "Need-less to say," remarked one researcher, "the motivation to read appears to fall far short of the motivation to publish."[9]

Recent evidence suggests that little has changed, except for evidence that some articles have literally zero readership. One study at Indiana University concluded that "as many as 50% of papers are never read by anyone other than their authors, referees and journal editors."[10] In other words, fully half the scientific papers *do not have a single reader* after they are published.

It is also possible to measure the influence of such articles by tracing the number of times they are cited by other scholars. Again, the numbers are hardly edifying. The Indiana study found that nearly 90 percent of the published articles are never cited by anyone. As critic Aaron Gordon noted: "That is, nine out of ten academic papers—which often take years to research, compile, submit, and get published, and are a major component by which a scholar's output is measured—contribute little to the academic conversation." Gordon was not surprised.

> Personally, I have witnessed paper presentations on 17th-century Scottish coins, obscure political parties in countries that no longer exist, and the definition of the word "capitalist." I distinctly remember focusing not so much on the hyper-specific nature of these research topics, but how it must feel as an academic to spend so much time on a topic so far on the periphery of human interest. It's not just a few academics, either; these esoteric topics are the rule in academia, not the exception.[11]

The problem of unread academic articles seems likely to get even worse as more go online. As one study concluded: "As more journal issues came online, the articles referenced tended to be more recent, fewer journals and articles were cited, and more of those citations were to fewer journals and articles."[12]

The same phenomenon of unread, uncited research seems to extend to the hard sciences as well. As in other fields, there are simply too many studies being published to be of much use to anybody. "The exponential growth in the number of scientific papers makes it increasingly difficult for researchers to keep track of all the publications relevant to their work," concluded one prominent study titled "Attention Decay in Science." As a result, many articles go unread, uncited, and are quickly forgotten. This attention deficit was becoming a problem, the study noted, because the number of citations an article received "is the main currency of the scientific community, and along with other forms of recognition forms the basis for promotions and the reputation of scientists."[13]

Despite this, the pressure on academics to publish seems to be ratcheting up, even in the humanities. Mark Bauerlein notes that publications in English and foreign languages and literatures (which includes books, essays, reviews, dissertations, editions, notes, etc.) exploded from 13,757 in 1959 to around 70,000 today. The number of journals publishing literary research and criticism more than tripled. And according to the Modern Language Association, more and more literature departments are insisting that faculty members fill those publications. Bauerlein noted that the percentage of departments that consider research more important than teaching has doubled since the 1960s.

Did this result in valuable additions to the store of our literary knowledge? Did it enhance our insight into important works of literature?

Bauerlein conducted a widely discussed investigation of the cost and impact of this flight to research, concluding that most of it was a colossal waste of time, effort, and money. This was, of course, tantamount to heresy: subjecting the latest effusions about symbolism in Melville's short stories to something as crude as a cost-benefit analysis. But it was quite revealing.

Bauerlein began by noting that universities invest a lot of resources in faculty research. Bauerlein examined the production of professors at four public universities, noting that "for example, from 2004 to 2009, University of Georgia English professors published 22 authored or coauthored books, 15 edited or co-edited books, and 200 research articles." Few of them drew any readers at all. "Once those books and essays are published, the vast majority of them attract meager attention from other scholars—for example, of 16 research articles published by University of Vermont professors in 2004, 11 of them received 0–2 citations, three received 3–6 citations, one received seven citations, and one 11."[14]

The hard reality was that the "research" had reached a point of diminishing returns. How many articles can even the most hardened scholar of Thomas Hardy absorb? After decades of mountainous publication, Bauerlein wrote, literary studies had reached a saturation point. "Who can read all of the 80 items of scholarship that are published on George Eliot each year?" he asked. "After 5,000 studies of Melville since 1960, what can the 5,001st say that will have anything but a microscopic audience of interested readers?"[15]

And yet universities continued to divert millions of dollars and thousands of faculty hours into the pursuit of the research grail. This led him to conclude that there "is a glaring mismatch between the resources these universities and faculty members invest and the impact of most published scholarship."

Bauerlein wrote, "Deep down, everybody knows this, but nobody wants to take the first step in reducing the demand."

CHAPTER 5

WHAT DO STUDENTS LEARN
(AND DOES ANYBODY CARE)?

SO AFTER ALL THE money, time, pomp, and circumstance what does a college diploma really mean? What do students learn in their four or five or six years of higher education? Apparently, not much.

In theory, higher education aims to shape and open minds. A liberal education consists of exposing students to a range of ideas, letting them explore the breadth and depth of their world. Ideally, this should include not only of the study of mathematics and science but also of the humanities—history, art, and literature.

But the last three decades have not been kind to the study of what Mathew Arnold called the "best that has been thought and said." The humanities have not only been besieged by hyper-specialization, budget cuts, and the flight from teaching; they have been dismantled from within. Indeed, what passes for the study of literature in many college classrooms today would be nearly unrecognizable to anyone who graduated before the new critical fads came to dominate academia. So it is hardly a surprise that students can graduate from college without ever having read Shakespeare.

But now the problem seems to run much deeper.

In both 1992 and 2003, the National Assessment of Adult Literacy found that most college graduates fell below proficiency in verbal and quantitative literacy. That meant that they could not "reliably answer questions that require the comparison of viewpoints in two different editorials, or compute the cost per ounce of food items."[1] The results were confirmed by the American Institutes for Research in 2006. The grim results were also consistent with Collegiate Learning Assessment Plus, which as previously noted found that 40 percent of students who graduate from college and universities lack complex reasoning skills. This includes an inability to "read a scatterplot, construct a cohesive argument or identify a logical fallacy."[2]

In 2015, the Educational Testing Service released a large scale study that concluded US millennials with a four-year bachelor's degree scored below their counterparts in nineteen of the twenty-one participating countries.[3] The ETS tried to sound an alarm: "A decade ago, the skill level of American adults was judged 'mediocre.' Now it is below even that."

The authors of the ETS report tried to put this in historic context:

In 1983, the National Commission on Excellence in Education issued a report that assessed the quality of education in the U.S. Authors of the report declared that the state of America's education made it "a nation at risk." The report went even further to assert that while the American people "can take

justifiable pride in what our schools and colleges have histori-
cally accomplished and contributed to the United States and
the well-being of its people, the educational foundations of our
society are presently being eroded by a rising tide of mediocrity that threatens our very future as a Nation and a people."
They concluded: "What was unimaginable a generation ago
has begun to occur—others are matching and surpassing our
educational attainments." From our current vantage point, it is
impossible not to see this statement as prophetic.

Despite lavish investment over the last several decades that have
made millennials "our best educated generation ever," the reality is that
"their skill levels are comparatively weak." The report warned against
assuming that "the conferring of credentials and certificates alone is
enough." Despite more young people attending college and getting the
degrees, the study found that adult literacy had declined since 1994,
while math abilities had declined since 2003.*

The results constitute an indictment of our entire educational
system, but they also raise obvious questions about the quality of education that colleges and universities are providing students. Perhaps
most troubling of all was the performance of our "best and brightest,"

---

*The study found that half of America's millennials failed to reach a minimal
level of proficiency in literacy while 64 percent failed to reach a minimum level
in mathematics. The numbers are brutal:

- In literacy, US millennials scored lower than fifteen of the twenty-two participating countries.
- In numeracy, US millennials ranked last, along with Italy and Spain.
- In PS-TRE [Problem Solving in Technology Rich Environments] US millennials also ranked last, along with the Slovak Republic, Ireland, and
  Poland.
- The youngest segment of the US millennial cohort (sixteen- to twenty-
  four-year-olds), who could be in the labor force for the next fifty years,
  ranked last in numeracy along with Italy and among the bottom countries
  in PS-TRE. In literacy, they scored higher than their peers in Italy and
  Spain.

including millennials who had costly four-year degrees. The ETS study found that millennials with bachelor's degrees "scored higher in numeracy than their counterparts in only two countries: Poland and Spain." In fact, the ETS report found that American young adults with bachelor's degrees "scored the same as the young adults with *only a high school education* in three of the top-performing countries: Finland, Japan, and the Netherlands." The declines were "in both comparative and absolute terms."

Meanwhile, even the very best-educated millennials—those with master's or research degrees—"only scored higher than their peers in Ireland, Poland, and Spain." In something of an epic understatement, the authors of the ETS study noted that "there is clear cause for concern."

AN EMPTY CREDENTIAL

Let's concede at the outset that many students find their college years enlightening and enriching. But something is rotten in the state of academia, and it is increasingly hard not to notice. There once was a time when employers could be reasonably certain that college graduates had a basic sense of the world and, as a minimum, could write a coherent business letter. That is simply no longer the case, as some academic leaders appear ready to admit.

Harvard's former president, Derek Bok, mildly broke ranks with the academic cheerleaders when he noted that, for all their many benefits, colleges and universities "accomplish far less for their students than they should." Too many graduates, he admitted, leave school with the coveted and expensive credential "without being able to write well enough to satisfy employers . . . [or] reason clearly or perform competently in analyzing complex, nontechnical problems." Bok noted that few undergraduates can understand or speak a foreign language; most never take courses in quantitative reasoning or acquire "the knowledge needed to be a reasonably informed citizen in a democracy."[4] Despite the massive spending on the infrastructure of higher education, he conceded, it was not at all clear that students actually learned any more than they did fifty years ago.

Indeed, a recent survey of the nation's top-ranked public universities by the American Council of Trustees and Alumni found that only nine of them required an economics course for graduation; just five required a survey course in American history; and only ten required that students take a literature course. Despite the lip service given to "multiculturalism" on campus, the study found that: "Fewer than half required even intermediate study of a foreign language."[5]

This knowledge deficit has been a long time coming. By 1990, the cost of four years at an elite private college had passed the median price of a house in the United States. But a survey sponsored by the National Endowment for the Humanities in 1989 found that a majority of college seniors would flunk even a basic test on Western cultural and historical literacy: 25 percent could not distinguish between the thoughts of Karl Marx and the United States Constitution (or between the words of Winston Churchill and those of Joseph Stalin), 58 percent did not know Shakespeare wrote *The Tempest,* and 42 percent could not place the Civil War in the correct half century. Most seniors were unable to identify the Magna Carta, Reconstruction, or the Missouri Compromise; they were "clearly unfamiliar" with Jane Austen's *Pride and Prejudice,* Dostoevsky's *Crime and Punishment,* and Martin Luther King's "Letter from the Birmingham Jail."[6]

These concerns now seem almost . . . quaint. The fact that college students had huge gaps in their knowledge was old news by the early 1990s. But today the question is no longer whether students have learned specific bodies of knowledge; it is whether they are learning anything at all.

In their widely cited book *Academically Adrift,* Richard Arum and Josipa Roksa concluded that 45 percent of students "did not demonstrate any significant improvement in learning" during their first two years of college. More than a third (36 percent) "did not demonstrate any significant improvement in learning over four years of college."[7]

Traditionally, the authors wrote, "teaching students to think critically and communicate effectively" have been claimed as the "principal goals" of higher education. But "commitment to these skills appears more a matter of principle than practice," Arum and Roksa found.[8] "An astounding proportion of students are progressing through higher education today without measurable gains in general skills," they wrote. "While they may be acquiring subject-specific knowledge, or greater self-awareness on their journeys through college, many students are not improving their skills in critical thinking, complex reasoning, and writing."[9]

But those are precisely the skills that employers increasingly expect from college graduates. A 2013 survey of employers on behalf of the Association of American Colleges and Universities found that 93 percent of employers say that a demonstrated capacity to think critically, communicate clearly, and solve complex problems is more important than a candidate's undergraduate major. More than three-quarters of the prospective employers of new college graduates said they wanted colleges to put more emphasis on such basic skills as "critical thinking, complex problem solving, written and oral communication, and applied knowledge."[10]

TRASHING THE CURRICULUM

So how could we spend so much for so little? The most obvious answer is that colleges and universities frankly don't care whether students learn much of anything. Once again, Harvard's Derek Bok is willing to admit that administrators have few incentives to worry about something as irrelevant as student achievement because student learning can't be monetized and doesn't do anything to advance academic careers. "After all," he writes, "success in increasing student learning is seldom rewarded, and its benefits are usually hard to demonstrate, far more so than success in lifting the SAT scores of the entering class or in raising the money to build new laboratories or libraries."[11]

There are, of course, other factors at work. The dumbing down of elementary and secondary education has made its way to the collegiate level; too many unprepared students are admitted despite their inability to do college-level work. Nearly four out of ten college faculty now agree with the statement "Most of the students I teach lack the basic skills for college-level work."[12] This inevitably contributes to the flight from teaching (few professors want to teach remedial courses) and the overall lowering of standards.

This general indifference to what if anything students learn is embodied in the modern curriculum that enables students to study just about anything, without necessarily learning much at all.

In *ProfScam*, I wrote:

> The university curriculum is the flip side of the academic culture's attitude toward teaching. . . . Indeed, it bears the unmistakable mark of the professorial touch. As absurd as it is, the curriculum keeps the universities well-stocked and the students reasonably pacified, while demanding as little as possible from either students or professors. No other explanation can account for the mélange of incoherence that confronts students at the modern university.[13]

The politics of academia's numbers game virtually dictates the destruction of traditional standards of performance and intellectual integrity. The proliferation of undemanding, unchallenging courses offering high grades is the inevitable by-product of the professoriate's desire to expend as little time and energy as possible on teaching, combined with the imperative of keeping classrooms stocked with warm tuition-paying bodies.

So students making their way through the academic shopping mall of the modern university's curriculum were tempted in the 1990s with options ranging from The Sociology of Sociability (the study of parties) at Vassar to Poets Who Sing at Washington University to Ultimate Frisbee at the University of Massachusetts and Dance Roller Skating at Kent State.[14] Not surprisingly, the curriculum is still littered with such courses. The American Council of Trustees and Alumni recently highlighted the University of Colorado–Boulder's Wops and Dons to Movers and Shakers: The Italian American Experience, and Indiana University's The Fame Monster: The Cultural Politics of Lady Gaga and Vampires, Ghosts and the Gothic in Popular Culture. The report's authors noted that one of the attractions of a course on Lady Gaga is undoubtedly the fact the "the most common grade awarded is an A+."

NOT EXACTLY A SWEATSHOP

The reality is that college students are not expected to work very hard and they respond accordingly. In *Academically Adrift*, Arum and Roksa note that "there is emerging empirical evidence that suggests that college students' academic effort has dramatically declined in recent decades."[15]

As recently as the 1960s, studies found that American college students spent around forty hours a week either attending classes or studying. That time spent learning has fallen drastically. Today, Arum and Roksa write, "full-time college students on average report spending only 27 hours per week on academic activities . . . that is, less time than a typical high school student spends at school."[16]

Researchers Philip Babcock and Mindy Marks looked back on a half century's worth of data, concluding that "in 1961, the average full-time student at a four-year college in the United States studied about twenty-four hours per week, while his modern counterpart puts in only fourteen hours per week. Students now study less than half as much as universities claim to require."[17]

This decline in time spent on study was across the board—in every major field of study and at every sort of four-year college, no matter what their level of selectivity or the sorts of degrees they offered.[18]

In 1961, more than two-thirds of college students (67 percent) reported that they spent more than twenty hours studying. Now only a fifth of students report putting forth that kind of effort. More than a third reported spending less than five hours a week studying for their classes. This limited effort reflected "the emergence of a college student culture focused on social life and strategic management of work requirements." As the pseudonymous author of *My Freshman Year: What a Professor Learned by Becoming a Student* wrote, the "art of college management" involves "controlling college by shaping schedules, taming professors and limiting workload."[19] For most students, this works quite well: They search out undemanding classes with professors who hand out generous grades. But this revolution in leisure time could not have occurred without a change in the overall standards of higher education. As Babcock and Marks concluded, "the observed ten-hour-per-week decline could not have occurred without the cooperation of postsecondary institutions."[20]

The decline and fall of writing illustrates the trend. Arum and Roksa found that fully half of the students in their study's sample "had not taken a single course during the prior semester that required more than 20 pages of writing, and one third had not taken one that required even 40 pages of reading per week." This does not seem to be an isolated problem:

> A national survey of approximately 300,000 college freshmen and seniors in 587 four-year colleges and universities found that while 83% of freshmen reported they had not written a paper during the current academic year that was 20 or more pages long, 51% of college seniors had not done so either.[21]

Even among elite schools, a third of seniors said they hadn't been required to write a lengthy paper (more than twenty pages) at any time in their last year. Even at the top 10 percent of schools in the study, 33 percent of college seniors reported they had not written a paper of this length during their last year of higher education.

The result is a lack of discernible effort among upperclassmen as well as underclassmen. Arum and Roksa note that one in five seniors and freshmen alike "report coming to class 'frequently' unprepared" but that this lack of effort "has had little impact on their grade point averages and often only modest effects on their progress towards degree completion."[22]

HIDING THE DECLINE

In an educational system obsessed with self-esteem and festooned with gold stars, happy faces, and participation trophies for even the most mediocre performances, it is probably not surprising that grade inflation has become rampant in higher education. A 2012 study found that 43 percent of all letter grades are now As. This is up 28 percent since 1960, and up by 12 percentage points since *ProfScam* was published in 1988. Less than 10 percent of the grades awarded in colleges and universities today are Ds and Fs.[23] In academia, nearly everyone is above average. Or at least they are told they are.

How inflated have grades become? Among private colleges, the average GPA has risen from 3.09 in 1991–1992 to 3.3 in 2006–2007.[24] At Harvard, administrators recently admitted that not only is the average GPA now an A-minus, but that A was now the grade most frequently given. Grade inflation has gotten so bad at Harvard that one prominent professor, Harvey Mansfield, has taken to giving his students two sets of grades: the official transcript grade and the grade they deserve—their true, uninflated grade based on the work they actually did. Mansfield argues that the inflated grades don't do the students any favors: "When good grades are easy, people don't become less concerned with grades; rather they become more concerned. Now in order to get into a good graduate school . . . you need to have a near perfect record, and that does induce more stress. You can't find a student who can take a C in stride anymore."[25]

As grades at the elite schools have exploded, less prestigious schools have joined in the race to inflate. Schools considered to be "modestly selective" are grading as generously as the "highly selective" schools did back in the 1980s. Meanwhile, the elite schools continued to pump up their grades. A 2012 study titled "Where A Is Ordinary: The Evolution of American College and University Grading, 1940–2009" concluded that grade inflation had gotten so bad that: "It is likely that at many selective and highly selective schools, undergraduate GPAs are now so saturated at the high end that they have little use as a motivator of students and as an evaluation tool for graduate and professional schools and employers."[26]

The inflation of grades has not, however, been even. For example, at the University of Colorado–Boulder, As and Bs accounted for 73 percent of the course grades awarded in 2007–2008. But as a study by the American Council of Trustees and Alumni found, all courses were not created equal:

> In Applied Math more students actually earned C's than A's, and in Economics under a quarter of students earned A's, while half of the students got an A in English. In the entire School of Education, A's represented 75% of the grades awarded while C's, D's, and F's combined only 5%. The same is true at the University of Wisconsin–Madison, where in the Spring 2013 term, 85% of the grades in the Counseling Psychology program were A's; 3.891 was the average GPA in the Education Department's Curriculum and Instruction courses; and over 64% of grades in Life Sciences Communication were A's. At the same time, A's made up less than a quarter of the grades awarded in Mathematics.[27]

Inevitably some academics have resorted to the usual techniques of denial, insisting that the higher grades reflect a better, smarter, harder-working student body. But this is so absurd that such claims are taken seriously only by a few scattered members of the boards of trustees. Stuart Rojstaczer, a former professor of geophysics at Duke who has studied grade inflation, dismisses the defenses as fiction. "There are no indications that college students are getting better nationally, and some indications that at the end of four years, they know less than a college graduate of the past," he says, citing studies showing that students now study substantially less than in the past.*

Rojstaczer is particularly critical of his old school, Duke, which has become a poster child for grade inflation. For at least four decades, he says, Duke's average GPA has been 0.2 points higher than that of its neighbor, the University of North Carolina at Chapel Hill. A consequence of the easy grades is the lack of motivations for students who realize they can simply go through the motions and still get good grades. He says, "I know this from personal experience. The energy in most of my classes couldn't have lit up a two-watt bulb. The funny thing is that in my student evaluations, students often remarked how energetic my classes were relative to others. I was always amazed by those comments. There must have been corpses instead of students in those other classes. Students simply did not prepare. They did not work. Not

---

*How did it happen? Or as Rojstaczer puts it; "How did we screw up so fast?" He says he put that question to the president of a prominent university. The answer:

1. Faculty cowardice (among some). Many faculty just do not want to argue with students about grades.
2. The quest for good teaching evaluations. I would guess that the correlation between high grades awarded and enthusiastic teacher evaluations is quite high almost everywhere.
3. Political correctness and the mania to support "self-esteem" of students.
4. Precipitous decline of honor codes almost everywhere, so that cheating is rampant.
5. The spread of "spinus dissaperanus," a viral disease that robs university leaders of whatever spine they had before becoming leaders.
6. Governing board failures, due partly to the fact that prospective board members eagerly seek the social status that comes with university board membership.
7. Growing lack of diversity in faculty philosophical views.

all students. But most. The average number of hours Duke students study is eleven per week. That's it. Eleven measly hours a week."

Though Duke's academic grandees exhibit occasional hand-wringing over the watered-down grades, Rojstaczer doesn't think they will touch the problem. "They don't want to do the work," he writes. "They are far more concerned with 'protecting the brand' than with solving substantive problems. As a result, the quality of education at Duke University continues to suffer."

The implications of this inflation for both grades and the value of college diplomas would seem to be obvious. Once the average grade becomes an A, Rojstaczer notes, it will mean that grades will be meaningless. "It also undoubtedly means that we will have severely discounted the value of higher education." He calls grade inflation "the greatest collective failure in education in America over the last twenty years."*

So why has grade inflation become so widespread and ingrained? The fundamental dynamics are relatively simple. Professors don't want the extra work that would come from insisting on higher standards and universities do not want to deal with the blowback that would result from grades that accurately reflected the mediocre work of their students. Given the lack of academic preparation of so many students, honest grading would be a political, public relations, and marketing nightmare. In a sense, colleges have been using the higher grades as a sort of marketing tool to keep their consumer base mollified and reasonably content with the rising price tag. Administrators have discovered that high grades ease the pain of writing out tuition checks.

---

* "One promising recent development is the 'honest transcript' movement. Dartmouth, Columbia, Indiana University, and the University of North Carolina–Chapel Hill have begun to use one or another version of this system, in which next to each grade is the average grade that the particular professor gave to the class. In Texas, legislation has been introduced to require all public colleges and universities to implement an 'honest transcript' system." ("ACTA, Getting What You Pay For?," 2014)

For faculty members, who have worked for decades to minimize the time they have to spend in the presence of undergraduates, inflated grades reduce the hassle and spare them the inevitable visits, interactions, and complaints that would result from handing out Cs, Ds, or heaven forfend, Fs. For members of the professoriate, awarding As for lousy, even illiterate work is actually the better part of valor in the modern academic culture. As Murray Sperber notes, professors who gave out grades that their students deserved would have to be prepared to "answer complaints from students and their parents, inquiries from department heads and deans, requests to appear before various student committees, and even lawsuits."[28]

Not surprisingly, faculty members choose instead to honor the unspoken bargain: "You don't ask much of me, and I won't ask much of you," which Sperber calls the faculty-student "nonaggression pact." This is especially true for junior or non-tenured faculty who teach lower division courses where they are most often likely to encounter students with shaky performance issues. As one department chair noted: "No junior instructor who wishes to gain tenure will flunk out 67 percent in an introductory course."

The result is what the late professor David Berkman called "rampant pandering." In *ProfScam*, I quoted a memo he had sent to faculty members:

> We pander to the ignorance. . . . We pander to student
> laziness—or to the past failures of colleagues to impose a
> challenging quantity of work—so that we pull back the first
> time seniors scream incredulously about the 20-page term
> paper, and in the future avoid ever opening ourselves to this
> reaction again. . . . And, perhaps worst of all, we pander to that
> high school-guidance-counselor-mentality with which so
> many of our students are imbued, which manifests itself as a
> demand that our judgments and our grading be grounded
> more in a superficial, psychotherapeutic support, than on the

professionalism in which the instruction and the kind of program we offer should be based.[29]

In other words, no matter how little they learned, the modern professoriate hands out more gold stars and happy faces.

CHAPTER 6

THE COLLEGE
FOR ALL DELUSION

DESPITE THE EVIDENCE THAT we already have too many students in higher education, many of them attending schools for which they are poorly prepared, the hot new idea among the political class is to double down by pushing for "free college for all."

Adam Green, cofounder of the Progressive Change Campaign Committee, for example, insists that the left needed a "big, bold economic message that tangibly impacts people's lives." And the issue he says that will motivate both young people and their parents to vote is a free guaranteed college education for everyone.[1] Another variation is the increasingly popular notion of having the government guarantee a "debt-free" college education for all.[2]

Not everyone was impressed. "This is exactly the kind of proposal which should make people skeptical of government," wrote columnist James Pethokoukis. "That's right, make no demands on the higher education industry to improve affordability and value. Just open the spigot of taxpayer money to full blast."[3]

That flood of money has already contributed significantly to the exploding cost of higher education; the more "free" money the government has provided, the easier it has been for colleges to raise their tuitions. Research by Stephanie Riegg Cellini and Claudia Goldin suggests that "institutions may indeed raise tuition to capture the maximum grant aid available."[4] Despite this, however, the political attractions of "free" tuition are obvious and were reflected in President Obama's largely symbolic proposal to make community colleges "free" to eligible students. In March 2015, Obama fully embraced the mantra, declaring that "two years of higher education should be as free and universal as high school is today."

The problem with the idea of "free college" is, however, not merely financial. It also reinforces the myth that college is appropriate or even possible for all students. That myth has destructive consequences for both the quality of higher education and for some of the students caught up in what has become a multibillion-dollar hoax.

As unrealistic as the idea of universal college education may be, the idea that everyone should attend college has been embraced by Americans. By 1992, 95 percent of high school seniors said they planned to go on to college, even though half of them lacked even basic ninth-grade math and verbal skills. These aspirations, however, had dramatic real-world consequences. In 1979, fewer than half of high school graduates enrolled in college. By 2012, that number had soared to more than two-thirds, and even with the dumbed-down curricula and inflated grades, many of these students would have a rude encounter with reality.[5]

How bad is it? Of the 1.8 million students assessed for college readiness in 2014, ACT found that only 26 percent met college-ready benchmarks in all four subjects (English, reading, math, and science).[6] Education critic Charles Murray notes that a study of forty-one institutions of higher learning shows that an SAT score of 1180 will give a college freshman a 65 percent chance of maintaining a 2.7 grade point average. But that is a score that only about one in ten eighteen-year-olds could achieve. "So," writes Murray, "even though college has been dumbed down, it is still too intellectually demanding for a large majority of students."[7] Even so, in recent decades, 30 percent of students with C grades in high school and 15 percent with a grade point average of C-minus or lower have been admitted into four-year colleges.[8] That has consequences both for the students and for the institutions, which often have to adjust their standards to the new demographic realities.

One result is that nearly one in five students in four-year institutions and more than half of students in two-year colleges end up in remedial courses.*

FAILURE FACTORIES

To put it bluntly, the push for "college for all" sets up students to fail. While the debate over a "college bubble" often focuses on the costs of student debt for students who have graduated, the reality is

---

*Student aid programs encourage this. Under the law, any student with a high school degree can use federal student aid, Pell Grants, and loans to pay for up to two semesters in remedial classes. As a recent Fordham Institute study noted: "States allow high school graduates to enroll whether they are college ready or not and spend billions on remedial coursework at four-year and *community* colleges." (Andrew P. Kelly, "Big Payoff, Low Probability: Post-Secondary Education and Upward Mobility in America," prepared for the Thomas B. Fordham Institute's Education for Upward Mobility Conference, December 2, 2014)

that somewhere between 40 and 45 percent of students who enroll in college drop out. The dropout rate among lower-income students is much higher. For those students the wage premium for attending college without getting a degree is basically zero.

This is inevitable when unprepared students, pumped up with unrealistic expectations, are fed into a system that is more interested in enrolling them than in giving them an actual education. Even as the number of students who aspire to college has exploded, the evidence suggests that not only are many of them utterly unprepared to do college-level work, they also have no realistic idea of what that even entails. In one survey of high school students in the Chicago area, nearly half agreed with the statement, "Even if I do not work hard in high school, I can still make my future plans come true."[9]

THE GREAT CON JOB

The push for "college for all" has become so ingrained in American education that sociologist James Rosenbaum has compared it to a massive con job. The key to a successful swindle, he wrote in *Beyond College for All,* is to give the "mark" the confidence that "they will gain a valuable reward at very little cost, and then lure them into an easy success strategy." That, unfortunately, describes much of what now passes for high school counseling. Writes Rosenbaum: "Like [a classic confidence scheme], students are promised college for very little effort. Lured by the prospect of easy success, students choose easy curricula and make little effort."[10]

Our obsession with "self-esteem" has come to dominate our educational system so thoroughly that high school students are neither warned of their educational inadequacies nor given reliable information about what the future holds. While high school counselors may not be intentionally misleading students, he writes, the high level of failure in community colleges is a result of high school esteem-ocrats offering "vague promises of open opportunity for college without spec- ifying the requirements for degree completion." At one time, counsel- ors were able to advise certain students that there were alternatives to college. But now, with the emphasis on personal growth and "college for all," writes Rosenbaum, the counselors "do not have to force the students to make tough decisions; they can encourage everyone to at- tend college."

Because the consequences of inflated and unrealistic expectations are not realized until years later, he notes, "high schools are rarely blamed for their graduates' failures in community college." But that is where the seeds of the future failure are planted. As a result, students drift through high school with no clear idea that they need to work harder or take courses that might prepare them for careers they would like to pursue. Many have no idea that their levels of achievement in high school might be relevant to their future plans and see no dire con- sequences for not working hard or getting low grades. So students with poor grades in math and science continue to indulge fantasies of pursuing careers in engineering or medicine.

Many schools go out of their way to avoid disabusing students of their unrealistic plans. Instead of providing a reality check, Rosenbaum notes, counselors convert the conversation "into an opportunity to build self-esteem rather than provide objective information about the world."[11] Instead of information that might lead them in a different di- rection, "many couch their advice in motivational platitudes," taking a warm, fuzzy approach without providing any useful information. Rosenbaum quotes one counselor as saying, "I just try to be soft and gentle with most people. . . . It's not really up to me what these kids could become." Another counselor says, "I counsel them all to believe in themselves." This is even the case when high school seniors "tell me they're going to be a doctor or a lawyer, and their grades in high school have been Cs and Ds. They don't seem to feel that there's any correla- tion between the two." Even then, Rosenbaum writes, counselors avoid blunt honesty. "Rather than deal with the unpleasant task of redirecting students' plans or explaining the need for meeting expectations and criteria for success," he writes, "counselors turn the discussion into a session on personal growth, vaguely soothing the student's ego."[12]

When pressed on the consequences of filling students' heads with unrealistic expectations, many counselors told Rosenbaum that "they have no alternative: they cannot make students confront difficult choices because students will not listen, parents will complain, and counselors themselves lack the authority to influence students' plans." So the result is a surrender of sorts, with the vague hope that things will somehow work out well. One counselor told Rosenbaum that even though he knew a certain student was not academically qualified, "I urged him to send in the application anyway. You know there's no harm."[13]

But of course there is a harm. Higher education is littered with the fallout from the mismatch between expectations and reality.

THE INEQUALITY MACHINE

Throughout this book, I've avoided the use of words like "tragedy," because it seems overblown. But there is something tragic about the false promise of higher education. As Andrew P. Kelly of the American Enterprise Institute wrote, few low-income students are getting degrees, and their economic benefit from their encounter with higher education is negligible, if not actually negative, especially if they take on any debt.

> For far too many disadvantaged high school graduates, access to college is a dead end rather than an on ramp to the middle class. Low-income students often graduate high school unprepared for college-level work, yet all of them are eligible to enroll in college and access federal financial aid. The majority of those who do enroll wind up in remedial courses that they

are unlikely to pass, and many of them wind up with little but debt and regret.[14]

Rather than being the instrument for shrinking inequality (as it so often claims), the modern academy often freezes it in place. Despite billions of dollars spent on K-12 education and massive and aggressive pushes for more "diversity," the educational gap between rich and poor seems to be widening. Research by Martha J. Bailey and Susan M. Dynarski of the University of Michigan finds that the disparity between rich and poor Americans earning bachelor's degrees has grown from a 31 percentage point gap thirty years ago to a 45 percentage point gap in 2012.[15] Those numbers mirror the growing gaps in test scores between rich and poor students. "Everyone wants to think of education as an equalizer—the place where upward mobility gets started," economist Greg J. Duncan told the *New York Times*. "But on virtually every measure we have, the gaps between high- and low-income kids are widening. It's very disheartening."[16]

Despite financial aid, soaring tuition costs create a formidable barrier for many low-income students. Also disheartening is what so many low-income students find when they arrive on campus: institutions that are often more interested in signing them up than in teaching them. The flight from teaching and the dumbing down of the curriculum have a negative effect on all undergraduates, but the implications are especially damaging for students who may fall between the cracks. The lack of structure in the curriculum, Andrew Kelly noted in his study, can lead many first-generation college students "to swirl, taking courses here and there but not making much progress toward a degree." Nor is the approach to teaching suited to ensuring academic success for students on the bubble. Kelly notes that "most PhD-trained professors were never taught how to teach students or assess learning," while higher education's support systems "are usually passive; students get help with academic support or career advising only if they walk into the office which houses those services on-campus." The utterly unsurprising result: "Students who are at risk of dropping out often simply stop showing up to class and are unlikely to take it upon themselves to get the help they need."[17]

As Arum and Roksa note, the failure of colleges to teach much of anything tends to perpetuate the differences between students with different levels of preparation. "These inequalities are largely preserved—or, in the case of African-American students, exacerbated," they write, "as students progress on their journeys through higher education." The failure to ensure that students make academic progress turns "college for all" into a cruel hoax, in which it becomes "little more than a policy designed for warehousing students during the years when they would otherwise face an elevated risk of unemployment and criminal behavior."[18]

FREE COMMUNITY COLLEGES?

All of this is what makes President Obama's proposal for free community college so problematic. Obama's idea was to provide free tuition to as many as 9 million students to attend community colleges at a cost to the federal government of $60 billion, plus another $20 billion from state taxpayers.

If the goal was to address the cost of higher education, Obama had chosen an odd solution. While there is a problem with higher education's being too expensive, community colleges are not a critical part of the problem, since tuition is generally around $3,800 a year. Nor are community colleges necessarily part of the solution.

While too many unprepared students are attending college, the numbers for community colleges are especially brutal. According to the Beginning Post-Secondary Students Survey, more than two-thirds (68 percent) of public community college students took at least one remedial course, and those students generally ended up taking three remedial classes. From there, the numbers get even uglier. A study prepared for the Fordham Institute notes that only about 60 percent of the community college students in remedial classes pass the classes, and just 22 percent of those students go on to pass courses that actually earn credits. Few of these non-college-ready students ever end up getting degrees. Overall, only one out of five community college students goes onto four year-colleges.[19]

If enacted, Obama's proposal would likely result in even more students entering college without sufficient preparation. Richard Vedder notes that this is a perverse result, since the numbers suggest we are already overinvested in higher education, resulting in a third to a half of recent graduates "taking jobs that usually go to high school graduates—they are 'underemployed,' many of them still living with their parents and dependent on parental financial support." Beyond that, the offer of "free" community college education flies in the face of strong evidence that "students do better in college when they have 'skin in the game,' that is, when they have to pay part of the cost."[20]

And, ironically, the proposal would likely make community colleges more expensive. Vedder notes: "[The] past large expenditures for federal student financial assistance, such as the Pell Grant and student loan programs, have contributed importantly to the tuition fee explosion. Community colleges have been less impacted by this, but it is likely the Obama proposal would lead to a fee explosion at the two-year schools."[21]

But if the proposal makes little educational sense, it makes perfect sense as a political ploy. Free stuff makes for good politics, especially when it aligns itself so well with other social/education pressure to get as many warm bodies into higher education as possible.

THE REAL WORLD

All of this is unnecessary. Despite the growing emphasis on getting as many students as possible into higher education, there are more than a few jobs that do not require a four-year bachelor's degree. Ironically, the "college for all" push comes even as employers report shortages in various skilled trades. Many of those jobs can pay more—and provide more stability and even personal satisfaction—than the jobs available to newly graduated BAs. And yet society and the educational system continues to divert students from such trades into institutions of higher education that (1) cost much more, (2) take an inordinate amount of time, and (3) provide little meaningful preparation for any livelihood.

Charles Murray argues persuasively that four years of study may make sense to get a well-rounded liberal education, which would include "a few dozen courses in philosophy, religion, classical and modern literature, the fine arts, classical and modern history (including the history of science), plus acquire fluency in a foreign language and take basic survey courses in the social sciences." But, Murray suggests, only about 10 percent of college students want that kind of an education. "For everyone else," he writes, "four years is ridiculous."

Murray also sees a more insidious consequence of the "college for all" movement. As more and more students have gone to college, "the more stigmatizing the failure to complete college becomes." Not only has that stigma become a huge impediment to students who might be better off choosing a more practical alternative, but it also contributes to the class division in American society. Now that the great majority of the country's smartest people have BAs, he argues, the lack of a degree now is taken to suggest that "you are too dumb or too lazy." Today, to be a mere "high school graduate" is "to label oneself in some important sense as a second-class citizen." Writes Murray: "No amount of protestations of egalitarianism by people who like the current system (i.e., people who do well in an academic setting) will change the reality—a reality fostered by a piece of paper that for most students in most majors is close to meaningless."[22]

In his valuable book *Real Education*, Murray proposed replacing the traditional emphasis on four-year degrees with certification tests—similar to the CPA exam for accountants—that would replace college degrees as signals of competence and tickets of admission. In this alternate universe, employers would rely more on evidence of what applicants know, and "less on where it was learned or how long it took."

"Imagine," he says, "if Microsoft announced it would henceforth require scores on a battery of certification tests for all of its programming applicants." That test would gain "instant credibility for programming job applicants throughout the industry."[23]

As we will see later in this book, that could also spell very big trouble for the status quo of higher education.

PART III

BLOAT

CHAPTER 7

OUR BLOATED COLLEGES

"I READILY ADMIT IT," said E. Gordon Gee, the president of Ohio State University. "I didn't think a lot about costs. I do not think we have given significant thought to the impact of college costs on families."[1]

On one level, Gee's admission was astonishing, but on another, not surprising at all. It is, after all, astonishing for one of the highest paid university presidents in the America to candidly admit that he was indifferent to the amount of spending on his watch. But it is not at all surprising, given the extraordinary bloat that has taken place across the higher education complex in recent years. Gee was merely acknowledging what has become known as academia's law of more.

Gee should know. Prior to leaving to become president of West Virginia University, Gee collected $6,057,615 in salary, bonuses, benefits, and deferred compensation from Ohio State University for the 2012–2013 fiscal year (and, as if that was not a sufficient parting gift, the university also agreed to what was described as a "generous" five-year contract for Gee to serve as president emeritus of Ohio State through 2018).[2] By that point of his career, Gee had been the president of several institutions, including the University of Colorado, Brown, and Vanderbilt.

Gee could be blithe about the costs because the spending—and his generous salary—were floated on an ocean of easy money, grants, subsidies, and of course, student loans. (The average debt of Ohio State graduates who took out student loans was about $26,000 and, according to the Institute for Policy Studies, the debt of OSU students grew 23 percent faster than the national average between 2010 and 2012.)[3]

But Gee was hardly an isolated case.

BUREAUCRATS EVERYWHERE

When confronted with rising costs or, occasionally, proposals to cut back on spending, the higher education complex trots out administrators who insist (1) that their budgets have already been cut to the bone, (2) that all of the spending increases of recent years—no matter how exorbitant or lavish—were absolutely, positively necessary, and (3) that any further cuts will mean the end of education as we know it.* The

---

*American universities have also managed to build up vast cash reserves that are seldom tapped to lower tuition for undergraduates. As the American Council of Trustees and Alumni noted: "Large endowments, however, have not held down the rising sticker price of a college education, a particular barrier to middle-class families that do not qualify for substantial levels of grant aid. To put this in context, 1% of the endowment of the University of Michigan would be enough to cut in-state tuition and fees in half for nearly 13,000 students. At the University of

case is usually made quite loudly, because there are so many administrators to make it.

Even as spending on instruction remained flat, colleges and universities ramped up spending on amenities, facilities, and non-teaching
bureaucrats.* The modern American university is characterized by hot
and cold running administrators of virtually every description, reflecting
the new obsessions and priorities of the higher learning.

What happened? Schools added layer upon layer of staffers who neither taught nor researched. New bureaucracies sprouted and new
titles proliferated. There arose in academia vice-presidents, provosts,
directors, and deans of every description. Even as colleges scrimped
on their education spending per student, academia was adding to the

---

Virginia, over 8,400 students would benefit, at the University of North Carolina,
over 6,100—yet these two schools still managed to raise in-state tuition over five
years by 27% and 30.1%."
*Where does money go? According to the Delta Project's *Trends in College Spend-
ing: 2001–2011*

Sharp declines in education and related spending per student that were
evident during the recession had ended by 2011; however, spending still
declined at the most and least selective institutions (research universities
and community colleges), which fared worse than other four-year
colleges.

- E&R spending per student decreased by roughly 1 percent at public
  and private research universities and community colleges in 2014,
  while increasing by less than 1 percent (or remaining unchanged)
  at nonresearch colleges. . . .
- Four-year institutions generally continued to invest in noninstructional student services while pulling back on institutional support;
  efforts to preserve instructional spending were mixed.
- Only public and private master's institutions and public bachelor's
  institutions boosted average instructional spending per student
  (by roughly 1 percent each); elsewhere per-student spending on
  instruction remained steady or declined.

The share of spending going to instruction also declined at private
institutions and public research universities.

(*Trends in College Spending: 2001–2011*, Delta Cost Project at American
Institutes For Research, July 2014)

ranks of its often generously compensated non-teaching staff.* From 1993 to 2009, according to the US Department of Education, the number of administrators in US universities rose by 60 percent—ten times the rate of growth of the tenured faculty.

The story was played out at schools across the country. By 2012, the number of administrative employees at Purdue University had risen by 54 percent in just a decade—a rate almost eight times the growth of the faculty.[4] Like other schools, Purdue's tuition had risen by roughly 60 percent and budget pressures were squeezing the budgets for the faculty members who were expected to actually teach undergraduates. But as Bloomberg reported in 2012, Purdue was able to find the cash for sixteen deans, eleven vice-presidents, along with six vice and associate provosts. The school had a marketing officer who was paid $253,000, a "chief diversity officer" who made $198,000, and a $313,000 acting provost.

This was, however, not at all unusual. Back in 1988, when I wrote *ProfScam*, the problem of administrative bloat was already evident, as universities hurried to build themselves into research palaces and multiversities. But the ballooning of bureaucracies had only just begun. When the New England Center for Investigative Reporting and the American Institutes for Research looked at the numbers, they found that from 1987 to 2011–2012, universities and colleges added 517,636 administrators and professional employees, *"or an average of 87 every working day* [emphasis added]."[5]

The report found that:

---

*A 2010 study of higher education costs at 198 leading public and private colleges and universities showed a 39.3 percent increase from 1993–2007 in expenditures per student for instruction, a 37.8 percent increase for expenditures in research and service, but a 61.2 percent increase per student for administration. It found that the ratio of faculty and staff positions per administrator has declined at public research universities from 3.5 in 1990 to 2.7 in 2000, and all the way down to 2.2 in 2012. ("Getting What You Pay For?," American Council of Trustees and Alumni, April 2014)

The number of non-academic administrative and professional employees at U.S. colleges and universities *has more than doubled in the last 25 years* [emphasis added], vastly outpacing the growth in the number of students or faculty, according to an analysis of federal figures.

The disproportionate increase in the number of university staffers who neither teach nor conduct research has continued unabated in more recent years, and slowed only slightly since the start of the economic downturn, during which time colleges and universities have contended that a dearth of resources forced them to sharply raise tuition.*

The result was that the ratio of nonacademic staffers to faculty doubled—in American higher education today there are "now two nonacademic employees at public and two and a half at private universities and colleges for every one full-time, tenure-track member of the faculty."

Just as dramatic were the swelling ranks of non-teaching bureaucrats in the central offices of state public university systems, which grew sixfold since 1987, and the number of administrators in them by a factor of more than thirty-four. In the California State University System, the central office alone had a larger budget than three of the system's twenty-three campuses. The University of Connecticut, which has seven vice-presidents and thirteen deans, also boasted thirteen vice, deputy, and associate vice provosts. The vice provost for "engagement" made $275,000 a year. The university's president was paid a half million dollars, but also had a chief of staff who made $199,000 a year. Without any apparent sense of irony, a spokesman for the university insisted that "UConn's administrative structure is an appropriately

---

*"The figures are particularly dramatic at private, nonprofit universities, whose numbers of administrators alone have doubled, while their numbers of professional employees have more than doubled."

sized, comparatively lean operation."[6] The key word here may be "comparative," because excess is often the new normal. Between 1993 and 2007, Arizona State University bloated its administrative ranks by 94 percent. The University of Minnesota layered on an additional thousand administrators in a decade.[7]

As Heather Mac Donald has noted, even as the University of California was being forced to cut back on many of its core programs, one of its campuses nevertheless chose to create a new full-time "vice chancellor for equity, diversity, and inclusion." As she notes, this was on top of "the Chancellor's Diversity Office, the associate vice chancellor for faculty equity, the assistant vice chancellor for diversity, the faculty equity advisors, the graduate diversity coordinators, the staff diversity liaison, the undergraduate student diversity liaison, the graduate student diversity liaison, the chief diversity officer, the director of development for diversity initiatives, the Office of Academic Diversity and Equal Opportunity, the Committee on Gender Identity and Sexual Orientation Issues, the Committee on the Status of Women, the Campus Council on Climate, Culture and Inclusion, the Diversity Council, and the directors of the Cross-Cultural Center, the Lesbian Gay Bisexual Transgender Resource Center, and the Women's Center."[8]

Andrew Hacker and Claudia Dreifus noted that at pricey Williams College (tuition $49,780), 638 out of 913 employees—more than 70 percent—"are doing something other than teaching." Along with a "babysitting coordinator," "queer life coordinator" and "spouse/partner employment coordinator," Williams also reported having "84 athletic coaches, 73 fund-raisers; a 42-member information-technology crew; a 29-person staff at its art museum . . . and 124 in dining services."[9] At Kenyon College, the construction of an elaborate athletics center meant the hiring of a sports information director, sports facilities director, coordinator for lifetime fitness, intramural and club sport coordinator, along with more than forty coaches. "Also," note Hacker and Dreifus, "its sushi bar requires chefs, and the coffee station needs baristas. Meanwhile, Kenyon's philosophy department has to get by with five faculty members."[10]

"In no other industry would overhead costs be allowed to grow at this rate," a 2012 analysis by Bain & Company noted, "executives would lose their jobs."[11] But higher education does not operate like any other industry. In fact, the greater the bloat, the higher the salaries of the top executives of the complex.

College presidents continue to be generously, if not lavishly, compensated. The American Council of Trustees and Alumni found that in 2012, the average university president at forty-nine institutions examined had a base salary of $431,986. As the ACTA report noted, "Generous packages for administrators have a price that may be passed on to students." In some schools those packages are generous indeed. In 2012, three dozen university presidents made more than $1 million a year, according to the *Chronicle of Higher Education*.

Many of the CEO salaries are enhanced by perks including free houses, cars, and lavish expense accounts even as students take on mountains of debt. One president of a large private university made more than $800,000 a year, but also charged the school for antiques, cashmere, $220,000 for the services of a personal chef, $44,000 for alcohol, birthday parties featuring pan-seared foie gras, Beau Soleil oysters, and caviar, as well as first-class tickets for trips abroad, a backyard waterfall, and chauffeurs who spent "much of their time running errands for his wife to jewelers, salons, and dry cleaners."[12] At the time, tuition at the school, American University, was nearly $28,000 a year and students provided more than 90 percent of the school operating budget. When this large living became controversial, the president was punished with a $3.75 million severance package that allowed him to resign from American University rather than be fired.[13]

MULTIVERSITY BLOAT

Much of the bloat has been in pursuit of what Clark Kerr had described as the "multiversity." His vision fired the imagination of the higher education complex because it provided a vision of academia that perfectly matched its ambitions and self-image.

In his 1963 book *The Uses of the University,* Kerr defined the multiversity as "not one community, but several—the community of the undergraduate and the community of the graduate; the community of the humanist; the community of the social scientist; and the community of the scientist; the communities of the professional schools; the community of nonacademic personnel; the community of the administrators."[14]

In other words, I wrote in *ProfScam,* "the multiversity was nothing more than a series of academic villages strung together under a single institutional name." Critics suggested that the new university would be marked by confusion, fragmentation, and indifference to undergraduate teaching. But Kerr's great contribution was to provide the vocabulary for the new leviathan.

One of the clearest signs of an institution's ambition to follow Kerr's vision was the multiplication of academic programs, centers, institutes, and interdisciplinary graduate programs. The case of a single school, the University of Minnesota, illustrates the trend. The University of Minnesota now has nearly three hundred "centers and institutes," each of course with its own director and infrastructure.[15] There are centers devoted to Spirituality and Healing, Minnesota Obesity, and Trans-Disciplinary Tobacco Use. There is a Center for Applied Research and Educational Improvement; Austrian Studies; the Central Minnesota Regional Sustainable Development Partnership; and the Center for Changing Landscapes. Minnesota has separate centers for the History of Information Technology, Child and Family Health Promotion Research, Girls and Women in Sport, Small Towns, Social Media and Business Analytics Collaborative, and so on.

In the new university, academic majors have also proliferated, covering virtually every possible area of interest. A recent study by the American Council of Trustees and Alumni found that universities across the country were bloated with expensive but underused programs. The study found four institutions—SUNY–Binghamton, the University of Delaware, the University of Nebraska, and the University of Vermont—where more than 40 percent of programs each produced fewer than ten graduates. The study found that 182 baccalaureate programs at fifty-two institutions produced not a single graduate in 2011–2012. This included 26 programs at the University of Minnesota, among them Actuarial Science and Technical Teacher Education. "The steady addition of new programs is an immense contributor to costs, and any efforts to reduce costs and enhance productivity must include prioritization and, where appropriate, the closing of programs," the study noted. At some point universities need to prioritize their programs, recognizing that adding extraneous programs results "in a substantial diminution of resources for existing programs," and the "price for academic bloat for all is impoverishment of each."[16]

But even as administrators and programs reproduce like aphids, the most dramatic and costly symbol of academia's addiction to bloat is its ongoing "edifice complex."

CHAPTER 8

ACADEMIA'S EDIFICE BLOAT

"My name is Ozymandias, King of Kings,
Look on my Works ye Mighty, & despair!"

—PERCY BYSSHE SHELLEY

THEY ARE GLEAMING, MASSIVE, expensive, and very much designed to make a statement.

In a post titled "Boy, I Wonder Why College Is So Expensive," blogger Freddie DeBoer marveled at Purdue's magnificent new $98 million, five-story, 338,000 square foot Gleaming Fitness Palace. "It really is lovely to look at," he wrote. "It looks like . . . money."[1] And indeed it did. The new Frances A. Córdova Recreational Sports Center—known as the CoRec—featured "row upon endless row of the latest fitness equipment, the cutting edge in treadmills and rowing machines and stair steppers and arc trainers and ellipticals" complete with built-in televisions and dozens of flat-screens to divert exercisers. Students could also make use of three saunas, two separate indoor running tracks, and a 55-foot climbing wall (not to be confused with the facility's bouldering wall), or play "racquetball in one of the half dozen courts. Or volleyball, or badminton, in spaces designated for those purposes. Or indoor soccer. Or indoor hockey."

For students who might prefer to relax, there are opportunities to schedule massages or visit the demonstration kitchen. "(Yes. A demonstration kitchen. Yes.)," DeBoer wrote. "Or perhaps what you need is a dip in the pool."

> Sorry, not *the* pool. *One* of the pools. The pool in the CoRec isn't the only pool; what kind of cow college do you think this is? The Boilermaker Aquatics Center, located on the other side of the CoRec, holds the competition pool, diving boards, heated diving well, its own locker rooms, etc. No, I'm talking about the CoRec's pool. The fabulous wrap-around pool that is overlooked by the atrium, one described in as having "three lap lanes, 26 person spa, vortex, two water basketball goals, water volleyball and much more." That spa has heated water and a Jacuzzi function. And, yes, you read correctly above: the pool has a vortex area, a feature that creates a downward suction that you can swim against for fitness.

In an inspired bit of flackery, Purdue's press release announcing the opening of the center referred to it as "a student-requested $98 million renovation and expansion of the nation's first general recreation center at a university." Of course few of the students who will be enjoying and/or paying for this colossus can actually be said to have asked for it, given that they were in grade school at the time the plans were laid. But the phrase "student-requested" helped feed the claim that all of this spending is really all *for the kids*.[2]

While critics were already decrying the spending boom, noting that colleges were plunging themselves into debt while driving up the sticker price of tuition, the boom was gathering momentum. By 2003 students at the University of Wisconsin–Oshkosh were getting massages, pedicures, and manicures, "while Washington State University boasts of having the largest Jacuzzi on the West Coast. It holds 53 people."[3]

Other schools had installed state-of-the-art golf simulators, ballrooms, art galleries, and aquariums, complete with live coral reefs. But these paled next to the edifice complex at E. Gordon Gee's Ohio State University:

> Ohio State University is spending $140 million to build what its peers enviously refer to as the Taj Mahal, a 657,000-square-foot complex featuring kayaks and canoes, indoor batting cages and ropes courses, massages and a climbing wall big enough for 50 students to scale simultaneously. On the drawing board at the University of Southern Mississippi are plans for a full-fledged water park, complete with water slides, a meandering river and something called a wet deck—a flat, moving sheet of water so that students can lie back and stay cool while sunbathing.[4]

These stately pleasure domes are seldom devoted to enhancing the academic experience of undergraduates, much less the writing of Shelley or Samuel Taylor Coleridge.* Indeed, few of these spectacular edifices do anything to enhance the actual quality of education that

---

* Perhaps, like Shelley, Coleridge was anticipating the ambitions of American higher education, when he wrote:

  In Xanadu did Kubla Khan
  A stately pleasure-dome decree:
  Where Alph, the sacred river, ran
  Through caverns measureless to man
    Down to a sunless sea.

the school is offering. Instead, they are designed to convince students and their families to sojourn for four (or more) years at an institution that is as undemanding as it is luxurious. Their main effect is to drive up the cost, while doing little or nothing to boost the underlying value of the degrees they confer. As a result, they inflate the bubble by driving the cost of a college degree further out of alignment with the underlying value of that degree.

THE BOWEN THESIS

Unfortunately, the extravagant spending is not a recent phenomenon. In 1980 Howard Bowen laid out his theory about what drove this sort of spending. An economist and former president of Grinnell College, Bowen argued that institutions of higher education will always spend all the money they can possibly raise. He summarized his theory in five rules:

1. The dominant goals of institutions are educational excellence, prestige, and influence.

2. There is virtually no limit to the amount of money an institution could spend for seemingly fruitful educational ends.

3. Each institution raises all the money it can.

4. Each institution spends all it raises.

5. The cumulative effect of the preceding four laws is toward ever increasing expenditure.[5]

Thus we not only got ever-expanding administrative superstructures, we also got the climbing walls, lazy rivers, Jacuzzis, and magnificent new campus structures that have popped up on campuses across the country.*

---

*Bowen's theory was examined empirically by economists Robert E. Martin of Centre College and Carter Hill of Louisiana State University, Baton Rouge—

TAJ MAHALS AND CLIMBING WALLS

Over the last two decades, higher education has embarked on an extraordinary construction binge—doubling spending since 1994 and peaking at a staggering $15 billion in 2006.[6]

In 2012, the *New York Times* again highlighted the Taj Mahal–ing of higher education, as schools spent heavily on "vast expansions and amenities aimed at luring better students: student unions with movie theaters and wine bars; workout facilities with climbing walls and 'lazy rivers'; and dormitories with single rooms and private baths."[7]

All of this spending, the paper noted, was taking place even as institutions were skimping on spending on instruction and students were being asked to carry more costs. "Students," the paper of record noted, "end up covering some, if not most, of the debt payments in the form of higher tuition, room and board and special assessments, while in some instances state taxpayers pick up the costs."

In the years since it began, the edifice boom was embraced by large and small schools alike and there is no sign that it is abating—if anything, excess seems to be piled on top of excess. At NYU, an undergraduate degree runs to more than $180,000 for tuition and fees (but not including books, food, or housing). But that price may still be heading upward as the university plans to spend around $5 billion to expand its facilities over the next two decades. Since that spending plan dwarfs NYU's $2.95 billion endowment, it likely means even higher tuition. In 2011, the school generated more student debt than any other school in the nation.

There is Texas A&M's $450 million renovation to its football stadium, Kyle Field, that will make it one of the loudest—and most costly—stadiums in collegiate sports. By boosting seating capacity from 80,600 to 102,512, Texas A&M has the largest stadium in the SEC.

Department of Economics. They confirmed his thesis: "As hypothesized by Bowen," they found, "revenues tend to drive costs higher in both public and private research universities." (Robert E. Martin and Carter Hill, "Baumol and Bowen Cost Effects in Research Universities" (March 2014); ssrn.com/abstract =2153122 or dx.doi.org/10.2139/ssrn.2153122)

The University of Oklahoma plans to spend $370 million on an upgrade to its Gaylord Family Memorial Stadium, complete with an 8,750-square-foot video board (to be called SoonerVision), 46,000-square-foot "fan zone," and work-out facilities that will feature a 30,852-square-foot "speed enhancement center." The University of California at Berkley spent $321 million upgrading its Memorial Stadium. The Universities of Washington and Michigan also gave their stadiums facelifts for $250 million and $226 million respectively.[8]

The over-the-top spending is not, however, confined to building sports palaces for football. The website Stack.com ran down "17 Insanely Expensive College Athletic Training Facilities" that begins with a description of the University of Oregon's new $69 million, 145,000-square-foot football training facility, "a building that looks more like a futuristic space station than a place where football players gather for meetings and workouts." Besides top-flight workout machines, the facility featured "flatscreen TVs, and even a barbershop— in case of a hair emergency."[9] The website noted the competitive impulse at work in the profligate spending: "Over-the-top training facilities are on the rise at campuses nationwide, and as each school attempts to outdo the others, the price tags attached to these training centers continues to skyrocket."

Oregon's lush facility actually cost less than half of what the University of Colorado was spending on its new athletic training facility—a $143 million, 120,000-square-foot practice center that included "an indoor football field and a 300-meter track. It also features a refurbished aquatics center with new locker rooms, an Olympic sports strength training room and a football locker room that's two and a half times the size of the one the Buffaloes currently inhabit." Not to be outdone, the University of Cincinnati built itself an entire athletic village that caters to the school's football, basketball, and baseball teams. The centerpiece of the $105 million extravaganza is the Lindner Center, "which aside from looking like a spaceship that took a wrong turn, contains locker rooms, offices, hydrotherapy pools and meeting spaces for each of Cincy's sports teams." The list goes on to include the University of Southern California's $70 million John McKay Center, Ohio State's $66.5 million Woody Hayes Athletic Center, the University of Iowa's $69 million Campus Recreation and Wellness Center, UCLA's $50 million Football Performance Center, and the University of Tennessee's $45 million Anderson Training Center.[10]

THE LAW OF EVEN MORE

Universities defend their spending on the amenities as competitive necessities to recruit students to their campuses. At least in the short run, there seems to be some anecdotal evidence that the lavish resort-like comforts are indeed attractive to students and their families, who might not be attracted to a school strictly based on its educational offerings. In the Midwest, for instance, pricey Carleton College opened a $42 million "Center for Creativity." Even if students never use it, explained one administrator, "it will be a useful tool for recruiting."[11] But it all comes at a steep cost.

By and large, colleges were putting the perks on their credit cards in the heady days before the 2008 Recession. In the first three-quarters of 2003, universities had issued $12 billion in bonds, up 22 percent from the previous year and triple what they had borrowed just three years earlier.[12] New Jersey's Ramapo College ran up $281 million in debt, building a new arena, dormitories, and a new business school. The school's debt payments now eat up 13 percent of its budget, and tuition has risen by 30 percent in the last decade.[13]

By 2012, the "decade-long spending binge" had more than doubled the debt levels of more than five hundred colleges and universities rated by Moody's. The enormous $205 billion in debt came at the same time universities were being forced to confront the increasing financial pressures from the recession and the looming student debt bomb. It was also hard not to conclude, as the *New York Times* did in

2012, that the "higher debt payments and other expenses have contributed to the runaway inflation of college costs, and the impact on students is real and often substantial."[14]

Larger and larger portions of university budgets have been diverted to pay the debt service on the lavish spending. At public universities, interest payments rose by 67 percent in the last decade; debt costs rose by 62 percent at private schools. For many of them, a reckoning is in the offing. As a study by Bain & Company found, debt costs were rising twice as fast as the cost of instruction. The Bain report documented the consequences of higher education's pursuit of the "law of more," concluding that "institutions have operated under the assumption that the more they build, spend, diversify and expand, the more they will persist and prosper . . . but instead, the opposite has happened: institutions have become overleveraged. . . . Their long-term debt is increasing at an average rate of approximately 12% per year, and their average annual interest expense is growing at almost twice the rate of their instruction-related expense. In addition to growing debt, administrative and student services costs are growing faster than instructional costs."[15]

From mid-2013 through the end of 2014, Moody's Investors Service downgraded the credit ratings of more than three dozen four-year colleges and universities. Only nine of roughly five hundred institutions received upgrades. In July 2014, Moody's issued a negative outlook for the entire higher education sector.[16]

In other words, the law of more was coming up against Herbert Stein's law, which posits that if "something cannot go on forever, it will stop." But perhaps not before the higher education bubble as a whole bursts.

THE GREAT COLLEGE SPORTS MYTH

Boosters often defend the athletic edifice complexes by arguing that athletic programs pay for themselves. They don't. While college athletics is a $10 billion industry, only about 10 percent of athletic departments at Division I schools break even—and the overall subsidies for the programs have exploded in recent years.[17] It is, in other words, simply a myth that athletics are either a cash cow or that they generally pay for themselves.

Despite the rosy claims that some programs provide support for other programs, Andrew Hacker and Claudia Dreifus wrote, "There's not a single college or university than can count on a revenue stream from their varsity teams." Even in cases where programs net big dollars (such as Texas), they note, "ways are found to use them within the athletics complex (a field house always needs refurbishing.)"[18]

In all of higher education, only twenty athletic programs—all in the so-called Football Bowl Subdivision (FBS)—operated in the black.[19] All of the rest of the 1,083 college sports programs ran deficits, requiring subsidies in the form of general funds, student fees, or government grants. While some football and basketball programs netted profits, those surpluses were generally eaten up by other sports programs— every one of which loses money. The bottom line, according to the NCAA, *is that the average loss among Division I collegiate athletic departments is $11.6 million a year.*[20]

Subsidies for athletic programs have been exploding. *USA Today* reported that in 2012, those subsidies for major-college sports programs in Division I athletics rose by nearly $200 million over 2011 levels.[21]

The NCAA itself noted that money-losing departments were forced to "close the gap through subsidies provided by their institutions." "But," the NCAA added, "at the median Division I school, the athletics budget rose more quickly than the institutional budget, requiring the athletics department to take a larger percentage of institutional funds."

In other words, increasing spending on sports was squeezing out spending on other priorities. "If the trend of athletic spending outpacing institutional spending continues," said NCAA chief financial officer Kathleen McNeely, "institutions will need to be able to justify that spending to the university community and the general public."[22] This will include some of the schools in elite athletic conferences.

In 2009, public institutions in the Atlantic Coast, Big East, Big Ten, Big 12, Pacific-10, and Southeastern conferences were forced to provide an average subsidy of $5.9 million in direct general-fund support and student fees. The average subsidy for other Division I conferences was $9.6 million in 2009. In some cases it was notably higher: Between 2005 and 2009 subsidies rose on average from $12 million to $16 million in the Mid-American Conference.[23]

The only schools to report no subsidies in 2012 were LSU, Nebraska, Ohio State, Oklahoma, Penn State, Purdue, and Texas.[24] Some of the biggest names in collegiate sports had to rattle the tin cup, drawing resources from elsewhere to pay for their programs. Among the losers was the University of Cincinnati, which built itself an entire athletic village. "Cincinnati has racked up wins with its deficits. Its men's basketball team made the NCAA tournament the last three seasons and its football team has played in four consecutive bowl games, including the Orange in 2009 and Sugar in 2010," noted USA Today. "All this while subsidies that the Bearcats athletics department receives, not adjusted for inflation, have nearly tripled since 2004–05, its final year in Conference USA."[25] Arizona State, a program in the elite Pacific-12, "fell more than $5.7 million short of covering its expenses—the fourth consecutive year in which it has had an overall annual operating deficit." Some schools had even larger deficits. Rutgers's athletic programs, for example, ran up a $28 million deficit in 2012, following a $28.5 million deficit in 2011. The red ink was covered by institutional funds and student fees. Even powerhouse Michigan reported receiving a small subsidy.

But these are the high-profile programs. For lesser programs, the picture is uniformly bleak, at least from a bottom line point of view. Not a single Division II or III program generates more revenue than it spends. A recent NCAA report found:

- The median cost for Division II institutions with football to subsidize their athletic departments was $4.8 million. At schools without football, the median cost to subsidize athletics was $3.8 million.

- The overall cost to institutions of running a Division II athletics program with football (the difference between generated revenues and expenses) has grown 103.4 percent through the past decade. It has jumped 92.5 percent over the same time frame for schools without football.[26]

The attraction of sports can hardly be gainsaid, and I speak here as a fan of both college football and basketball. The annual NCAA men's basketball tournament is justifiably one of the nation's most popular (and well-funded) sporting events. For colleges, especially those with impressive athletic pedigrees, the programs not only provide marvelous spectacles but also give students a sense of community and alumni a reason to feel attached to and therefore generous to their alma mater. The identity of some institutions is indissolubly tied to their athletic teams (Roll Tide, Fighting Irish, Hoosiers), which also provide the schools a national profile that even the best biology department could never generate.

But the role of sports in higher education raises persistent and nagging questions not just about costs, but also about priorities and the degree to which universities will undermine their core missions to field winning teams. None of these questions are new, but the financial pressures on higher education—and on students—give them a new urgency. At many top universities, athletic spending has grown much faster than their instructional spending, and many of them have passed on the costs directly to students. As the American Council of Trustees and Alumni noted, student athletic fees have risen sharply in recent years "by as much as 413.3% at the University of California–Santa Barbara and 318.3% at Auburn University."[27]

Meanwhile, a study by the Delta Cost Project titled *Academic Spending Versus Athletic Spending: Who Wins?* found that Division 1 schools now spend *three to six times* as much per capita on athletes as they do on non-jock students and that spending on sports was growing at least twice as fast as spending on academics on a per-capita basis.[28] For anyone who has watched the growth of college sports, this should not come as a surprise, but the numbers are nevertheless revealing.

At top-tier schools—those with teams that compete in the Football Bowl Subdivision (FBS)—the median spending per student for academics was less than $14,000. But at these same schools, the Delta study found, the median spending was $92,000 per athlete in 2010. "Overall," the study found, "median academic spending per full-time student in the other Division I subdivisions was about $11,800 in 2010, while athletic spending per athlete ranged from $37,000 to $39,000." The 2008 Recession changed very little. The Delta study found that of the three subdivisions of the NCAA's Division I, "only the FBS reined in escalating athletic spending per athlete in 2010; nevertheless, athletic subsidies per athlete continued to increase in all subdivisions despite these financial constraints."[29]

The Delta report noted that "very few" Division I athletic departments were self-funded and that most relied on subsidies from institutions and students. But the study noted that the biggest subsidies per athlete came in the second-and third-tier programs that had the lowest actual total spending per athletes. These were generally schools that could not count on revenue from lucrative broadcast deals or bowl games. "Without access to other large revenue streams," the Delta study found, "these programs have increasingly turned to their institutions to finance additional athletic spending."[30]

The result is that runaway athletic spending not only further squeezes, but also continues to drain resources from other parts of the university. As an ACTA report "Getting What You Pay For" noted: "More broadly, athletic spending has a negative impact on institutions' abilities to grow in areas pertinent to their academic mission." Investing adequately in undergraduate teaching (or even research) "can be difficult when the highest paid state employee is a school's head football or basketball coach—as was the case in 2011 in Oklahoma, Connecticut, and Maryland."[31]

PART IV

JUNK
SCHOLARSHIP,
HOAXES, AND
SCANDALS

CHAPTER 9

DOES THE EMPEROR HAVE ANY CLOTHES?

FOR SEVERAL MONTHS IN 2010, a scientist named Ike Antkare was one of the most prominent academic scientists in the world. The author of 102 academic papers, including one on "Developing the Location-Identity Split Using Scalable Modalities," Antkare quickly became one of the most widely cited scientists of modern times. As measured by Google Scholar and a program that tracks how often a researcher is cited by others, Antkare ranked twenty-first in the world—behind first-place Sigmund Freud, but ahead of Albert Einstein, who ranked thirty-sixth. "Best of all," a commentator later noted, "in regards to the [citation index], Ike Antkare is in sixth position, out-classing all scientists in his field (computer science)."

Computer scientist Cyril Labbé cited the numbers in declaring that Antkare had become one of the "great stars in the scientific firmament."[1]

The only problem was that Antkare did not exist. He had been invented by Labbé, who also fabricated all of the 102 fake academic papers, using a computer program that had been designed to produce scientific-sounding gibberish.

As Labbé explained, the computer program known as SCIgen "is an automatic generator of amazing and funny articles using the jargon of the computer science field." The program also exposed the soft underbelly of academia. Since published research is the coin of the realm in academia—the essential currency of reputation, prestige, and tenure—the integrity of the process of publications goes to the heart of the academic enterprise. With the explosion of academic journals and the increasing pressure on academics to publish anything, anywhere, skeptics began to wonder how much of what was being published was simply junk scholarship? How reliable were the claims of rigorous "peer review" that underpinned the research culture? How much of the impenetrable jargon was actually gibberish in fancy clothes?

In 2005, three students at the Massachusetts Institute of Technology (MIT) created their own test. Computer science graduate student Jeremy Stribling and two colleagues, Daniel Aguayo and Maxwell Krohn developed SCIgen, a computer program designed to create nonsense articles. Their goal was to create "maximum amusement" by generating ludicrous papers and attempting to get them accepted at international science conferences. Indeed, in 2005, Stribling and his coauthors succeeded spectacularly. Their utterly bogus paper, "Rooter: A Methodology for the Typical Unification of Access Points and Redundancy," was accepted for the Ninth World Multi-Conference on Systemics, Cybernetics and Informatics (WMSCI).[2]

This was hardly the first hoax that embarrassed academia. And it would not be the last.

THE HOAX

On May 18, 1996, the front page of the *New York Times* carried a remarkable story: The high-profile journal *Social Text* had published a lengthy postmodernist critique of science, unaware that the whole thing was a parody, a complete spoof of academia's "self-indulgent nonsense."[3]

The article, written by a physicist named Alan Sokal, was "a hodgepodge of unsupported statements, outright mistakes, and impenetrable jargon," wrote the editors of *Lingua Franca,* the journal that exposed the prank.[4] Somehow the editors of *Social Text,* the fashionable and oh so au courant journal of postmodernist thought, had been duped into publishing an article replete with "unreadable prose, mistaken claims about scientific theories, and a general failure to give the scientific method its due." Filled with references to "hip theorists" like Jacques Derrida, it was "full of nonsense and errors." But it had been published nonetheless.[5]

Hilarity ensued as the implications of the prank became clear, not least because it seemed to confirm suspicions that beneath the academic gibberish lurked . . . well, just gibberish. There was, in fact, no there there.

Sokal explained that he had resorted to the hoax/parody for what he called a "simple pragmatic reason."

The targets of my critique have by now become a self-perpetuating academic subculture that typically ignores (or disdains) reasoned criticism from the outside. . . . But how can one show that the emperor has no clothes? Satire is by far the best weapon; and the blow that can't be brushed off is the one that is self-inflicted.[6]

Deploying the full panoply of post-structuralist jargon, he submitted a paper titled "Transgressing the Boundaries: Toward a Transformative Hermeneutics of Quantum Gravity."[7] In the article, Sokal wrote that "'postmodern science' has abolished the concept of objective reality." As he later pointed out: "Nowhere in all of this is there anything resembling a logical sequence of thought; one finds only citations of authority, plays on words, strained analogies, and bald assertions." But he struck all the right political notes, insisting that in order for science to be "liberatory," it had to be "subordinated to political strategies."

But, Sokal wondered, was it possible that the academic rock stars would not realize that he was writing a parody? Would they really accept his stew of nonsense and spoofery as a legitimate contribution to critical theory?

Yes, they did.

Afterward, the author of the hoax could hardly conceal his incredulity. Throughout the article, he had used "scientific and mathematical concepts in ways that few scientists or mathematicians could possibly take seriously." But even more surprising (at least to Sokal) was "how readily they accepted my implication that the search for truth in science must be subordinated to a political agenda, and how oblivious they were to the article's overall illogic."

The obvious implication was that because the editors of *Social Text* liked the political agenda and conclusions, they felt "no need to analyze the quality of evidence, the cogency of the arguments, or even the relevance of the arguments to the purported conclusion." This suggested, Sokal wrote, that "some fashionable sectors of the American academic left have been getting intellectually lazy."

Sokal later published an annotated version of the parody article, in which he pointed out the errors, incomprehensibility, and illogic of the statements in the article. "I am very proud of this sentence," he wrote in one note, "which makes utter nonsense sound plausible." In another note he writes that he was inspired by a quote from Derrida "to produce . . . a perfectly crafted crescendo of meaninglessness."

The physicist explained that he had to work carefully so as not to be caught out and so leavened his nonsense with lavish citations of fashionable academic names, shamelessly flattered the editors, and of course parroted their ideological and political points of view. Because he worried that some of his scientific colleagues might believe he was actually serious, he later wrote:

> One of my worries when I wrote this article was that some physicists and mathematicians . . . might conclude that "this time Sokal's really gone mad." To avoid this fate, I sprinkled throughout the article some assertions that are *so* preposterous that no physicist—even one who had already gone mad—could possibly have invented them with a straight face.[8]

One example of his intentional absurdity was his citation of the New Age concept of the "morphogenetic field," which he said "constitutes a cutting-edge theory of quantum gravity." The connection, wrote Sokal, was "pure invention. No competent physicist or mathematician would fail to recognize the spoor." But, wrote Sokal, "the editor of *Social Text* felt comfortable publishing an article on quantum physics without bothering to consult anyone knowledgeable in the subject."

Some defenders of the journal's editors lashed out at Sokal, claiming "that a right-wing campaign was under way to discredit the social critique of science, or that know-nothing scientists were misrepresenting the work of the humanities." But the hoax was no right-wing plot. Sokal was himself a man of the left; he had once taught math in Nicaragua when the Sandinistas were in power. And even left-leaning commentators ridiculed the way *Social Text* had been taken in by the hoax.

Writing in *The Nation*, Katha Pollitt had some good advice for the editors: "When one has been duped so incontrovertibly and so publicly there's only one thing to say: Is my face red!"[9] The editors did not take her advice. Instead, their reactions were hurt feelings, indignation over the supposed ethical breach, ideological blowback, and an altogether insufficient amount of embarrassment.

In other words, the usual academic response to criticism/exposure.

THE WHISTLEBLOWERS

But as amusing as such stories were, they did not answer the question: Were the hoaxes aberrations or evidence of a deeper rot? Jeffrey Beall was determined to find out.

An academic librarian at the University of Colorado in Denver, Beall had become increasingly suspicious about the explosion of new academic journals. While many of them boasted titles with words like "global" and "international," Beall told *Nature*, he became fascinated with the fact that so many of the emails he got from the new journals were riddled with grammatical errors. He suspected that many of them were what he called "predatory publishers," who preyed upon the obsessive desire of academics to publish, but had weak or nonexistent standards.[10]

Beall became a one-man watchdog, creating a blog cataloging the hundreds of publishers whose academic journals seemed questionable. At the same time other skeptics continued to test the academic publishers. In 2009, a graduate student at Cornell submitted another fake computer-written article to *The Open Information Science Journal*. Philip Davis, a graduate student, and Kent Anderson, executive director of international business and product development at *The New England Journal of Medicine,* wanted to see whether the journal would "accept a completely nonsensical manuscript if the authors were willing to pay." It did. For a mere $800, publisher Bentham Science Publishing, told the authors, it would publish the fake paper. The two authors promptly withdrew it and the editor of the journal later resigned.[11]

Echoing some of the reaction to Sokal's hoax, the director of publications for the publisher lashed out at the whistleblowers, telling *Nature* in an email that "submission of fake manuscripts is a totally unethical activity and must be condemned." The publisher also insisted (in the face of rather obvious and dramatic evidence to the contrary) that "a rigorous peer review process takes place for all articles that are submitted to us for publication. Our standard policy is that at least two positive comments are required from the referees before an article is accepted for publication."[12] He insisted that these things had happened in this case as well, although obviously he was unable to explain how the reviewers failed to note that the paper was computer-generated gibberish.

Worse was yet to come. Jeffrey Beall told *Nature* that the problem seemed to be getting worse. "2012 was basically the year of the predatory publisher," he said. "That was when they really exploded." Not surprisingly, Beall is unpopular with many academic publishers, who accused him of exaggerating the problem. To determine how bad the problem really was, someone would have to run a large-scale test of the standards of the journals—not just a Sokal-like experiment with a single journal, but a test that would involve hundreds of academic journals.

And that is precisely what journalist John Bohannon did in 2013.

THE STING

Like Sokal, Labbé, and the MIT students before him, Bohannon set out to create "credible but mundane" scientific papers filled with errors so obvious that any genuine peer review would recognize them as "flawed and unpublishable." Since he planned to submit the fake papers to hundreds of publications, he wanted the papers to be roughly comparable. "So," he wrote in *Science,* "I created the scientific version of Mad Libs."[13]

To ensure that they would be utterly bogus, he sought help from molecular biologists at Harvard to pre-review the papers. The scientists helped Bohannon "fine-tune the scientific flaws so that they were both obvious and 'boringly bad.'" Concerned that his native-sounding English might give him away, Bohannon used Google to translate all of the papers into French "and then translated the result back into English," which gave them the "idiom of a non-native speaker."

He also generated fictitious author names, such as Ocorrafoo M. L. Cobange, "by randomly permuting African first and last names harvested from online databases, and then randomly adding middle initials." Bohannon then "randomly combined Swahili words and African names with generic institutional words and African capital cities," to come up with fictional institutional affiliations.

Bohannon's sting involved sending out 10 fake papers a week. By October 2013, the results were in: 157 journals had accepted a fake article for publication; 98 had rejected the paper. "Of the 255 papers that underwent the entire editing process to acceptance or rejection, about 60% of the final decisions occurred with no sign of peer review," Bohannon wrote. "Of the 106 journals that discernibly performed any review, 70% ultimately accepted the paper."

The results were an indictment of the publishers, but also a vindication of Jeffrey Beall. "The results show that Beall is good at spotting publishers with poor quality control," Bohannon wrote. "For the publishers on his list that completed the review process, 82% accepted the paper."

NO, THEY HAVEN'T

Given the importance of academic publishing for higher education, the Bohannon sting should have been a fire bell in the night for academia. But has academia cleaned house? Apparently not.

In the years since its creation, the paper-writing computer program SCIgen has been made available for free downloads and its nonsense papers have continued to show up at various conferences. In 2014, Cyril Labbé informed publishers Springer and IEEE that they had published more than 120 papers that had been written by computers rather than actual human beings.

Labbé developed software that spots the gibberish, but publishers continued to be taken in by the hoaxes. As *Nature* reported:

> Over the past two years, computer scientist [Labbé] has catalogued computer-generated papers that made it into more than 30 published conference proceedings between 2008 and 2013. Sixteen appeared in publications by Springer, which is headquartered in Heidelberg, Germany, and more than 100 were published by the Institute of Electrical and Electronic Engineers (IEEE), based in New York. Both publishers, which were privately informed by Labbé, say that they are now removing the papers.[14]

This is not to suggest that a majority—or even a large minority—of academic papers are actual frauds. But given how many academic papers are published every year in obscure journals and how few of them are read by anyone, it is frankly anybody's guess how many are merely gobbledygook.

Skepticism seems warranted.

CHAPTER 10

A SCANDAL RECONSIDERED

IN THE FALL OF 2009, the academic counselors for football players at the University of North Carolina at Chapel Hill knew they had a problem, a huge one.

Many of the athletes were woefully unprepared and/or unmotivated for academic work, much less course work at an elite school like Chapel Hill. Some of them read at an elementary school level and many struggled to maintain a grade point average that enabled them to remain eligible to play. But for years the university was able to finesse the problem.[1] Until now.

In November 2009, the academic counselors put together a succinct slide presentation for the football coaches.[2]

WHAT WAS PART OF THE SOLUTION IN THE PAST?

- We put them in classes that met degree requirements in which
  - They didn't go to class
  - They didn't take notes, have to stay awake
  - They didn't have to meet with professors
  - They didn't have to pay attention or necessarily engage with the material

How did this work? The slide presentation explained the courses that the football players had been taking:

- AFAM/AFRI SEMINAR COURSES
  - 20–25 page papers on course topic
  - THESE NO LONGER EXIST.

Lest the magnitude of this be lost on the coaches, the counselors also displayed the grade point averages of their players in the bogus classes compared to the grades they were getting in other classes.

Fake classes 3.61, compared with average GPA of 1.917 in other classes

---

The immediate crisis was triggered by the planned retirement of a woman named Deborah Crowder, who was a secretary in the Department of African and American Studies (AFAM). For years Crowder had presided over the classes that required no attendance, no actual instruction, and no faculty involvement, investigators later found. The classes required only a single paper, which was graded by Crowder, who freely handed out As and Bs, investigators later found, "with little regard for the quality of the student's work." This was actually an understatement, since many of the papers were either plagiarized or packed with "fluff."*

Now, however, Crowder was leaving and the academic counselors worried that UNC's vaunted student athletes would no longer be getting the grades they needed to remain eligible. One of the counselors warned the school's football operations coordinator to make sure that they got their homework in before someone other than Crowder graded them.

> Ms. Crowder is retiring at the end of July . . . if the guys papers are not in . . . I would expect D's or C's at best. Most need better than that. . . . ALL WORK FROM THE AFAM DEPT. MUST BE DONE AND TURNED IN ON THE LAST DAY OF CLASS.

As it turned out, the academic counselors need not have panicked, because the fake paper classes continued at UNC even after Crowder's departure, according to the Wainstein report.

But the full extent of the use of the fake courses wouldn't be known for years. In 2013, the fake courses resulted in criminal charges against department chair Julius Nyang'oro, charges that were later dropped in partial exchange for his cooperation.

The scam had gone on for eighteen years, involving hundreds of courses, and thousands of students. And when it was finally exposed, administrators at UNC insisted they were shocked! shocked! to learn that something of this magnitude had been going on.

---

* The following account is based largely on the extensive investigative report by Kenneth L. Wainstein, A. Joseph Jay III, and Colleen Depman Kukowski, of the law firm Cadwalader, Wickersham & Taft LLP on behalf of the university: "Investigation of Irregular Classes in the Department of African and Afro-American Studies at the University of North Carolina at Chapel Hill," October 16, 2014. It will hereafter be referred to as the Wainstein report.

DUKE, STANFORD, AND HARVARD, TOO

The University of North Carolina is far from the only school to experience academic cheating. Stories of schools pampering student athletes are legion, and even elite schools have seen large-scale breakdowns of honor codes.

In 2014, Duke launched an investigation into alleged cheating in its Computer Science 201 class, a class that enrolled more than two hundred students. In early 2015, a letter from Stanford provost John Etchemendy about widespread cheating roiled the campus. One faculty member, the provost wrote, "reported allegations that may involve as many as 20 percent of the students in one large introductory course."[3]

Like other campuses, Stanford was also known to steer athletes toward notoriously easy classes, at one point providing them a list of undemanding, high-grading courses. The closely guarded list included Beginning Improvising and Social Dances of North America III. The classes, one student athlete told the student newspaper, the *Stanford Daily*, were "always chock-full of athletes and very easy As."[4]

Confronted with the existence of the easy-course list, some Stanford faculty defended the practice because they believed that students athletes should, indeed, get special handling. The professor who taught Social Class, Race, Ethnicity, Health—one of the courses highlighted on the list given to the athletes—argued that "(Stanford) accommodates athletes in the manner that they accommodate students with disabilities."[5]

One of the highest profile cheating cases involved Harvard, where dozens of students were caught up in a cheating scandal involving one of the school's notoriously undemanding courses. In 2013, Harvard began investigating reports that nearly half of the 279 students enrolled in Introduction to Congress had plagiarized answers on the final take-home exam. As the *New York Times* later reported, the scandal "was a heavy blow to sports programs, because the class drew a large number of varsity athletes, some of them on the basketball team."[6]

Many of those athletes felt they had been caught in the academic equivalent of bait and switch. The government class, taught by Professor Matthew B. Platt, had a reputation for being stress-free and highly graded. One student later quoted the professor telling students: "I gave out 120 As last year, and I'll give out 120 more." But suddenly, they complained, the course became more difficult, especially the take-home exams. Students complained that "many of the exam questions were designed to trick you rather than test your understanding of the material," while another wrote that the course "went from being easy last year to just being plain old confusing." Many of them turned for help to the teaching assistants who "readily advised them on interpreting exam questions." The results in many cases were answers that were identical, including even typos, triggering the cheating investigation.[7]

But what set the University of North Carolina scandal apart was both its scope and its extraordinary duration.

WHAT SORT OF SCANDAL?

After the UNC story broke, it was widely described as the worst-ever scandal of its sort in the modern history of higher education. This is both hyperbole and unfair. It is far more accurate to say that what came to light at UNC was only the worst scandal that was *actually discovered*.

Critics have also debated whether it was an academic scandal or a collegiate athletic scandal. In reality it was both, but also something larger: It was a scandal that cut to the heart of the culture of higher education. The chancellor of Chapel Hill, Carol Folt, seemed to acknowledge as much when she said "I think it's very clear that this is an academic, an athletic, and a *university problem*."[8]

UNC's scandal cast an unflattering light on the role of college athletics in the modern university. But the UNC scandal suggests that athletic scandals may not simply be an isolated or a one-off problem.

Indeed, a *majority of the students who benefited from the fraudulent "paper" courses were not athletes.*[9] So something else was happening there; and for critics of higher education, much of it had a familiar feel: the chronic grade inflation; the mismatch of students and schools; the unspoken bargain between students and faculty; the obsession with diversity and the burgeoning bureaucracy of nonacademic "helpers"; and perhaps most striking of all, the disconnect (at best) of the university's administration from what was actually happening in the curriculum, academic departments, and classrooms of its campus.

The fake classes at UNC went on for nearly two decades, and word spread throughout the campus that they provided high grades for little or no effort. And yet little or nothing was done about it. An investigative report later determined that Deborah Crowder had not acted alone: Her plan to help student athletes and other underprivileged students escape the rigors of actual college work was actively supported by "a network of like-minded women in various roles on campus who took it upon themselves to support those students who were struggling with school." These advisers knew what was going on. They "knew about the paper classes; they knew that Crowder controlled enrollment; and they often referred academically-challenged students to Crowder for placement in those classes."[10]

But the full network of enablers extended far beyond the group of "like-minded women." It also included coaches, tutors, academic advisers, and other faculty members who found it convenient for themselves, and as a way to lighten the burden on some students, and administrators who appeared to have worked heroically to ignore what was happening on their campus. Ultimately, it is hard to come up with more dramatic evidence that universities are not focused on undergraduate learning than the area of student athletics—a term that is an ironic oxymoron at many universities.

AN OPEN SCANDAL

Despite the ritual professions of indignation and surprise, the reality is that scams involving student athletes are a scandal in plain sight. In January 2015, former Tar Heel women's basketball player Rashanda McCants, the sister of former men's star Rashad McCants, and football player Devon Ramsay filed a lawsuit against the school alleging that "the NCAA's history is replete with examples of student-athletes receiving far less than the valuable academically sound instruction they were promised and for which they contracted with member schools." The suit claims that the NCAA has known for decades that "academic fraud is pervasive among its member schools and that the NCAA's initial and ongoing eligibility requirements do little to ensure academic success (particularly for student-athletes in need of remediation) and even incentivize academic fraud."[11]

The lawsuit could pose a significant challenge to collegiate athletics, especially because the process of discovery could be quite messy and the reality behind the "student athlete" is widely known. In order to keep teams well stocked with athletes who can compete on the national stage, schools routinely admit students who are not remotely able to do college-level academic work. This inevitably sets many of them up to fail, but the payoff for the bottom line is simply too great. As the lawsuit against UNC notes, the NCAA pulled in "$913 million in total revenue in fiscal year 2013, more than two-thirds of which was derived from the 'March Madness' basketball tournament."[12] UNC's role in the all of this was considerable.

The lawsuit noted that in 2010, TBS and CBS agreed on a fourteen-year, $10.8 billion broadcast deal for the NCAA tournament. As a result, from 1992 to 2011, revenues from March Madness exploded from approximately $143 million to more than $750 million per year. "This growth was at least partially attributable to the success of UNC's athletic program," the lawsuit noted, especially since the men's basketball team won three times in 1993, 2005, and 2009—and went to the national semifinals on five other occasions.[13]

With a payoff that huge, why not admit students who were academically unprepared . . . or even students who could not read at all?

One study of Chapel Hill athletes found that 60 percent of them could only read between fourth- and eighth-grade levels. Worse yet, some read below a third-grade level. In 2014, Mary Willingham, a former academic adviser to UNC athletes, told CNN that she once had to work with a basketball player who could neither read or write. But, she said, he was not an anomaly. Willingham said that one "student athlete" was not able to read polysyllabic words, so she had to help him sound out words like *Wis-con-sin*. "So what are the classes they are going to take to get a degree here? You cannot come here with a third-, fourth- or fifth-grade education and get a degree here," she told CNN. The network reported that Willingham—who worked at UNC–Chapel Hill from 2003 to 2010—"admits she took part in cheating, signing her name to forms that said she witnessed no NCAA rules violations when in fact she did. But the NCAA, the college sports organizing body, never interviewed her. Instead, it found no rules had been broken at Chapel Hill."[14]

In the wake of the UNC academic scandal, the student newspaper, the *Daily Tarheel,* declared bluntly: "For better or for worse, student-athletes are not like most students, especially those competing in men's basketball and football."[15] That is certainly true not just for UNC, but for schools around the country.

The same CNN report that quoted Willingham reported that data they had collected through open records requests from schools across the country showed a "staggering achievement gap between college athletes and their peers at the same institution." While experts suggested that an SAT score of at least 400 on the critical reading or writing test was necessary for college-level work, the report found many athletes were admitted with scores in the 200s and 300s on the SAT critical reading test, "a threshold that experts told us was an elementary reading level and too low for college classes." And while academic experts said the threshold for college-level work was a score of 16 on the ACT, "we found some students scoring in the single digits, when the highest possible score is 36 and the national average is 20."[16]

WHAT HAPPENED AT UNC–CHAPEL HILL

The scandal at UNC–Chapel Hill grew out of a kind of corruption peculiar to institutions like the academy, compounded of "good intentions," a commitment to diversity and equity, compassion, and professional self-interest.

According to the Wainstein report, the most thorough investigation of the eighteen-year-long fake courses, the architect of the fraud was Deborah Crowder, who saw herself as a virtual Mother Teresa of academic opportunity, especially for struggling athletes. Crowder was a passionate sports fan who "was occasionally unable to come to work for a day or two after the Tar Heels lost a basketball game." But her motivations extended beyond simply helping out the sports teams. The Wainstein report noted that "Crowder was known throughout campus as a 'do-gooder' who was always willing to help out a student who was struggling. This compassionate approach derived from her firm belief that Chapel Hill should be a school that welcomes and supports students of all types—and 'not just the best and the brightest.' "[17]

For years, she was prevented from "cutting corners" for the students because her department was run by faculty members who tried to maintain some semblance of academic standards. That all changed with the appointment of a new chair, Professor Julius Nyang'oro. In something of an understatement, the report describes Nyang'oro's administration of AFAM as "more hands-off than his predecessors." In reality, he was an absentee professor who essentially turned the department over to its secretary, Deborah Crowder. "He acquiesced, in part," the report found, "because he was happy to cede decision-making authority to her, especially since his busy consulting and personal schedule kept him away from campus for long periods of time."[18]

Moreover, he shared her "sympathy" for students who were unable to do traditional college work. According to the Wainstein report, "Crowder took advantage of the more permissive environment under Nyang'oro and started to implement a plan to offer classes that awarded high grades with little regard for the quality of a student's work."[19] In effect, they created a "shadow curriculum" which operated from 1993 to 2011 by creating "paper" classes that were taught on an independent study basis. Later they created lecture-style classes, which were similarly fake.

GUTS

Such notoriously easy courses have been a familiar feature in higher education for decades, often (but not exclusively) associated with the need to maintain the fiction of the student-athlete. In *ProfScam,* I had described some of the "great guts" that were littered across academia.* Other schools referred to them as "micks," an apparent homage to Mickey Mouse. At Yale, for instance, self-appointed "gutmasters" would steer unmotivated undergrads in search of an easy A to Introduction to Interpersonal and Group Dynamics, which was described as having "lots of in-class fun and games. No tests. Very little reading. And a paper or two (one of which, purposely, is a group exercise)." Not to be outdone, Harvard boasted courses known among the student body by such nicknames as "Heroes for Zeroes," "Nuts and Sluts," "Snowmobiles," and "Spots and Dots."[20]

---

*The origin of the term is murky, although the *New York Times* once took a stab at it by quoting etymologists who speculated that the term "guts" might refer to courses that could be passed with nothing more than "gut instinct."

But the AFAM department at Chapel Hill took the concept of the nondemanding gut class to a whole new level. As the Wainstein report later described them:

> These were classes that involved no interaction with a faculty member, required no class attendance or course work other than a single paper, and resulted in consistently high grades that Crowder awarded without reading the papers or otherwise evaluating their true quality. . . .
>
> Over the 18 years these classes existed, Crowder and Nyang'oro were responsible for offering 188 different lecture classes as well as hundreds of individual independent studies in the "paper class" format—with no class attendance or faculty involvement, and with Crowder managing the class and liberally grading the papers. Through this scheme, over 3,100 students received one or more semesters of deficient instruction and were awarded high grades that often had little relationship to the quality of their work [emphasis added throughout].[21]

Student-athletes accounted for a "disproportionately high percentage of enrollments" in the fake courses, but a majority of the students who took the "paper classes" were nonathletes.* Word of the bogus classes spread widely throughout campus, especially among fraternities.†

---

* "Of the identifiable enrollments in the lecture paper classes, 47.4% were student-athletes, even though student-athletes make up just over 4% of the Chapel Hill undergraduate student body. Of those student-athlete enrollments, 50.9% were football players, 12.2% were men's basketball players, 6.1% were women's basketball players, and 30.6% were Olympic and other sport athletes." (Wainstein report, 3–4)

† "With up to 400 enrollments in some semesters, their existence was hardly a secret. As with any course that offers an easy path to a high grade, word of these classes got around. . . . Over the course of ten years, there were 729 enrollments in the paper classes by members of fraternities (and some sorority sisters)." (Wainstein report, 51–52)

But knowledge of the "paper classes" wasn't merely spread by the fraternity grapevine. It had become increasingly institutionalized: Academic counselors in the athletic department steered students to the AFAM classes. "At least two of those counselors went so far as to suggest what grades Crowder should award to their players who were taking her paper classes," the Wainstein report found. The counselors' enthusiasm *suggests* that the fake courses had become a well-known part of the system of keeping athletes eligible.

Word also got out that even the minimal class requirements could be avoided. The Academic Support Program for Student-Athletes made tutors available to all student-athletes, and those tutors often helped the student-athletes with their paper-class papers. While most conducted themselves appropriately, several of the tutors crossed the line between permissible and impermissible assistance and drafted parts of the papers that the student-athletes submitted for credit in these classes.

One basketball player, Rashad McCants, later claimed:

> I didn't write any papers, but I know that the tutors did help guys write papers—as far as help them through the grammar, the structure, paragraphs, so on and so forth. But for some of the premier players, we didn't write our papers. It was very simple. When it was time to turn in our papers for our "paper classes," we would get a call from our tutors, we would all pack up in one big car, or pack up in two cars, and ride over to the tutor's house, pick up our papers and go about our business.[22]

Other players and coaches have disputed McCants's story. The Wainstein investigators were unable to contact or interview McCants and professed themselves agnostic on his claims, but said they were "able to identify other occurrences of analogous misconduct through our interviews with several of the tutors." Of the nine tutors they investigated, "only three admitted to going over the line and 'feeding' text to the student-athlete they were tutoring."[23]

Not that it mattered since "it was common knowledge that Crowder simply skimmed the introduction and conclusion of each paper, and rarely, if ever, looked at the material in between." Not surprisingly, some students "took advantage of Crowder's lax grading process by filling their papers with 'fluff' that often included material that they blatantly copied from sources on the Internet."* A later review found that:

- In over 40% of the 150 papers (61 papers), 25% or more of the text was deemed unoriginal.

- In 17% of the papers (26 papers), 50% of the text was deemed unoriginal.

Of those 61 papers with 25% or more of unoriginal content, the average grade was 3.69 (or almost an A–).[24]

The Wainstein report stated the obvious: "If it turned out, however, that the student's paper was plagiarized, then it is hard to see how his experience with a paper class held any educational value at all for him."[25] But obviously "educational value" was not the point at all. And pretty much everyone involved knew that.

---

* Some students made no attempt to disguise the fact that they were turning in faux papers.

> For example, in one paper that was ostensibly about the life and work of Nikki Giovanni as it related to larger dynamics in African-American culture, the student had simply written a two-page introduction and a last page of text, and the entire rest of the paper in-between those pages is almost nothing other than transcriptions of poems and other texts by Giovanni, formatted to take up maximal space. In a way, such papers are even more telling than the plagiarized papers, because, while plagiarism is not always easy to detect, students who used large amounts of "filler" quotes did nothing whatsoever to hide the fact that they were turning in mostly unoriginal work. The quote marks and citations are there, making it clear to the reader that most of the paper was not written by the student. (Wainstein report, 60)

The fake courses were also championed by advisers not affiliated with the sports teams. Here we come to Deborah Crowder's "network of like-minded women," in the very heart of the university's advising system.

> Over her 30-year tenure, Crowder became a part of what was affectionately called "the good old girls network," which was a network of like-minded women in various roles on campus who took it upon themselves to support those students who were struggling with school. Some of these women were Steele Building academic advisors. These advisors knew about the paper classes; they knew that Crowder controlled enrollment; and they often referred academically chal-lenged students to Crowder for placement in those classes. For years, advisors . . . sent struggling students to Crowder, in the hope that these classes would alleviate the pressure on them.[26]

Ironically enough, the fake courses proved convenient even for members of the faculty who otherwise objected to the lowered stan-dards and dishonesty of the courses.

> One particularly popular class was the third level of Swahili, which was offered in this irregular format specifically so that students—and particularly student-athletes—who struggled in lower levels of Swahili could satisfy their foreign language requirement by writing a paper about Swahili culture *in English* rather [than] completing a regular Swahili 3 paper class *in Swahili*.[27]

According to the Wainstein investigators, the professor in the course often clashed with Crowder, who objected to his policy of requiring actual work from his students. They argued frequently, especially when Crowder objected to the professor's refusal to give out higher grades for students who refused to do course work.

> At one point, the behavior of student-athletes in his Swahili 3 course was so unruly that [a tutor] wrote about it in an email to her supervisors. In a letter attached to her email, [she] wrote, "Their behavior is so rude and juvenile that from across the room I was trying to get them to shut up. "Later in the letter, [she] noted that one student-athlete had learned so little in his two-plus semesters of Swahili instruction that he could not even say the word "hello" in Swahili.[28]

In the professor's defense, the tutor wrote, all he was "asking for is a little respect. These kids owe [the professor] for even being put in a level 3 Swahili course, but I have the feeling that he will flunk them right out of there if they can't do the minimum amount of work necessary."

The situation created a dilemma for professors who were faced with choosing between having uninterested, unprepared, and occasionally disruptive students in their class or "off-loading the behavior problem to Crowder's paper class." Not surprisingly, some of them chose the latter. And not just in the African Studies department.

"It was widely known among the faculty that the AFAM Department offered some of the easiest classes on campus," the Wainstein report later found. In fact, a number of them acknowledged that they would occasionally recommend AFAM classes to students looking for a less rigorous course. One professor admitted that "he would advise science majors to take what he understood to be less-rigorous courses, such as those in the AFAM or Communications Departments, during semesters when they were taking particularly challenging and time-consuming science courses in order to balance difficult course schedules."[29]

So entrenched had the fake "paper courses" become, that they even managed to survive the departure of Crowder in 2009. Despite the near panic among the academic counselors, they were able to pressure Nyang'oro into continuing the practice. During Crowder's tenure, the academic counselors kept up "a steady drumbeat of requests for paper classes and student-athlete enrollments." When he announced her retirement, investigators found, there was a "demonstrably concerted effort" by the counselors to persuade Nyang'oro to continue the classes, "an effort that is clearly laid out in the email traffic between them and that paid off with three addi- tional paper classes that Nyang'oro agreed to offer between 2009 and 2011."[30]

The only change was that instead of Crowder's grading the papers, Nyang'oro now did. Investigators found that the chairman graded the papers

> with an eye to boosting student GPAs, regardless of paper quality. Prior to deciding on the grades in each of these classes, Nyang'oro asked Crowder's successor . . . to look up each student's GPA. This information, along with the occasional request from an academic counselor for leniency with a particular student-athlete who needed a GPA boost, informed Nyang'oro's grading and allowed him to make sure that any grade he assigned would not lead to academic ineligibility for any students or student-athletes.[31]

So the system continued. And yet no one noticed. Or at least no one noticed enough to intervene. But it was not lack of opportunities or warnings. "Despite fairly widespread knowledge about them on the Chapel Hill campus," the Wainstein report noted, "these paper classes continued without much interruption for years."[32]

But how and why did that happen? Why did no one in a position of responsibility notice? Or take action?

Over the years, school officials repeatedly blew off or ignored warning signs. In 2006, after the story broke that football players at Auburn had been given inflated grades for attending essentially non-existent courses (a story very similar to what had been happening for more than a decade at UNC), there was a twinge of interest in whether something similar could happen at Chapel Hill. The concerns appear to have been brushed off. Former chancellor James Moeser (2000–2008) told investigators that after the Auburn story broke, campus administrators had "lively discussions, but no one raised a concern that there might be similar issues with independent studies at Chapel Hill, likely due to the commonly held—but naïve—belief that Chapel Hill was 'above' such academic improprieties."[33]

This naïveté is puzzling because concern over "illicit methods" of keeping players eligible had been an issue at UNC since at least 1989. That year, UNC's Ad Hoc Committee on Athletics had concluded that "all intercollegiate athletic programs of NCAA Division 1-A, including our own, are in varying degrees of conflict with the purposes and standards of universities, in general." Specifically, the committee had noted that "some student-athletes are not students and do not genuinely represent the student bodies, of which they are nominally members, that the effort to enroll them and keep them eligible results frequently in a corruption of the academic process." The Ad Hoc Committee called out the coalitions of coaches, administrators, faculty members, trustees, and boosters "who intimidate or manipulate administrators and faculty members" to "maintain by illicit methods the eligibility of student-athletes who would otherwise have become ineligible to play."[34]

Investigators identified only two other attempts to look into the problem; neither went anywhere.

In its November 2006 and January 2007 meetings, three of the school's top athletics officials raised concerns about the AFAM paper classes with members of the Faculty Athletics Committee. But they said "the FAC members responded by citing the professor's prerogative to choose the right teaching method in a class and instructing them not to pursue their concerns any farther."[35]

In other words, the members of the committee actively chose not to know what was going on. As administrators later acknowledged, "No examination of the syllabus of any of these [independent study] courses was made since they are approved by the faculty in the respective departments."*

This active not-wanting-to-know is also reflected, investigators found, in a "telling email in the wake of the Auburn University independent studies scandal, in which [one athletic department official] acknowledges that Chapel Hill has independent studies and then asks rhetorically 'Do I or anyone in the Department of Athletics have any say in how departments structure their courses—NO!'"[36]

In one other instance, some time in 2005 or 2006 a senior associate dean gently raised concerns about the extraordinary number of "independent studies courses" that Professor Nyang'oro was supposedly handling. At a luncheon with Nyang'oro, she pointed out that it was implausible that any faculty member could be responsible for more than three hundred such courses a year. Nyang'oro was told to reduce the number of independent courses and to "get [Crowder] under control." Returning from his lunch with the dean, Nyang'oro told Crowder that the administration was concerned about the classes and told her to scale back enrollment, which she did. According to investigators, the dean noticed the decline and sent Nyang'oro an email with the subject line "Ind Studies," thanking the department chair and noting that "it has gotten quieter from your side of campus."[37] The Wainstein report raised the obvious question here. While the dean's intervention resulted in a cut in the number of students taking the

---

*The Wainstein report concluded: "This assumption—that a course is academically legitimate based upon the mere fact that it was offered by a department— prevented further scrutiny by the FAC in 2002 and served as the justification for much of the reticence to scrutinize the paper courses in the AFAM Department for so many years thereafter." (Wainstein report, 83)

fake classes, why did she let the matter drop? The report noted point-edly:

> She never asked how he or his small department could possibly teach 300 different independent studies in a single year and never challenged him on the quality of instruction these students were or were not receiving in these independent studies. If she had, she would have learned that the students were effectively getting no instruction and that these were largely paper class students who were writing papers for Debby Crowder. The administrator's inexplicable decision not to press this obvious issue allowed the paper class scheme to continue for another five years.[38]

But the administrator's indifference is "inexplicable" only if one does not understand the underlying academic culture that made the scandal possible in the first place and allowed it to persist for so many years. And here we get the reconsideration of the UNC scandal as a window on the structure, culture, and priorities of the modern university.

At this point, the Wainstein report makes for especially interesting reading. It is a thorough, outsider look inside the academic culture; unlike the usual academic doublespeak, it employs language that is clear and direct; and at times does not try to conceal its bemusement at what it had discovered about the academic culture.* While seeming

---

*In contrast, an earlier report by former North Carolina governor James Martin reads like a whitewash. While documenting many of the problems with the "paper courses," Martin did not have access to all of the investigative materials that the Wainstein report had. The Martin report, while perhaps well intentioned, was also quite convenient for the university, because it sought to isolate the problem by pinning the blame for the fake courses on two staffers (Nyang'oro and Crowder) in a single department, while appearing to absolve the rest of the school. Many of its conclusions were refuted by the Wainstein report.

to accept the top administration's "plausible deniability" that it knew anything about the scandal, the report laments

> a woeful lack of oversight of the AFAM Department and Chairman Nyang'oro that made it possible for him and Crowder to carry out their paper class scheme. As far as we could tell, there was almost no structured oversight of the AFAM Department's operations during Nyang'oro's tenure from 1992 to 2011. Despite the fact that these classes involved thousands of students and coordination between Crowder and numerous University employees, the Chapel Hill administration never scrutinized AFAM's operations or the academic integrity of their course offerings. It was only when media reports raised questions about AFAM classes in 2011 that administration officials took a hard look at the AFAM Department. They were shocked with what they found.[39]

But this was not an aberration. It's the way things work in American higher education: For the most part, no one pays attention to an awful lot of what happens.*

> We have attempted to diagnose why the academic oversight at Chapel Hill was so lacking for so many years, and we have identified both cultural and structural reasons. Culturally, *the minimal oversight can be attributed to* the same value that was

---

* "Like many universities, the Chapel Hill administration took a loose, decentralized approach to management of its departments and department chairpersons, on the theory that strong management in the college environment unduly constrains the academic independence that fosters creative instruction and research. As a result of this approach, the University failed to conduct any meaningful oversight of the AFAM Department and ASPSA, and Crowder's paper class scheme was allowed to operate within one of the nation's premier academic institutions for almost two decades." (Wainstein report, 6)

allegedly expressed by the faculty in the 2007 FAC meeting—
*the cherished academic independence that professors enjoy in elite
institutions.*

As former Dean Kalleberg explained to us, *the ethos of
Chapel Hill's administration revolved around trust and a resistance
to structured management* [emphasis added throughout].[40]

In other words, no one was minding the store, because no one cared
enough to pay attention. Despite some feeble attempts to spin the university's obliviousness as a matter of high academic principle, the indictment is nonetheless revealing. In the end, the Chapel Hill scandal
was more than just another collegiate sports scandal. It exposed higher
education's capacity for enabling and ignoring mediocrity, fraud, and
failure—as long it involves undergraduate education.

PART V

VICTIM U.
(TRIGGER
WARNING)

CHAPTER 11

GRIEVANCE U.

Safe Places, Triggers, and Microaggressions

"[We] want to create an atmosphere where both students and faculty feel comfortable voicing a single homogeneous opinion," said Abrams, adding that "no matter the subject, anyone on campus is always welcome to add their support to the accepted consensus."

—THE ONION*

A FAMOUS PLAQUE AT the University of Wisconsin declares "Whatever may be the limitations which trammel inquiry elsewhere," universities should be devoted to "fearless sifting and winnowing by which alone the truth may be found." But the reality of the modern university is often quite different, reflected not merely in campus "speech codes," but in an often stultifying, conversation-ending

*A parody. Sort of. ("College Encourages Lively Exchange of Idea," *The Onion*, April 27, 2015)

atmosphere of ideological conformity. None of this seems designed to teach students either how to *think or learn,* much less fearlessly sift and winnow.

Despite the frequent invocation of terms like "diversity" and "inclusion," higher education today involves carefully navigating complex mazes of identity and gender politics that at some schools now include "trigger warnings," "microaggressions," and "safe places." The pressure for ideological conformity has turned college campuses into places so intolerant and unfunny that prominent comedians—Jerry Seinfeld, Chris Rock—have learned to avoid them.

A caveat is in order here: not all colleges have embraced such hair-trigger sensitivities and there have been eloquent (if infrequent) dissents to the regimes of brow-beating and enforced sensitivity. But the trend is not encouraging as more administrations embrace the notion that universities can micromanage even the most benign of human interactions. The results are regimes of sensitivity crafted with delicate, almost byzantine complexity that can discover racism or sexism in the most casual of interactions, the angle of an eyebrow or the tone of the voice, or an innocent-seeming question.

Across academia, those special identities and their accompanying grievances are encouraged, nourished, and even institutionalized in ways that are often difficult to keep up with, even for au courant academics.

At Wesleyan University of Middletown, Connecticut (tuition and fees $62,508), for example, the campaign to be inclusive and supportive of sexual minorities has led the school to set up a separate residence, known as the Open House, for students who want a place of their own. Wesleyan explains that the Open House is intended as a "safe place" for the "LGBTTQQFAGPBDSM communities." The acronym stands for: "Lesbian, Gay, Bisexual, Transgender, Transsexual, Queer, Questioning, Flexual, Asexual, Genderfuck, Polyamourous, Bondage/Disciple, Dominance/Submission, Sadism/Masochism," all which are now considered "communities" in need of special recognition on campus. Lest this not be sufficiently inclusive, Wesleyan hastens to add that the Open House is also open to "people of sexually or gender dissident communities" who are otherwise not included in the list above.[1]

"The goals of Open House," the university explains on its housing website, "include generating interest in a celebration of queer life from the social to the political to the academic. Open House works to create a Wesleyan community that appreciates the variety and vivacity of gender, sex and sexuality."

Recognizing that other groups might also need separate residences, Wesleyan also offers students the option of Malcolm X House, for African-American upperclassmen interested in "the exploration and celebration of the cultural heritage of the African Diaspora, both for themselves and for the larger Wesleyan community."[2] There is also Earth House, which is committed to creating a "community based on love, peace, sustainability, cooperative communalism, and human values as opposed to one based on concern for material goods." Residents "espouse the values and principles of social ecology, deep ecology, and ecofeminism" and challenge "traditional social structures and replacing them with new, creative and egalitarian alternatives."[3]

There is, however, no house devoted to free speech.

So it was perhaps not surprising that Wesleyan was one of the first schools to witness the distinctive intolerance of the Snowflake Rebellion of 2015–2016.

At Wesleyan, it began with an opinion piece in the student newspaper, the *Wesleyan Argus,* which offered criticism of the Black Lives Matter movement.[4] The student author did not question claims that some police were racist, but he wondered about the movement's tactics and rhetoric, including its tendency to demonize police officers. The writer asked, "is the movement itself actually achieving anything positive? Does it have the potential for positive change?"

The reaction on campus was dramatic. Rather than respond to the opinion article with another viewpoint, activists began a campaign to boycott and defund the newspaper, claiming that it "neglects to provide a space for the voices of students of color . . ." When the school's president, Michael S. Roth, offered a defense of free speech on campus, activists responded with an open letter declaring that "We do not have the time, nor luxury, to be caught up in this smokescreen of free speech."

> Freedom of speech, in its popular understanding, does not protect Black Lives Matter advocates who are trying to survive in a racist world, but instead protects the belief systems of dominant people—despite the extent of their heightened ignorance. . . . By focusing on the freedom of speech instead of students' lives and ability to safely exist on this campus, you are practicing censorship and you are partaking in racism.[5]

Despite apologies for the offending column from the newspaper's editors, the student assembly voted unanimously to study whether to slash the *Argus*'s annual funding. But this was just the beginning of the push back against free speech on campuses across the country. The protests at Wesleyan were quickly followed by high-profile controversies at Yale, the University of Missouri, Amherst, Claremont McKenna, Smith College, and then throughout academia. As the campus rebellion spread, it became clear that many of the protesters were not simply indifferent to principles of free speech and intellectual tolerance— they were actively hostile to them.

INTOLERANCE U.

Cardinal John Henry Newman argued that the university should be devoted to "universal learning," unhindered by any doctrine or dogma, thus setting the ideal for liberal education. But Newman might be hard pressed to recognize what passes for liberalism and tolerance at modern institutions of higher learning. Academia's tolerance and commitment to the free exchange are tested every spring when, invariably, activists demand the silencing of one or another commencement speaker.

In 2014 alone, student and faculty protests induced Christine Lagarde, the head of the International Monetary Fund, to withdraw from speaking at Smith College's graduation; protests led former secretary of state Condoleezza Rice to skip Rutgers' commencement; and Dr. Ben Carson dropped plans to speak at Johns Hopkins.[6] In May 2014, Brandeis University announced it was withdrawing its offer of an honorary degree to Ayaan Hirsi Ali, who had been critical of Islam's treatment of women. Reported the *New York Times:*

> "We cannot overlook that certain of her past statements are inconsistent with Brandeis University's core values," the university said in a statement released eight days after it had announced that Ms. Hirsi Ali and four other people would be honored at its commencement on May 18.[7]

It apparently did not occur to the timid administrators that their refusal to allow Ali to speak was also "inconsistent with Brandeis University's core values," perhaps because such tolerance is often honored more in theory than in practice in the modern academy.* Not only have controversial figures such as Ann Coulter been disinvited from speaking on campus, so have major figures like Supreme Court chief justice

---

*In contrast, after protests at Haverford led to the withdrawal of Robert J. Birgeneau, former chancellor of the University of California–Berkeley, his stand-in, former Princeton president William G. Bowen, used the occasion to chastise the protesters' approach, calling it "immature" and "arrogant," and to maintain that the withdrawal of Birgeneau was "defeat" for the Quaker college and its ideals. "I am disappointed that those who wanted to criticize Birgeneau's handling of events at Berkeley chose to send him such an intemperate list of 'demands.' In my view, they should have encouraged him to come and engage in a genuine discussion, not to come, tail between his legs, to respond to an indictment that a self-chosen jury had reached without hearing counter-arguments." (Susan Snyder, "Haverford College Commencement Speaker Lambastes Students," *Philadelphia Inquirer,* May 18, 2014)

John Roberts, who was considered "too controversial" to speak at Butler University in 2010. The rising tide of political intolerance on campus is a test of moral courage of academic leaders, and the results are unfortunately not encouraging.

Even so, this assault on free speech has generated some notable resistance. After upheavals at Yale and the University of Missouri, Purdue University President Mitch Daniels sent out a campus-wide email reaffirming the school's commitment to remain "steadfast in preserving academic freedom and individual liberty."[8] With admirable bluntness, the American Association of University Professors argued that: "The presumption that students need to be protected rather than challenged in a classroom is at once infantilizing and anti-intellectual. It makes comfort a higher priority than intellectual engagement. . . ."[9]

Equally impressive, a "Committee on Freedom of Expression" at the University of Chicago, declared that: "It is not the proper role of the University to attempt to shield individuals from ideas and opinions they find unwelcome, disagreeable, or even deeply offensive." Rather, the Chicago committee declared:

> In a word, the university's fundamental commitment is to the principle that debate or deliberation may not be suppressed because the ideas put forth are thought by some or even by most members of the university community to be offensive, unwise, immoral, or wrong-headed. It is for the individual members of the university community, not for the university as an institution, to make those judgments for themselves, and to act on those judgments not by seeking to suppress speech, but by openly and vigorously contesting the ideas that they oppose.[10]

The intolerance on campus has become so flagrant and widespread that it even drew the notice of some on the left, including President Barack Obama, who was moved to remark on the movement to "coddle" undergraduates by protecting them from uncomfortable ideas.

I've heard some college campuses where they don't want to have a guest speaker who is too conservative or they don't want to read a book if it has language that is offensive to African-Americans or somehow sends a demeaning signal towards women. . . . I gotta tell you I don't agree with that either. I don't agree that you, when you become students at colleges, have to be coddled and protected from different points of view. . . . You shouldn't silence them by saying, "You can't come because I'm too sensitive to hear what you have to say." That's not the way we learn either.[11]

His remarks appear to have little effect on his fellow progressives on campus, who seem to be accelerating their efforts to turn academia into a fever swamp of enforced sensitivity.

VICTIM U.

At one time, it was generally understood that campuses were places where free debate was not merely tolerated, but encouraged, and where academic rigor was respected, not seen as a form of covert racism. It was also understood that while academic freedom meant the right to express unpopular views, there was no right "not to be offended." As I have written elsewhere, a willingness to be offended at the smallest slight "is not a sign of superior consciousness—it is a decision to be a whiner and an emotional bully."[12] Being easily offended ought not to give anyone license to silence, censor, or harass people with whom they disagree.*

---

* "This may come as a surprise, but living in a free country does not mean that you are free from annoyance or immune to things that offend you. . . . If you want to avoid being offended, you should probably try a Buddhist monastery rather than, say, public transportation or a modern university." (Sykes, *50 Rules Kids Won't Learn in School*, 73)

This has all changed with the rise of the notion that in order to be inclusive, campuses need to shelter minorities and others from words, ideas, or even images that might offend them. Despite herculean efforts to make campuses more diverse places, the attempt to sanitize campuses has fallen short; in practice it has meant that speech is only as free as the most hypersensitive activist on campus will allow. The competition is quite fierce for the position of "most offended." Who is a more oppressed victim, the Chicana lesbian or the African-American woman? Or perhaps the transgendered Native American?

Since the invocation of victim status on campus confers both authority and immunity, activists have managed to find more and more things to be offended about and have refined their grievances with exquisite subtlety. Compliant administrations often willingly hand the perpetually offended a veto over what is acceptable and what needs to be subject to remediation and reeducation.

For students this often means learning to keep their heads down and avoiding the many invisible trip wires of grievance that crisscross the modern university community.

TRIGGERS

One of the more dramatic manifestations of the culture of victimization on campus is the embrace of so-called trigger warnings. The idea is simple enough. Because there are so many frail, damaged, or easily offended students on campus, literature professors ought to post warnings about the books students are reading, lest they stumble on scenes of passages that might be provocative or disturbing.

As Rutgers student Philip Wythe explained in a column making the case for the trigger warnings:

> "The Great Gatsby" possesses a variety of scenes that reference gory, abusive and misogynistic violence. Virginia Woolf's famous cerebral narrative, "Mrs. Dalloway," paints a disturb-

ing narrative that examines the suicidal inclinations and post-traumatic experiences of an English war veteran. And Junot Diaz's critically acclaimed work, "This Is How You Lose Her," observes domestic violence and misogynistic culture in disturbing first-person narrations.[13]

He explained that the triggers can cover a "variety of topics—from graphic violence to drug abuse." *The Great Gatsby,* for instance, could carry warnings for "suicide," "domestic abuse," and "graphic violence." Wythe suggested that professors could use the triggers in various ways. They could put them in the course syllabus, "informing students which books possess triggering material and which books are trigger-free." (He does not, by the way, explain how a professor could be certain that a book would not contain any material guaranteed not to offend any student under any circumstances.) Professors could also "dissect a narrative's passage, warning their students which sections or volumes of a book possess triggering material and which are safer to read. This allows students to tackle passages that are not triggering but return to triggering passages when they are fully comfortable." The use of such warnings, Wythe wrote, "fosters positive and compassionate intellectual discussion within the collegiate classroom."

Actually, the trigger warnings turn the classroom into an emotional and psychological minefield and the job of teaching into a low-rent center for the detection and avoidance of emotional trauma. They also inevitably lead to demands that the already battered humanities curriculum be molded around the delicate sensibilities of the victimized students. This policy, of course, treats them not as inquiring minds, but as delicate snowflakes. As Todd Gitlin notes, "it's hard to resist the thought that overwrought charges against the trigger-happy curriculum are outgrowths of fragility, or perceptions of fragility, or of fears of fragility running amok."[14]

But, as Gitlin suggests, we are no longer dealing with your garden-variety political correctness. "I'm old enough," Judith Shulevitz wrote in the *New York Times,* "to remember a time when college students objected to providing a platform to certain speakers because they were deemed politically unacceptable. Now students worry whether acts of speech or pieces of writing may put them in emotional peril."[15]

"SAFE PLACES"

This concern for the emotional fragility of students has caused campuses to create "safe places," for groups that wish to avoid certain troubling ideas, talks, or debates. When author Christina Hoff Sommers, for example, was invited to speak on the campus of Georgetown on the topic "What's Right (and Badly Wrong) with Feminism?" her appearance was met with trigger warnings. One read: "Trigger warning: this event will contain discussions of sexual assault and may deny the experiences of survivors." Another warned: "Trigger warning: antifeminism." A subsequent visit by Sommers to Oberlin sparked protests that her very presence on campus could lead to the creation of "a really unsafe space for people who attended."[16] At both Oberlin and Georgetown feminists created what they called "safe places" for students to seek shelter from her remarks.

Similarly, faced with the prospect of a debate over campus sex assault, Brown University created a refuge for students who might find the discussion too traumatic. The result was a safe room—a refuge from any "troubling" or "triggering" ideas—that was equipped "with cookies, coloring books, bubbles, Play-Doh, calming music, blankets, and a video of frolicking puppies, as well as students and staff members trained to deal with trauma."[17]

Yes, academia sometimes is beyond parody.

But this is a new wrinkle on the old ideological intolerance. The use of the hashtag #Notsafe to protest lectures and the creation of safe places to avoid campus speakers is meant to equate ideas with acts of violence and debates with the threat of assault or other injury. By invoking federal civil rights laws, including Title IX, campus victimologists have in effect weaponized their grievances (as we will see later). Those laws are now used to force colleges dependent on federal money to respond aggressively to any suggestions that they have created a hostile environment for members of protected groups.

But treating words as threats turns our understanding of the role of language and ideas upside down, while also transforming students from liberal learners to potential victims. Colleges thus feel compelled not only to affirm the grievances of hypersensitive undergraduates, but to encourage students to think of themselves as snowflakes. One Columbia student objected to the campaign to transform the campus into "safer spaces," noting that "I don't see how you have a therapeutic space that's also an intellectual space."

Some critics were tempted to dismiss the whole thing as silly. "What is the -ism that refers to discrimination against relatively sane people who can read 'The Merchant of Venice' without a therapist on speed dial? Normalism?" asked columnist Kathleen Parker. She suggested that institutionalizing such angst may be "misplaced in an institution of higher learning where one is expected to be intellectually challenged and where one's psychological challenges are expected to be managed elsewhere. . . . Then again, if reading 'The Great Gatsby' causes one undue angst owing to its abuse, classism, sexism and whatever-ism, then one might consider that college is not the right place at the right time."[18]

THE ASSUMPTION OF FRAGILITY

But where does this new assumption of fragility come from? Why is there a push to infantilize our best and brightest?

Like the speech codes and other policies, the trigger warnings and safe places fit in well on the modern campus because they draw their inspiration from the culture of victimization, where students are presumed to be either a member of an oppressed group or somehow damaged psychologically. The triggers embody the notion prevalent in modern education that students are delicate plants whose self-esteem and psyche needed to be treated with more than normal caution. On campus, this is reinforced by strains of feminist thought and political and legal pressure to make campuses offense-free zones.* But the new emphasis on sensitivity also marks the rise of the therapeutic approach to both politics and learning. The very term "sensitivity," after all, owes more to the world of psychology than to, say, Marxism. But it is consistent with the deeply ingrained educational philosophy that insists on bubble-wrapping children, protecting them from all of the bumps, bruises, and setbacks of life, in the belief that by shielding them from adversity and offensive ideas that they will somehow be empowered to face the world.

Indeed, there is evidence that we have created a nation of snowflakes—students who are unprepared to handle even the routine vicissitudes of daily life, much less the challenges posed by collegiate life. College counselors increasingly bemoan the neediness and lack of resilience among the students they encounter. A recent article in *Psychology Today* recounted the complaints of college counselors who noted that emergency calls had risen dramatically in recent years:

> Students are increasingly seeking help for, and apparently
> having emotional crises over, problems of everyday life. Recent
> examples mentioned included a student who felt traumatized
> because her roommate had called her a "bitch" and two

---

* "Universities are in a double bind," Judith Shulevitz explains. "They're required by two civil rights statutes, Title VII and Title IX, to ensure that their campuses don't create a 'hostile environment' for women and other groups subject to harassment. The theory that vulnerable students should be guaranteed psychological security has roots in a body of legal thought elaborated in the 1980s and 1990s and still read today. Feminist and antiracist legal scholars argued that the First Amendment should not safeguard language that inflicted emotional injury through racist or sexist stigmatization." (Judith Shulevitz, "In College and Hiding from Scary Ideas," *New York Times,* March 21, 2015)

students who had sought counseling because they had seen a mouse in their off-campus apartment. The latter two also called the police, who kindly arrived and set a mousetrap for them.[19]

When the sighting of a mouse triggers a call for counseling, is it really any wonder that so many schools think that they have to bubble-wrap their students? Not surprisingly, some academics use this fragility as an excuse for the policies that infantilize their students.

University of Chicago law professor Eric Posner actually makes the case for bubble-wrapping college students by arguing that college students are in fact intellectually and emotionally infants and therefore should be treated as such.[20] Posner suggests that the current generation of students may be uniquely unprepared for the rough and tumble of collegiate life.

> Perhaps overprogrammed children engineered to the specifications of college admissions offices no longer experience the risks and challenges that breed maturity. Or maybe in our ever-more technologically advanced society, the responsibilities of adulthood must be delayed until the completion of a more extended period of education.
>
> If college students are children, then they should be protected like children.

Posner was merely making explicit what is usually left implicit in the policies that infantilize students. Such policies may make campuses kinder and gentler places. But they decidedly will not make them institutions of *higher learning*. The point of a college education, after all, is to push students out of their comfortable bubbles. "You're at school to be disturbed," notes Gitlin. "Universities are very much in the business of trying to get you to rethink why you believe what you believe and whether you have grounds for believing it."[21] Walter Russell Mead notes that given the increasingly dangerous world we live in, this is perhaps the wrong time to coddle the next generation. While the assault on free speech is a horrible betrayal of academic values, there is an even worse result from treating students as frail flowers: "the catastrophic dumbing down and weakening of a younger generation that is becoming too fragile and precious to exist in the current world— much less to fight the real evils and dangers that are growing."[22]

But both Gitlin's and Mead's attitudes are increasingly quaint notions on many campuses.

"If I were a junior faculty member looking at this while putting my syllabus together, I'd be terrified," Oberlin professor Marc Blecher told the *New York Times*. "Any student who felt triggered by something that happened in class could file a complaint with the various procedures and judicial boards and create a very tortuous process for anyone."[23]

Blecher made his comments after Oberlin (tuition and fees $61,780 a year) not only embraced the trigger but put out a guide for faculty to use in developing warnings for anything that might "cause trauma" or be otherwise disruptive. In crafting their trigger warnings, Oberlin told members of the faculty:

> Be aware of racism, classism, sexism, heterosexism, cissexism [transgender discrimination], ableism, and other issues of privilege and oppression. Realize that all forms of violence are traumatic, and that your students have lives before and outside your classroom, experiences you may not expect or understand.

Oberlin's Trigger Guide specifically singled out Chinua Achebe's classic novel of life in colonial-era Nigeria, *Things Fall Apart*, as a book that could "trigger readers who have experienced racism, colonialism, religious persecution, violence, suicide, and more."

What was not clear was how schools like Oberlin would handle other classic works. Would *War and Peace* carry a warning of "scenes of violence"? Would *Crime and Punishment* be flagged for axe murder? Or elder abuse? And where would you even start with *Macbeth*? Or *Hamlet*? What about the possible trigger warnings for *A Portrait of the Artist as a Young Man, Brave New World, Lolita,* or *The Grapes of Wrath*? Would a class that included *Old Yeller* have to include a warning about his demise at the end of the book (a moment many readers have found especially traumatic)? Would even Jane Austen be immune? Might readers with inappropriately behaving mothers require triggers before reading *Pride and Prejudice*?

Sadly enough, these are not rhetorical questions.

OVID, THAT SEXIST BASTARD

The crusade against triggering classics is waged with a grim humorlessness matched only by its dogged literalism. At Columbia University, several students took it upon themselves to quantify—complete with pie charts—every single incidence of rape, assault, "or other nonconsensual activity" in the university's humanities curriculum. Their chart helpfully broke down the world's great literature into "Women Raped" and "Women Not Raped."[24] Ovid was a particular problem:

> In the first semester, a quarter of the characters were women and about 20% of those women were raped, which is on par with conservative estimates of rape on college campuses. The second semester had a much higher figure than the first, around 50%, mostly due to Ovid's *Metamorphoses* (which has roughly 80 instances of assault). Even this number is an underestimate, though, as I treated many of the instances of mass rape on the syllabus as a single data point for simplicity. It's worth noting that these mass rapes were almost always

directed at a conquered group—think about the "victory tour" after the Trojan War portrayed in *The Odyssey*. . . . these tactics are still used in imperialist warfare today.

This critique of Ovid inspired Todd Gitlin to ask, "Why stop with Ovid? Has anyone taken a look at the Old Testament recently?"* But the Columbia activists would probably not have gotten the joke. Grimly, they insisted that universities that celebrated diversity should "stop assuming that we will all share neutral responses to often violent and triggering material." In other words, Columbia students simply could not be expected to handle the insensitivities that ran rampant through Homer, Augustine, Ovid, Shakespeare, Cervantes, Dostoevsky, Sophocles, Euripides, Herodotus, much less Genesis.

A university that uncritically accepts rape in its foundational literature class, without any thoughtful discussion directly addressing rape and sexual assault, must question its ability to firmly reject rape and sexual assault on campus. The same can be said of Lit Hum's other violences: a campus with this syllabus at its core will never be proactive in addressing the needs of students of color, queer and trans students, disabled

* "Lot's two daughters slept with him in order to continue his line (Genesis 19). Joshua slaughtered 12,000 Canaanites in one day (Joshua 8) and soon thereafter 'smote all the country of the hills, and of the south, and of the vale, and of the springs, and all their kings: He left none remaining, but utterly destroyed all that breathed, as the Lord God of Israel commanded' (Joshua 10:40). In the Holy Book, no one is judged harshly for war crimes. Is the Bible a manual for righteous massacres? Should trigger warnings be mandated? Should the Columbia Core print up a new edition of the Bible with a frontispiece warning the tender reader against the gruesome stories to be found therein?" Gitlin asks the question as a kind of reductio ad absurdum, but there is no reason to think that the response by the folks who advocate triggers would not be . . . yes. (Todd Gitlin, "Please Be Disturbed," *The Tablet,* March 13, 2015)

students, low income students, or any other marginalized groups.

Not all students or academics are willing to concede the need for triggers on works of literature. The push for the warnings became the subject of considerable debate at the University of California at Santa Barbara, where the student government urged the school to add triggers to course syllabuses to protect students from being exposed to material that might trigger a traumatic reaction.[25]

Some critics on campus questioned whether students really needed to be protected from material that might be outside of their comfort zone. "The learning process necessarily involves exposing people to ideas that will challenge their beliefs and make them feel uncomfortable," a political science major named Jason Garshfield pointed out to the student newspaper. "People who attend college are implicitly agreeing to be pushed outside their intellectual and emotional comfort zones. . . . I would like to see the [Student] Senate have a higher regard for the fortitude and resilience of the students of this university, as well as the discretion of our professors to teach their students at the level they feel is appropriate."

The school's dean of humanities and fine arts, David Marshall, also tried to point out that "thousands of years of art and literature have been provocative and disturbing." This was what made them valuable and worth studying. "Think of 'Oedipus Rex,' which contains scenes of violence, patricide, incest, and death. In addition, there are many works of art, film, and literature that contain disturbing images in order to prevent social ills, such as violence against women," Marshall said in an email to the student paper. "Finally, I would note that our university adheres to the principles of academic freedom."[26]

But in the modern university, academic freedom goes only so far, because the politics of sensitivity change the rules of discourse. A culture built on hypersensitivity will be one without any mutually agreed upon standards of justice and fairness. Political sensitivity means if I'm a victim, you must attune yourself to all of the shifting shades of emotional grievance that I might feel, and because only a victim can understand a victim's pain, only I can define it. As a pseudonymous liberal professor wrote: "Hurting a student's feelings, even in the course of instruction that is absolutely appropriate and respectful, can now get a teacher into serious trouble."[27]

This has led to what he called "higher ed's current climate of fear," which he described as "a heavily policed discourse of semantic sensitivity in which safety and comfort have become the ends *and* the means of the college experience."

There is an inherent contradiction in some of these policies because they assume that while some students and professors can be permitted to engage in vigorous debates and exchanges of ideas, certain victim groups, either women or minorities, are to be considered frail psychological groups—so frail that they could be blighted or their self-esteem destroyed by the slightest word or expression or idea that they might find uncongenial.

This is the double-edged sword of victimization. While the ostensible goal is to enhance the self-esteem of and to empower members of the victim groups, some universities now go to great lengths to explain to sensitive students all of the ways in which they are unable to function in a normal environment.

So students may come to an elite university thinking, "Life is treating me pretty well; I'm at one of the finest universities in the country," only to find that extraordinary steps are taken to convince them that despite their middle-class background, despite having scholarships, despite living on a wonderful campus, they are in fact victims who are subject to indirect and unseen forms of racism and sexism, known as microaggressions.

MICROAGGRESSIONS

The campaign to eradicate microaggressions has given an entirely new vocabulary and set of weapons that can be wielded against uncompliant students and faculty alike.

Faculty and staff in the University of California system, for instance, were treated to training in the nuances of "Recognizing Microaggressions and the Messages They Send." The handout defined microaggressions as "the everyday verbal, nonverbal, and environmental slights, snubs, or insults, whether intentional or unintentional, that communicate hostile, derogatory, or negative messages to target persons based solely upon their marginalized group membership."[28]

"The first step in addressing microaggressions is to recognize when a microaggression has occurred and what message it may be sending," the training document declared, listing "themes" of various microaggressions in a helpful chart.

For example, faculty were warned against saying such things as "America is the land of opportunity." Other proscribed comments included:

"I believe the most qualified person should get the job."

"Men and women have equal opportunities for achievement."

"Gender plays no part in who we hire."

"Everyone can succeed in this society, if they work hard enough."

All of those statements, the University of California training document explained, sent racist and sexist messages because they embraced what it called the "Myth of Meritocracy," which includes any statement that race or gender does not play a role in life successes, for example in issues like faculty demographics. Specifically, remarks about hard work and opportunity are microaggressions because they send the messages that "The playing field is even, so if women cannot make it, the problem is with them." And "people of color are lazy and/or incompetent and need to work harder."

There is, or ought to be, a vigorous debate over whether America is, or should be a meritocratic society. But by labeling the question "microaggression," the speech police have shifted the question from an idea to be discussed and debated to an offensive utterance that may create a hostile or unsafe environment. The myth of meritocracy is not refuted, it is merely stigmatized on ideological, racial, gender, and therapeutic grounds.

The University of California document took a similar tack with other possible comments, labeling as microaggressions such seemingly innocuous remarks as:

"When I look at you, I don't see color."

"There is only one race, the human race."

"America is a melting pot."

"I don't believe in race."

These statements, the training document explains, are also racist because they "indicate that a White person does not want to or need to acknowledge race." By denying the central role of race, they send the message that the speaker is "denying the experiences of students by questioning the credibility/validity of their stories," suggesting that minorities "assimilate to the dominant culture" and deny "the individual as a racial/cultural being."

Even innocent questions that reflect curiosity are transformed into microaggressions, including "Where are you from or where were you born?" Rather than seeing such a question as a genuine attempt to learn more about another person, the California "tool" explained that such queries were hurtful because they sent the messages that "you are not a true American," "you are a perpetual foreigner in your own country," and "your ethnic/racial identity makes you exotic."

Similarly, an attempt to encourage more class participation by Asian, Latino, or Native American students can also be offensive. Faculty members who say "Why are you so quiet? We want to know what you think" or "Speak up more" may imagine that they are trying to constructively engage their students in the pedagogical experience. But according to the University of California trainers, they are in fact guilty of "Pathologizing Cultural Values/Communication Styles," which is the "notion that the values and communication styles of the dominant/White culture are ideal/'normal.'"*

---

*Faced with criticism/ridicule, the University of California denied that its training in microaggressions involved any censorship:

> To suggest that the University of California is censoring classroom discussions on our campuses is wrong and irresponsible. No such censorship exists. UC is committed to upholding, encouraging, and preserving academic freedom and the free flow of ideas throughout the University. As such, the media characterization of voluntary seminars for UC deans and department heads about campus climate issues—similar to seminars at university campuses throughout the country—is inaccurate.
>
> Contrary to what has been reported, no one at the University of California is prohibited from making statements such as "America is a melting pot," "America is the land of opportunity," or any other such statement. Given the diverse backgrounds of our students, faculty and staff, UC offered these seminars to make people aware of how their words or actions may be interpreted when used in certain contexts. Deans and department heads were invited, but not required, to attend the seminars.

Blogger Eugene Volokh was unpersuaded by the university's defense, noting that administrators had previously defined microaggressions as "one form of systemic everyday racism." Commented Volokh: "But apparently instructors—including untenured ones—are somehow expected to feel uncensored, and free to express their ideas, including ones UC has labeled racist, aggressive, and hostile. Really?" ("UC Teaching Faculty Members Not to Criticize Race-Based Affirmative Action, Call America 'Melting Pot,' and More," The Volokh Conspiracy Blog, *Washington Post*, June 16, 2015)

TARGETING GRAMMAR

Even progressive faculty members struggle to accommodate the brittle psyches of their pupils. One left-leaning university professor wrote that he knows full well that he would not get fired "for pissing off a Republican, so long as I did it respectfully." But the same could not be said of his more progressive students.

> All it takes is one slip—not even an outright challenging of their beliefs, but even momentarily exposing them to any uncomfortable thought or imagery—and that's it, your classroom is triggering, you are insensitive, kids are bringing mattresses to your office hours and there's a twitter petition out demanding you chop off your hand in repentance. . . .
>
> There are literally dozens of articles and books I thought nothing of teaching, 5–6 years ago, that I wouldn't even reference in passing today.[29]

One of the most dramatic casualties of the new "inclusiveness" was Professor Val Rust, a widely respected, honored, and award-winning emeritus professor of education at UCLA. For forty-five years, Rust has been a leading figure in the study of education reform, the role of education in social change, as well as the international role of higher education. He is listed as the author or coauthor of more than a hundred books and articles. In late 2013, the elderly Rust became the target of a celebrated protest against racial "microaggression."*

What had the seventy-nine-year-old professor done to deserve this? In a letter to his colleagues, Rust wrote: "I have attempted to be rather thorough on the papers and am particularly concerned that they do a

---

*After the student newspaper the *Daily Bruin* published an article about the protests, one reader posted this online comment: "We endured 'microaggression' when I was in college too, only we didn't call it that. We called it 'life.'"

good job with their bibliographies and citations, and these students apparently don't feel that is appropriate."[30]

UCLA student Josh Hedtke later explained:

> Among the . . . professor emeritus's alleged transgressions are repeatedly requiring students to write "Indigenous" in lowercase form instead of uppercase form . . . requiring students to capitalize "white" if they also choose to capitalize "black," and my personal favorite: requiring the students to use the Chicago Manual of Style instead of the style standards of the American Psychological Association.[31]

In the education school where Rust taught, criticizing poor grammar was apparently regarded as quite inflammatory. Said one former teaching assistant, the climate was "You have to give an A or you're a racist." But the disagreements over style and capitalization were merely the occasions of a broader conflict. Heather Mac Donald described what happened:

> Val Rust's dissertation-prep class had devolved into a highly charged arena of competing victim ideologies, impenetrable to anyone outside academia. For example: Were white feminists who use "standpoint theory"—a feminist critique of allegedly male-centered epistemology—illegitimately appropriating the "testimonial" genre used by Chicana feminists to narrate their stories of oppression?[32]

When Professor Rust changed the capitalization of "indigenous" in one of the papers, it was taken as a sign of "disrespect for the student's ideological point of view." Practitioners of critical race theory were especially strident in Rust's classes. During one of these highly charged discussions, Mac Donald writes, "Rust reached over and patted the arm of the class's most vociferous critical race-theory advocate to try to calm him down—a gesture typical of the physically demon-strative Rust, who is prone to hugs. The student, Kenjus Watson, dra-matically jerked his arm away, as a burst of nervous energy coursed through the room."

Protests followed. On November 14, 2013, the class's five "students of color," accompanied by other students of color, staged a dramatic entrance into Rust's classroom, forming a circle around the elderly pro-fessor and the class's other five students to read what they called a "Day of Action Statement."

The text of that statement suggests what Rust and other professors had been up against. As Mac Donald noted, the "Day of Action State-ment contains hardly a sentence without some awkwardness of gram-mar or usage." This is putting it rather kindly. The statement by these graduate students in education—presumably poised to become the leaders of America's schools—was a hot mess. The declaration ac-cused Rust of "racial microaggressions" that were "directed at our epistemologies, our intellectual rigor and to a misconstruction of the methodological genealogies that we have shared with the class." It continued:

> The silence on the repeated assailment of our work by white
> female colleagues, our professor's failure to acknowledge and
> assuage the escalating hostility directed at the *only* Male of Color
> in this cohort, as well as his own repeated questioning of this
> male's intellectual and professional decisions all support a compla-
> cency in this hostile and unsafe climate for Scholars of Color.

Worse was yet to come:

> It is, at its most benign, disingenuous to the next generations
> of Scholars of Color to not seek material and systematic
> changes in this department. It is a toxic, unsafe and intellectu-
> ally stifling environment at its current worse.

Mac Donald notes that the writing in the manifesto should have alarmed administrators because of what it said "about their own pedagogical failure to prepare students for scholarly writing and advising." Instead, the administration launched a campaign of all-out appeasement of the protesters. In an email to staff and students, Dean Marcelo Suárez-Orozco legitimized the disruption, saying that he was aware of "a series of troubling racial incidents," including those in Rust's class. "Rest assured," he wrote, "I take this extremely seriously. . . . As a community, we will work toward just, equitable, and lasting solutions. Together, we shall heal." The healing included announcing that Professor Rust would no longer teach the class by himself, but would be joined by three other faculty members including "the school's leading proponent of microaggression theory and critical race theory."

Other students of Rust came to his defense, including student Stephanie Kim, who wrote an op-ed article describing the protest as "a deliberately mean-spirited circus that creates exactly the hostile and toxic environment split along unsettling racial lines that the demonstrators claim to be fighting against. . . . As a woman of color, I am deeply saddened that my adviser and mentor for the last five years, Rust, was unjustly demonized as the symbol of white male oppression as a cheap way of arousing public support."[33]

But with the tacit support of the administration, the situation disintegrated. Activists launched an online petition demanding more vigorous action against "white supremacy, patriarchy, heteronormativity, and other forms of institutionalized oppression." A town hall meeting was convened to discuss the "hostile and toxic atmosphere for students of Color." Perhaps thinking naïvely that the session was intended to actually resolve the misunderstanding, rather than to be a mere airing of alleged injustices, Professor Rust attended the town hall meeting. Afterward, when Rust tried to talk to one of the students who had denounced him for failing to ask for forgiveness for his racism, the elderly professor reached out once again to touch the young man. Once again, the reaction was dramatic: the student filed battery charges against the professor and the university told Rust to stay off campus for the rest of the academic year or face disciplinary charges.

Administrators doubled down by forming a special committee to examine the school's embedded racism. Not surprisingly, the committee's report opened by heaping praise on the student protesters, who, it said, had "courageously challenged us to reflect on how we enact [the school's social-justice] mission in our own community. We owe these students a debt of thanks."[34]

Undoubtedly, UCLA professors will think long and hard before correcting their students' grammar again.

Indeed, the new politics of victimology occasionally draws sharp lines about what students are and are not allowed to talk about, even in classes that are presumably devoted to the exchange of ideas. What is most striking about this new intellectual intolerance is that it has spread to private, even traditionally Catholic colleges.

SHUT UP, THEY EXPLAINED

An undergraduate student at Milwaukee's Marquette University discovered the limits of acceptable discourse during an after-class discussion with his philosophy instructor. He told her that he was disappointed that she quickly passed over the issue of gay marriage in class, since the student wanted to argue against the policy. The instructor, a graduate student teaching assistant, told him that he would not be permitted to make any comments opposing gay marriage because they would be "homophobic" and would "offend" any gay students in the class. The student recorded the conversation with the instructor, Cheryl Abbate:

> STUDENT: Regardless of why I'm against gay marriage, it's still wrong for the teacher of a class to completely discredit one person's opinion when they may have different opinions.

ABBATE: Ok, there are some opinions that are not appropriate that are harmful, such as racist opinions, sexist opinions, and quite honestly, do you know if anyone in the class is homosexual?

STUDENT: No, I don't.

ABBATE: And don't you think that that would be offensive to them if you were to raise your hand and challenge this?

STUDENT: If I choose to challenge this, it's my right as an American citizen.

ABBATE: Ok, well, actually you don't have a right in this class, as—especially as an ethics professor, to make homophobic comments, racist comments, sexist comments—

STUDENT: Homophobic comments? They're not. I'm not saying that gays, that one guy can't like another girl or something like that. Or, one guy can't like another guy.

ABBATE: This is about restricting rights and liberties of individuals. Um, and just as I would take offense if women can't serve in XYZ positions because that is a sexist comment.

STUDENT: I don't have any problem with women saying that. I don't have any problem with women joining anything like that.

ABBATE: No, I'm saying that if you are going to make a comment like that, it would be similar to making a—

STUDENT: Absolutely.

ABBATE: How I would experience would be similar to how someone who is in this room and who is homosexual who would experience someone criticizing this.

STUDENT: Ok, so because they are homosexual I can't have my opinions? And it's not being offensive towards them because I am just having my opinions on a very broad subject.

ABBATE: *You can have whatever opinions you want but I can tell you right now, in this class homophobic comments, racist comments, and sexist comments will not be tolerated. If you don't like that you are more than free to drop this class.* [Emphasis added.][35]

Advised that he could complain about the gag rule, the student took the issue to the office of the dean of Arts and Sciences, which referred him to the chairperson of the philosophy department. According to the *College Fix,* the student was merely seeking to have the school acknowledge that the instructor was wrong to tell him he couldn't bring up gay marriage, "and ensure that students in the future will be allowed to speak in similar classroom situations."[36]

Unable to get any such response, he took his story (and the tape recording of the conversation with the instructor) to one of the most senior members of the Marquette faculty, political science professor John McAdams. In addition to being a respected political scientist, McAdams also publishes a blog called the *Marquette Warrior,* which had long been an irritant to the school's administration because of his trenchant criticism of political correctness and what he saw as the school's failure to uphold Catholic values.

In November 2014, McAdams published a blog post on the incident.[37] In the blog post, McAdams put the incident in the wider context of academic intolerance. "Abbate, of course, was just using a tactic typical among liberals now," he wrote. "Opinions with which they disagree are not merely wrong, and are not to be argued against on their merits, but are deemed 'offensive' and need to be shut up."

As McAdams later recounted, "The post created a firestorm of controversy. First, people were appalled at the instructor's actions weighed in," and then came the backlash from the left and Marquette's administration, who felt he had been unfair in criticizing the teacher. The next month, the dean of the School of Arts and Sciences informed McAdams that he was suspended from his teaching duties and banned from campus. The initial letter gave no specific grounds for the action, but it soon became clear that he was being disciplined solely for what he had written on his blog.[38]

If members of the Marquette community thought that McAdams's suspension was simply a one-time overreaction, they were quickly disabused. The next month, despite support for the professor from the

American Association of University Professors and even some left-leaning members of the Marquette faculty, the same dean sent McAdams a letter telling him that "we are commencing as of this date the procedures for revoking your tenure and dismissing you from the faculty." The dean's letter leaned heavily on the fact that the instructor had been a graduate student and that much of the criticism she had received had been harsh, imputing the responsibility for the attacks to McAdams's original blog posts.[39]

Marquette's administrators—and McAdams's leftist critics—were, in effect accusing the veteran professor of "cyberbullying" a graduate student. McAdams pointed out that his blog was factually accurate, his language was restrained, and that the "student" was acting as a faculty member. Technically, Abbate was not a teaching assistant, but rather held a "lectureship." McAdams explains: "For practical purposes, she was the professor. She contrived the syllabus. She taught the class, she assigned the grades; she conducted all of the classes. It was her class."[40]

The decision to suspend McAdams and ban him from campus drew sharp criticism from both the right and left. One of Marquette's most prominent left-wing academics, Daniel Maguire (who has himself tangled with McAdams in the past) called the decision to ban McAdams from campus over something he had written "bizarre, demeaning, and unjust.

"In almost half a century in the academe," Maguire wrote, "I have never seen a similar punishment imposed on a professor in this 'blunt instrument' fashion."[41]

McAdams admits that he was shocked. "I was appalled, I was thinking, 'How the hell, do they think they can do this?'"

Even though he had poked the bear for years, he admits that he did not expect the administration to take such a draconian step. "No," he says. "Because, it's never happened before. Usually protections of academic freedom are pretty strong.

"I mean, Holocaust deniers routinely have their academic freedom protected," he says, "9/11 Truthers routinely have their academic freedom protected. There's a guy in Florida who believes that the Sandy Hook massacre was a government operation to gin up support for gun control. He's been widely denounced. Fair enough. But no one has tried to take his tenure away from him."

Marquette, however, seemed oblivious to the implications of their decision to fire a tenured professor for something he had written. In a masterpiece of academic doublespeak, Marquette's president Mike Lovell issued a statement insisting that the attempt to fire McAdams for a blog post had nothing whatever to do with academic freedom:

> The decisions here have everything to do with our Guiding
> Values and expectations of conduct toward each other and
> nothing to do with academic freedom, freedom of speech, or
> same-sex marriage. . . .

McAdams was not impressed. "In real universities," McAdams later wrote, "administrators understand (or more likely grudgingly accept) that faculty will say controversial things, will criticize them and each other, and that people will complain about it. That sort of university is becoming rarer and rarer. Based on [the administration's] actions, Marquette is certainly not such a place."[42]

The attempted firing drew national attention and much of the criticism was withering. The *Atlantic* magazine called the move "an attack on academic freedom," and ridiculed Marquette's argument that McAdams should be held responsible for harassing and insulting emails that Abbate had received from critics. By that logic, writer Conor Friedersdorf noted, no academic could criticize anyone because they could be stripped of tenure based on "nasty emails" written by third parties. "Only myopia can account for failure to see the threat to academic freedom."[43]

The case also drew the attention of the Foundation for Individual Rights in Education (FIRE). "If Marquette can fire a tenured professor for criticizing a fellow teacher on a blog, then tenure at Marquette is worthless, as are freedom of speech and academic freedom," declared executive director Robert Shibley. "While this is more than likely just an excuse to get rid of McAdams, the fact that McAdams's supposed offense was criticizing a teacher for squelching dissenting opinions in class only makes Marquette's utter contempt for dissenters more obvious."[44]

In fact, McAdams's case appears to be exceptionally strong—based on Marquette's own written policies.

According to Marquette's Faculty Statute a tenured professor can be subject to "discretionary" dismissal only for "serious instances of illegal, immoral, dishonorable, irresponsible, or incompetent conduct." But the university's rules make it clear that a tenured professor cannot be fired for anything that is protected by academic freedom:

> In no case, however, shall discretionary cause [for dismissal] be interpreted so as to impair the full and free enjoyment of legitimate personal or *academic freedoms of thought, doctrine, discourse, association, advocacy, or action* [emphasis added].[45]

In case this is not explicit enough, the statute that lays out the causes of termination reiterates the school's commitment to protecting academic freedom: "Dismissal will not be used to restrain faculty members *in their exercise of academic freedom or other rights guaranteed them by the United States Constitution* [emphasis added]."[46] In other words, even though the school is a private institution, Marquette's professors are contractually entitled to the full breadth of First Amendment protections.

But Marquette's handling of McAdams was consistent with the tone of Marquette's sweeping speech code, which sharply limited the sorts of things that could be said on campus. As FIRE later noted, "While Marquette's policies impermissibly restrict a variety of student speech, the university's Harassment Policy stands out in particular." It reads:

> Harassment is defined as verbal, written or physical conduct directed at a person or a group based on color, race, national origin, ethnicity, gender or sexual orientation where the offensive behavior is intimidating, hostile or demeaning, or *which could or does result in mental, emotional or physical discomfort, embarrassment, ridicule or harm* [emphasis added].[47]

That prohibition is so vague and so sweeping that it would seem to rule out a good deal of the discussions that one would normally expect to find on campus. "How on earth are students expected to discuss anything remotely controversial when they can be charged with harassment for causing another person 'emotional discomfort'?" asked writer Samantha Harris. "Almost any discussion of a difficult or sensitive issue inevitably causes someone some discomfort."

For his part, McAdams is careful to distinguish the source of the attempt to fire him. "I think we've got to distinguish between old-style liberals and leftists and the politically correct types," he said. "Old-style liberals wanted to argue and stand up and make their case. New-style liberals don't necessarily want to make their case, they simply want to shut people up."[48]

In retrospect all of this was merely prologue for the campus uprisings that exploded in late 2015.

THE SNOWFLAKE REBELLION

The protests at Yale were emblematic of the new climate on college campuses across the country. The initial explosion of grievance at the Ivy League school was not caused by any overt racist act, but rather by an email that sought to make the case for tolerance on campus. On October 30, 2015, Erika Christakis, an associate master of Silliman College, a residential college at Yale, wrote a response to a campus email warning students against inappropriate Halloween costumes. An expert in early childhood education and lecturer at the Yale Child Study Center, Christakis took issue with the overwrought and paternalistic tone of the costume warning.

> When I was young, adults were freaked out by the specter of Halloween candy poisoned by lunatics, or spiked with razor blades (despite the absence of a single recorded case of such an event). Now, we've grown to fear the sugary candy itself. And this year, we seem afraid that college students are unable to decide how to dress themselves on Halloween.

Yale students had been specifically warned to avoid costumes that "appropriated" another culture. But, she wrote, as a former preschool teacher, "it is hard for me to give credence to a claim that there is something objectionably 'appropriative' about a blonde-haired child's wanting to be Mulan for a day." She wondered, "what is the statute of limitations on dreaming of dressing as Tiana the Frog Princess if you aren't a black girl from New Orleans? Is it okay if you are eight, but not 18?" She wasn't sure. But that was the point. "I don't, actually, trust myself to foist my Halloweenish standards and motives on others."

She concluded with a commonsense suggestion for Yale students.

> Nicholas [her husband, the master of the residential college] says, if you don't like a costume someone is wearing, look away, or tell them you are offended. Talk to each other. Free speech and the ability to tolerate offence are the hallmarks of a free and open society. . . .

> In other words: Whose business is it to control the forms of costumes of young people? It's not mine, I know that.

Her email, in short, was thoughtful, nuanced . . . and met with an explosion of rage. In a scene captured on video, students surrounded

Erika Christakis's husband, Nicholas, as he tried to explain why the university should not infantilize students by censoring their costumes. As he tries to explain his opposition to censorship, one young woman screams: "Be quiet! In your position as master it is your job to create a place of comfort and home for the students that live in Silliman. You have not done that. By sending out that email, that goes against your position as master, do you understand that?"

When Nicholas Christakis tries to explain why he does not agree, she shrieks:

> Then why the f*** did you accept the position? Who the f*** are you? You should step down. If that is what you think about being a master you should step down. Do you understand? It is about creating a home here. You are not doing that. . . . You should not sleep at night. You are disgusting.[49]

If anything, the incident emboldened Yale's protesters. When the William F. Buckley Jr. Program at Yale sponsored a forum on free speech on campus, activists attempted to disrupt the event. A report in the student newspaper reported that "several attendees were spat on as they left. One Buckley fellow said he was spat on and called a racist. Another, who is a minority himself, said he has been labeled a 'traitor' by several fellow minority students. Both asked to remain anonymous because they were afraid of attracting backlash."[50]

Yale's response to all of this would become a template for other schools—almost complete capitulation. Nicholas Christakis later offered a public apology for his insensitivity and within weeks of the controversy over the email, Yale President Peter Salovey declared his determination to "build a more inclusive Yale." While paying lip service to the ideal of free speech, Salovey acceded to many of the activists demands, including expanding financial support for the Afro-American Cultural Center, the Asian American Cultural Center, La Casa Cultural, and the Native American Cultural Center. In addition, despite decades of sensitivity training and multiple "diversity" programs on campus, he announced plans to launch a campus-wide plan to reeducate the university "about race, ethnicity, diversity, and inclusion," and announced that: "I, along with the vice presidents, deans, provosts, and other members of the administration, will receive training on recognizing and combating racism and other forms of discrimination in the academy."[51]

At the University of Missouri Columbia, protesters issued a grammatically challenged demand that administrators confess to their racial "privilege":

> We demand that University of Missouri System President, Tim Wolfe, writes a hand-written apology to [the] demonstrators and holds a press conference in the Mizzou Student Center reading the letter. In the letter and at the press conference, Tim Wolfe must acknowledge his white privilege, recognize that systems of oppression exits, and provide a verbal commitment to fulfilling [protester] demands. . . ."[52]

After members of the football team joined with activists and threatened to go on strike, the school's president and chancellor were forced to resign. Even after achieving that victory, however, campus protesters escalated their tactics, leading to a confrontation between a faculty member and a student reporter trying to cover a protest on the public, taxpayer-funded campus. After telling the reporter he had to leave the protest, Professor Melissa Click, a professor of communications, was caught on videotape trying to grab the student's camera and then calling for "muscle" to forcibly remove the reporter. Click later apologized, and resigned her "courtesy appointment" in Mizzou's journalism school, and was later fired by the university.[53]

Apparently hoping to avoid a similar incident with journalists, protesters at prestigious Smith College (tuition and fees, $63,950 a year) came up with their own twist: they demanded that any journalist who wished to cover their events would first have to pledge to support "and articulate their solidarity with black students and students of color." Only reporters who explicitly pledged their support for the movement would be allowed to attend.

The reaction from Smith College's administration?

Stacey Schmeidel, Smith College director of media relations, said the college supports the activists' ban on media.

"It's a student event, and we respect their right to do that, although it poses problems for the traditional media," Stacey Schmeidel said.

Schmeidel went on to say that the college reserves the right to remove reporters from the Student Center because it's a private campus.[54]

Even at normally quiet Amherst College (tuition and fees, $62,940 a year), activists angrily demanded the school discipline students who had put up signs lamenting the demise of free speech on campus. The protesters' demands were a word salad of victimism, calling on the school's president to apologize for Amherst's "institutional legacy of white supremacy, colonialism, anti-black racism, anti-Latinx racism, anti-Native American racism, anti-Native/indigenous racism, anti-Asian racism, anti-Middle Eastern racism, heterosexism, cis-sexism, xenophobia, anti-Semitism, ableism, mental health stigma, and classism."

More specifically, the group calling itself the Amherst Uprising demanded that the administrators "not tolerate the actions of student(s) who posted the 'All Lives Matter' posters," and posters that lamented the demise of free speech on campus. The activists demanded that the college apologize not only for allowing the posters, but should also search out those responsible, and subject them to "extensive training for racial and cultural competency."[55]

CHAPTER 12

RAPE U.

KARL MARX WAS WRONG. "History repeats itself," he said, "first as tragedy, second as farce."

But as it turns out, what begins as farce can become deadly serious, even tragic, the second time around.

In the early 1990s, Antioch, a small college in Ohio, unveiled a new policy for sexual assault that required participants to ask for and receive affirmative assent to each and every separate act in a sexual encounter. The policy was widely ridiculed, including a skit on *Saturday Night Live* that parodied the policy by presenting it as a television game show called *Is It Date Rape?*[1]

ANNOUNCER: Live, from Antioch College in Antioch, Ohio . . . it's time to play . . .

AUDIENCE: *Is . . . It . . . Date Rape?!*

ANNOUNCER: with your host, the dean of intergender relations, Dean Frederick Whitcomb! [*played by Phil Hartman*]

Contestants in the SNL skit included a "major in Victimization Studies" (played by Shannen Doherty) and a football player/frat boy (played by Chris Farley). The dean (Hartman) begins the show by defining the rules:

Okay, for those of you not familiar with the rules to our game, it's quite simple. Antioch College defines date rape *as:* any sexual contact or conduct between two or more persons, in which consent of such contact, which includes: the touching of thighs, genitals, buttocks, or the breast/chest area is not expressly obtained in a verbal manner. If the level of sexual intimacy increases during an interaction: i.e., if two people move from kissing while fully clothed to undressing for direct physical contact, and the people involved do not express their clear verbal consent before moving to that level, that too is . . . date rape.

After running through a series of scenarios ("It is the last day of school, a female student asks a male student to help her move her futon": Date Rape!), the Phil Hartman character introduces the Antioch College Date Rape Players to help explain the rules to the contestants.

MALE DATE RAPE PLAYER 1: May I compliment you on your halter top?

FEMALE DATE RAPE PLAYER 1: Yes. You may.

MALE DATE RAPE PLAYER 1: It's very nice. May I kiss you on the mouth?

FEMALE DATE RAPE PLAYER 1: Yes. I would like you to *kiss* me on the *mouth*.

[*They kiss on the mouth.*]

MALE DATE RAPE PLAYER 1: May I elevate the level of sexual intimacy by feeling your buttocks?

FEMALE DATE RAPE PLAYER 1: Yes. You have my permission.

[*Male touches female's buttocks.*]

MALE DATE RAPE PLAYER 1: May I raise the level yet again, and take my clothes off so that we could have intercourse?

FEMALE DATE RAPE PLAYER 1: Yes. I am granting your request to have intercourse.

[*Scene ends.*]

DEAN FREDERICK WHITCOMB: Contestants?

VICTIM STUDIES MAJOR: [*buzzes in*] Date Rape!

DEAN FREDERICK WHITCOMB: Ohhhh . . . sorry! Mark, what do you say? Is it date rape?

FRAT BOY: Uhhh . . . oh, man! [*beats himself up*] Uhhh . . . Date Rape?

DEAN FREDERICK WHITCOMB: Ohhhh . . . sorry! We were looking for "It is *not* date rape." *Not* Date Rape.

The skit is funny and politically incorrect. But it was also prophetic.

What was farce in 1993 *is now the law in states like California and campuses across the country.* Call it Antioch's revenge.

In 2014, California state law not only shifted the burden of proof to the accused in sexual assault cases on campus, but also required that participants show affirmative consent for all of their sexual acts. Consent is defined in the law as "an affirmative, unambiguous, and conscious decision by each participant to engage in mutually agreed-upon sexual activity." The law specifies that this consent must be "ongoing." Unless the accused student can show that such consent was explicit and "ongoing," they will be found guilty of violating the school's sexual assault policy.[2]

The new rules—a conflation of High Victorian prudery and radical feminist theory—read as if they were written by people who have never actually had sex. George Washington University law professor John Banzhaf notes that the standards are unreasonable, because

> it just isn't the way things work. How would this work in practice? Suppose the guy asks, 'May I touch your breast?' Does that mean through her shirt? Over her bra? Does that mean he can touch her bare breast? Does it mean he can touch it with his hand or his lips? What if this all happens in succession? As things escalate, is he supposed to ask before each of the 20, 30, 40 steps? Nobody talks like that, not even lawyers.[3]

As Robert Carle noted, the rules apply only to college students—not faculty or administrators—and are potentially draconian in their application. "For example," he wrote on the Federalist website, "if a student throws her arms around her boyfriend and kisses him without his permission, even if she has done this dozens of times before, she has violated affirmative consent policies."[4]

Nor should she count on the campus adjudicators of the charge to show much concern for her due process rights or to anything approaching traditional notions of evidence. In a statement opposing the California law, the Foundation for Individual Rights in Education (FIRE) warned:

> [There] will be no practical, fair, or consistent way for colleges (or, for that matter, courts) to ensure that these newly mandated prerequisites for sexual intercourse are followed. It is impracticable for the government to require students to obtain

affirmative consent at each stage of a physical encounter, and to later prove that attainment in a campus hearing. Under this mandate, a student could be found guilty of sexual assault and deemed a rapist simply by being unable to prove she or he obtained explicit verbal consent to every sexual activity throughout a sexual encounter."[5]

YES, YOU TOO COULD BE A RAPIST

Indeed, the new rules seem to rewrite the grammar of sexual encounter so thoroughly that a host of sexual contacts could be redefined into "sexual assault." Yale's new policy, for instance, demands that any sexual contact can be considered a rape if consent is not "positive," "specific," and "unambiguous." Under that new standard, notes Jed Rubenfeld, a professor of criminal law at Yale's Law School, "a person who voluntarily gets undressed, gets into bed and has sex with someone, without clearly communicating either yes or no, can later say—correctly—that he or she was raped. This is not a law school hypothetical. The unambiguous consent standard requires this conclusion."[6]

David Bernstein, a professor of law at George Mason University, agrees that the affirmative consent standards are absurd in practice. "Just leaning over to give your date (or your spouse) a kiss without asking first and receiving a yes comes within stated definition of sexual assault," he notes, "regardless of how many times you've done it before without objection."

But Bernstein also notes the new rigorous policies raise two obvious questions: (1) Why are the new rules applied only on college campuses, not to society as a whole, and (2) why are they applied just to students, but not to faculty or administrators?[7]

"The answer," writes Bernstein, "is that it's not a good idea, and it's a product of the current moral panic over the hookup culture." But that panic is already rapidly reshaping American campus life.

WHEN FARCE BECOMES REALITY

Colleges are not, of course, merely places where students go to study. As Tom Wolfe has so graphically chronicled, the modern university can be "a hedonistic playground of nonstop drinking and rampant casual sex."[8] His account in *I Am Charlotte Simmons* of the interplay of drinking, drugs, and casual hookups can be unsettling reading for parents sending their offspring away to what looks like a four-year binge/party. But overblown or not, the reality is that the modern campus often revolves around the age-old twin obsessions of booze and the opposite sex. It can also be a very scary place both for the victims of sexual assault and for those accused of it.

Of course, sexual assault can never be tolerated and colleges need to confront it with the utmost seriousness. But on the modern alcohol-soaked college campus, the cases may not always be so simple. Can consensual sex become nonconsensual (rape) retroactively? What if one or both of the parties has second thoughts, days or even months afterward? Because they sobered up? Or because their mom found their diary? And what about due process? Unfortunately, in addition to the pain suffered by actual victims, too many students have been caught up in higher education's newly hatched Kafkaesque system. Many of them have been forced to file lawsuits against schools who have suspended or expelled them despite shaky or nonexistent evidence.

"The legal filings in the cases brought by young men accused of sexual violence often begin like a script for a college sex farce," wrote Emily Yoffe in *Slate*, "but end with the protagonist finding himself in a Soviet-style show trial."[9] Or sometimes with no trial at all. This new regime represents the intersection of media hype (a la *Rolling Stone*'s discredited account of an alleged gang rape at the University of Virginia), political opportunism, government coercion, and gender politics on campus. The results are sometimes bizarre.

Harvard law professor Janet Halley recounts how she had assisted a young man who had found himself caught up in an investigation by the administration at the liberal arts university he attended in Oregon. He was subjected to interrogation about his campus relationships, "seeking information about his possible sexual misconduct in them (an immense invasion of his and his friends' privacy)." Despite being innocent of any wrongdoing, Halley wrote, the young man was also "ordered to stay away from a fellow student (cutting him off from his housing, his campus job, and educational opportunity)—all because he *reminded her* of the man who had raped her months before and thousands of miles away."[10]

But in the new environment on campus, not even total innocence was a sufficient defense. Even after he was "found to be completely innocent of any sexual misconduct," the "stay-away order remained in place, and was so broadly drawn up that he was at constant risk of violating it and coming under discipline for *that*." As Halley later wrote in the *Harvard Law Review*: "When the duty to prevent a 'sexually hostile environment' is interpreted this expansively, it is affirmatively indifferent to the restrained person's complete and total innocence of any misconduct whatsoever."

But this is what happens when the presumption of innocence and the centrality of due process is replaced with an ideological, legal, and bureaucratic imperative to believe the victim and to take the swiftest and most draconian action as quickly as possible.

A RAPE IN VIRGINIA. OR NOT.

Among the highly publicized campus incidents that was seized upon to call attention to the "rape culture" allegedly prevalent on campus, no incident received more attention than the horrifying account in *Rolling Stone* of a 2012 gang rape at a University of Virginia fraternity. The article by writer Sabrina Rubin Erdely described in vivid detail how the victim ("Jackie") was "brutally assaulted by seven men at a frat party." The magazine piece was also a blistering indictment of the university for failing to respond adequately. "When she tried to hold [her attacker] accountable," the headline read, "a whole new kind of abuse began."[11]

The response: a firestorm of indignation, rallies, protests, and swift action by University of Virginia administrators, who seemed intent on not appearing to underreact to the article. University of Virginia president Teresa Sullivan went so far as to suspend all fraternity activities—even those of fraternities that were not implicated in the story at all. Sullivan issued a statement to the university community that seemed to prejudge the case:

> The wrongs described in Rolling Stone are appalling and have caused all of us to reexamine our responsibility to this community. Rape is an abhorrent crime that has no place in the world, let alone on the campuses and grounds of our nation's colleges and universities. We know, and have felt very powerfully this week, that we are better than we have been described, and that we have a responsibility to live our tradition of honor every day, and as importantly every night.[12]

Sullivan said that the university had asked the local police to investigate, but she did not wait for that investigation to pledge actions that implicitly assumed the allegations were true:

> I write you today in solidarity. I write you in great sorrow, great rage, but most importantly, with great determination. Meaningful change is necessary, and we can lead that change for all universities. We can demand that incidents like those described in Rolling Stone never happen and that if they do, the responsible are held accountable to the law. This will require institutional change, cultural change, and legislative change, and it will not be easy. We are making those changes.

But there was a problem: Jackie's story quickly unraveled. A series of articles in the *Washington Post* documented inconsistencies, errors, and what appeared to have been outright fabrications by the alleged victim, including her apparent invention of an imaginary boyfriend. There had been no party at the fraternity the night she claimed to have been assaulted. Other students came forward to deny her claims, while some of her friends told the paper they had come to doubt her story. This led *Rolling Stone* to make an extraordinary admission. Erdely confessed that she had never even attempted to check the accuracy of Jackie's story by talking with any of the male students she had accused of assaulting her. "Because of the sensitive nature of Jackie's story, we decided to honor her request not to contact the man who she claimed orchestrated the attack on her nor any of the men who she claimed participated in the attack for fear of retaliation against her."[13]

The magazine—and the university—would come to regret that decision to suspend what amounted to journalistic due process as it became apparent that Jackie's accusations had fallen apart.* The article had been thoroughly discredited by the time the Charlottesville Police Department issued a final investigative report that concluded that there was "no substantive basis to support" the magazine's account.[14]

Despite the furor surrounding the article and the seriousness of the charges she had leveled against fellow UVA students, the police report said, Jackie refused to cooperate with them in any way—she

---

* After *Rolling Stone* retracted the story, President Sullivan in effect retracted some of her own earlier comments, issuing a statement that said in part:

> Irresponsible journalism unjustly damaged the reputations of many innocent individuals and the University of Virginia. Rolling Stone falsely accused some University of Virginia students of heinous, criminal acts and falsely depicted others as indifferent to the suffering of their classmate. The story portrayed University staff members as manipulative and callous toward victims of sexual assault. Such false depictions reinforce the reluctance sexual assault victims already feel about reporting their experience, lest they be doubted or ignored.

declined to provide any statement or answer any questions. She also refused to give police consent to view records that might aid in the investigation. "Despite numerous attempts to gain her cooperation," the report said, "'Jackie' has provided no information whatsoever to investigators."*

Police also found that many elements of Jackie's story turned out to have been flatly untrue. "In short," police concluded, "we cannot find any basis of fact to conclude that there was any event at the Phi Kappa Psi Fraternity house on the evening of September 28, 2012." While they were careful to avoid flatly saying that Jackie had fabricated the entire story,† the report found "no substantive basis of fact to conclude that an incident occurred that is consistent with the facts as described in the November 19, 2014, *Rolling Stone* magazine article."

The story may have been discredited, but the damage at Virginia was very real: to the students who were falsely accused and whose lives were disrupted, the organizations whose reputation was attacked, the administrators who were unfairly portrayed, and the school itself, which had become known as the "Rape School." But the greatest setback may have been to the genuine victims of sexual assault. The *Columbia Journalism Review* (CJR) analysis of the botched story quoted one rape survivor saying that at UVA, "It's going to be more difficult now

---

*The police statement said that the University of Virginia provided investigators access to relevant members of the Office of the Dean of Students who had knowledge of "Jackie's" previous contacts with their office, along with redacted copies of documents that reflect Dean Eramo's previous meetings with "Jackie"; specifically those documents referencing the sexual assault, physical assault, and an anonymous sexual assault report. "None of the documents we were given or had access to revealed any facts similar to what was disclosed in the Rolling Stone article."

†The department's statement acknowledged that it could not prove a negative: "The department's investigation cannot rule out that something may have happened to 'Jackie' somewhere and at some time on the evening of September 28, 2012. Yet, without additional evidence we are simply unable to reach a definitive conclusion."

to engage some people . . . because they have a preconceived notion that women lie about sexual assault."[15]

How did it happen? The magazine believed Jackie's story because it wanted to believe it. "Erdely and her editors had hoped their investigation would sound an alarm about campus sexual assault and would challenge Virginia and other universities to do better," the *Columbia Journalism Review* analysis found. "Jackie's story seemed a powerful candidate for such a narrative." In other words, the story had a preconceived agenda and the writer and editors set aside normal standards of skepticism because the story fit the narrative they set out to prove. Like many of the new adjudicators of sexual assault on campus, the magazine became invested in believing the victim's allegations, despite the holes and contradictions. Inconvenient facts and evidence that might have called the entire story line into question were ignored. The report found that *Rolling Stone* "set aside or rationalized as unnecessary essential practices of reporting that, if pursued, would likely have led the magazine's editors to reconsider publishing Jackie's narrative so prominently, if at all."[16]

The Virginia story ought to be a cautionary tale for academia, illustrating as it does the danger of policies that undermine due process or that accept victims' allegations at face value. But it is far from clear that the collapse of the false narrative will do much to change the way higher education continues to respond to the issue. Some of that intransigence is legal—the federal government's edict remains in force—and some is frankly ideological. In the world of victimology, the specific details of a case are treated as less significant than the "larger truths" that they reveal. Even if a given case turns out to be a hoax, advocates still insist that it serves to raise our consciousness and is therefore useful. "Accurate or not," one news account insisted, "the *Rolling Stone* article heightened scrutiny of campus sexual assaults amid a campaign by President Barack Obama to end them."[17] In other words, the larger agenda can trump the inconvenient details of the smaller lie.

THE DEAR COLLEAGUE LETTER

Political correctness on college campuses is not a recent phenomenon, but the spread of the new disciplinary regimes largely can be traced to a letter from the Obama administration, now known as the "Dear Colleague" letter. In the April 4, 2011, letter to schools across the country that received federal aid (which almost all colleges do), Russlynn Ali, the assistant secretary for civil rights in the US Department of Education, spelled out instructions for new systems and procedures for handling sexual assault cases. The letter carried a heavy hammer: Henceforth federal funds would be linked to compliance with the new edict. Declaring that "the likelihood that [female students] will be assaulted by the time they graduate is significant," the Office of Civil Rights insisted that schools adjust their standards for judging the guilt or innocence of students accused of assault.[18]

Before the "Dear Colleague" letter, schools had relied on a standard of "clear and convincing evidence" (as opposed to the criminal court standard of "beyond a reasonable doubt") to judge guilt or innocence in sexual assault cases. But the OCR said that this would no longer be good enough. Instead, institutions were instructed to rely on "a preponderance of evidence" standard when deciding on discipline. As Emily Yoffe noted, "This is the lowest evidentiary standard, only requiring a smidge more than 50 percent certainty" for cases that could result in life-changing punishments.

The OCR letter also mandated other changes. In cases where the accused was found "not responsible," accusers were also given the right to appeal, opening the possibility that acquitted students would face what amounted to double jeopardy on the charge. Under the new rules, accused students are often not allowed to speak with their lawyers during disciplinary hearings and the parties are not permitted to either question or cross-examine one another, "a prohibition recommended by the federal government in order to protect the accuser."[19]

But as Yoffe noted in her widely debated piece in *Slate*, "bad policy" was being "made on the back of problematic research, and will continue to be unless we bring some heathy skepticism" to the question of the prevalence of sexual assault on campus. In making sexual assault on campus one of his administration's signature initiatives, President Obama has frequently claimed that one in five women on campus has been sexually assaulted.

That makes for a good sound bite and a powerful justification for the federal government's crackdown. But is it true?

Obama's number is based on the Campus Sexual Assault Study, or CSA, which administered an online survey to 5,466 female students at two public universities (one in the Midwest and one in the South). The participants were asked a series of questions that took fifteen minutes to complete, after which they were given a ten-dollar Amazon.com gift card for filling out the questionnaire.[20] As Yoffe points out, the survey defined sexual assault rather broadly—including not just unwanted intercourse, but also "forced kissing," "fondling," and "rubbing up against you in a sexual way, even if it is over your clothes."*

---

*In 2014, the two researchers who conducted the online survey wrote a piece for *Time* magazine, which tried to set the record straight:

> As two of the researchers who conducted the Campus Sexual Assault Study from which this number was derived, we feel we need to set the record straight. Although we used the best methodology available to us at the time, there are caveats that make it inappropriate to use the 1-in-5 number in the way it's being used today, as a baseline or the only statistic when discussing our country's problem with rape and sexual assault on campus.
>
> First and foremost, the 1-in-5 statistic is not a nationally representative estimate of the prevalence of sexual assault, and we have never presented it as being representative of anything other than the population of senior undergraduate women at the two universities where data were collected—two large public universities, one in the South and one in the Midwest.

(Christopher Krebs and Christine Lindquist, "Setting the Record Straight on '1 in 5,'" *Time*, December 15, 2014)

But other statistical measures paint a vastly different picture. For example, for the years 1995 to 2011, the National Crime Victimization Survey, which is conducted by the federal government, found that around 0.8 percent of women aged eighteen to twenty-four *who did not attend college* said that they were victims of threatened, attempted, or actual rape/sexual assault. That compared to 0.6 percent of *college* females in that age group who said they experienced such attempted or actual assaults. As Yoffe notes, "that finding diverges wildly from the notion that one in five college women will be sexually assaulted by the time they graduate," which is the number used to justify the new enforcement diktats.[21]

The result of the new federal mandates and the campus policies they have spawned has been a steady stream of stories and lawsuits of students who claimed they had been railroaded by questionable claims of assault. In a 2014 article headlined "Presumed Guilty," the *Chronicle of Higher Education* examined the complaints of male students who said that the scales had been tipped against them.[22] The *Chronicle* article included the account of a sophomore astronomy major from the University of Massachusetts who was accused of sexual assault even though he says the sex was consensual. Identified as "John Doe," the student said that a female classmate invited him to her apartment. While they both had been drinking, neither was intoxicated and the woman's consent was explicit.

> "She said yes to everything I asked, and immediately prior to having sex, she said, 'Put on a condom.' At one point I had stopped, and she asked me why, and I said, 'I'm sorry. I'm a little nervous.' And she said, 'OK, don't worry about it.'"
>
> The next day, says Mr. Doe, he sent the woman a text message, asking her if what had happened was a one-night stand or the beginning of a relationship. Her answer: a one-night stand. Later that day, he says, he got a call from the

dean's office: The young woman was alleging that Mr. Doe had sexually assaulted her.[23]

Following the new federal rules, university officials gave him just six hours to vacate his dorm. "They treated me with such hostility," he told the *Chronicle*, "like I was already a criminal." University officials ultimately decided that his partner had been too drunk to consent to sex and he was expelled. "They undermined all of the hard work I had done," Doe told the *Chronicle*. "It was humiliating and degrading." Like dozens of others, the student filed a suit challenging the school's treatment of him.

The University of Michigan also faced a federal lawsuit from a student named Drew Sterrett, who was accused of sexual assault months after the incident, and only after the female student's mother found a diary recounting her sexual activity. Prior to the incident in March 2012, according to his lawsuit, Sterrett "had an excellent reputation, zero involvement with law enforcement and conducted himself in a manner that was completely respectful of women at all times." The alleged victim filed her complaint against Sterrett in August 2012—five months after the sexual encounter.

Yoffe recounts Sterrett's ordeal in detail, including Michigan's apparent decision to ignore much of the evidence in his favor. The alleged victim—called CB in court documents—insisted that she had been asleep when she was assaulted, a claim contradicted by time-stamped social media at the time of the incident. Throughout the incident, Sterrett's roommate was in the upper bunk above the couple having sex.

Their sex became so loud and went on for so long that Sterrett's roommate, unable to sleep in the upper bunk, sent Sterrett a Facebook message around 3 a.m.: "Dude, you and [CB] are being abnoxtiously [sic] loud and inconsiderate, so expect to pay back in full tomorrow."[24]

The case is also notable because of the role of the alleged victim's mother. According to CB's sophomore-year roommate, she received a phone call from an "emotionally upset" CB who said that her mother had found a diary that "contained descriptions of romantic and sexual experiences, drug use, and drinking." The roommate later filed a deposition saying that: "It is my belief, based on my personal observations and conversations with CB, that it is possible CB manufactured a story about a sexual assault in response to the conflict CB described occurring between her and her mother in the summer of 2012."

None of this, however, was of much help to Sterrett, who was suspended from Michigan after officials "determined that [he] engaged in sexual intercourse with [her] without her consent and that that activity is so severe as to create a hostile environment," according to his suit in federal court.[25] In September 2015, three years after he was forced to leave school, the University of Michigan vacated the charges against Sterrett and cleared his transcript of any disciplinary action. In an email to Yoffe, he described his three-year-long fight to clear his name as "emotionally difficult, debilitating and crushing at times."

Similar lawsuits have been filed against Vassar College, Duke University, Occidental College, Columbia University, Xavier University, Swarthmore College, and Delaware State University among other schools. "The common thread is really egregious due process violations," attorney Andrew Miltenberg told the *Los Angeles Times*. The overall effect of the OCR's "Dear Colleague" policies, said FIRE's Robert Shibley, "has been a significant amount of pressure on universities to treat all of those accused of sexual misconduct with a presumption of guilt."[26]

SHUT UP, THEY EXPLAINED. AGAIN.

Despite the fragile foundations of the new regimes, daring to question them can be risky, even for someone not employed by an institution of higher education.

In June 2014, conservative columnist George Will drew the wrath of feminist enforcers by writing a column in the *Washington Post* that questioned the spreading culture of victimization on college campuses. Will's column touched on the rise of the notion of "microaggressions" and "trigger warnings," noting that victims tend to "proliferate" when campuses "make victimhood a coveted status that confers privileges."[27]

But what generated the backlash was Will's critique of the new approaches to sexual assault mandated by the Obama administration. The new rules, Will wrote, promised to sort out all of the "ambiguities of the hookup culture, this cocktail of hormones, alcohol and the faux sophistication of today's prolonged adolescence of especially privileged young adults." He questioned the Obama administration's claim that one in five college women are assaulted, and cited a case at Swarthmore where a female student waited six weeks to report an assault that had taken place under decidedly ambiguous circumstances.

The federal's government's demand that schools adopt a minimal "preponderance of the evidence" standard when adjudicating sexual assault charges was combined, Will wrote, "with capacious definitions of sexual assault that can include not only forcible sexual penetration but also nonconsensual touching," as well as the doctrine "that the consent of a female who has been drinking might not protect a male from being found guilty of rape." The result, Will noted (quite accurately), was a flood of litigation.

Outrage ensued.

The reaction to Will's column became itself a case study in academia's new culture of intolerance. Faculty members at Miami University worked themselves into a state of high dudgeon, accusing Will of "hate speech" that "amount to the sort of vitriol that potentially encourages violence against women." Objecting to Will's planned appearance on campus, the director of the Women's Gender and Sexuality program at the Oxford, Ohio, campus professed herself "disappointed that a speaker who clearly does not respect women, or take the issue of sexual assault seriously, is being given a platform to speak, particularly because such inflammatory rhetoric has the potential to re-victimize and re-traumatize some of our students."[28] (Implicit in this was the suggestion that Will's words should be flagged with a "trigger warning.")

Going even further, Scripps College canceled its speaking invitation to Will. President Lori Bettison-Varga said that Scripps had revoked the invitation because Will had "trivialized" sexual assault."[29] In a statement, Bettison-Varga declared:

> Sexual assault is not a conservative or liberal issue. And it is too important to be trivialized in a political debate or wrapped into a celebrity controversy. For that reason, after Mr. Will authored a column questioning the validity of a specific sexual assault case that reflects similar experiences reported by Scripps students, we decided not to finalize the speaker agreement.*

In case there was any doubt that Will had strayed into forbidden territory, four United States senators—Richard Blumenthal, Dianne Feinstein, Tammy Baldwin, and Robert P. Casey, Jr.—censured Will for trivializing the "scourge of sexual assault," and insisting that the new federal rules "have received positive feedback."[30] While the *Washington Post* stood by Will, pointing out that his column was "within the realm of legitimate debate," other media outlets disagreed. The *Chicago Tribune* declined to publish the offending column, while the *St. Louis Post-Dispatch* went further, apologizing for allowing Will's "offensive and inaccurate" comments to be printed in its pages and announcing that it was henceforth dropping his syndicated column.[31]

---

*After the decision to cancel Will's appearance, Christopher DeMuth, a former president of the American Enterprise Institute, resigned in protest from the school's speaker selection committee.

Ironically, Will pointed out, many of his critics seemed to miss the underlying point of his column: that sexual assault was in fact too serious a crime to be politicized or handled by academic kangaroo courts. In an interview with radio host Dennis Prager, Will explained: "My argument was that sexual assault is so serious—we rank it in our Western law as just shy of murder . . . and we have lots of laws against it. And if someone is accused of rape, it's serious business and should be put in the hands of professionals, that is the criminal justice system, instead of jerrybuilt, due-process-challenged semi-courts on campuses."[32]

The reaction to Will's column sent a rather stark message: dissent on this issue was hazardous to one's professional health, for conservative columnists but even more so for academics themselves. So it is not surprising that the most vocal critics of the new sexual inquisitions tend to be lawyers for those who are being disciplined or tenured faculty members at elite schools with the clout to push back.

THE HARVARD BACKLASH

Harvard law professor Janet Halley created a considerable stir when she sounded the alarm over the violence that the new policies on sexual assault did to the principle of due process. Critiquing Harvard's new OCR-compliant harassment policies, she concluded that they were tilted "in favor of the complainant and an irrebuttable presumption against the respondent."[33] One central problem was that Harvard—along with other schools—was putting the Title IX office in charge of adjudicating charges of sexual assault and harassment. Critics pointed out that Title IX offices were unsuited to such a role, since they were designed for compliance monitoring and were, after all, focused exclusively on sex discrimination, not on the careful balancing of the many issues involved in he-said-she said, often drunken sexual encounters.

Harvard's required training program for staff members, for example, emphasized the trauma involved, which may cause victims to tell stories that "may come out garbled or 'sketchy.'" This can cause investigators to conclude that the victim may be lying. The intention of the training program, wrote Halley, was "100% aimed to convince them to believe complainants, precisely *when* they seem unreliable and incoherent. . . . Meanwhile, the immense social, cultural, and psychological differences that can affect the credibility and coherence of *both* parties' accounts" went unmentioned.

Harvard's policy also glossed over other complications: for instance, why might someone change their minds about whether the sex was consensual? Many of the cases pose thorny evidentiary and credibility problems. Sometimes the change of heart is attributed to heavy drug or alcohol use or memory loss.

> Do we want to say that the sex assented to and engaged in by
> a person who forgets most or all of the details the next day
> was—for the reason of memory loss alone—done by a person
> who was morally or legally incapacitated? Sometimes we will
> say yes, for instance when we think that memory loss was
> caused not by drinking or drug use but by psychological
> dissociation from intensely aversive experience. But what if it
> is selective; what if it is self-serving; what if it is motivated by
> unconscious racial bias or by a felt need to disavow shame,
> avert a *crise de conscience,* or pacify an angry parent, spouse,
> or partner?

Halley was skeptical that officials in the Title IX office would be able to sort all of that out.

Halley was not alone in her discomfort with the erosion of due process rights. Perhaps the strongest—and in some ways the most surprising—response to the new sexual assault regime came from her colleagues in the Harvard Law School. In October 2014, Halley and twenty-seven of her colleagues (including some the biggest names on the faculty) signed a statement objecting to the university's new policy.[34]

The law professors concluded by calling on Harvard to withdraw the new policy and "begin the challenging project of carefully thinking through what substantive and procedural rules would best balance the complex issues involved in addressing sexual conduct and misconduct in our community."

What is unclear is whether even Harvard Law will be able to stem the tide. Pressure on schools to comply with the federal government are immense. When Tufts University briefly sought to push back against the OCR, it was slapped down—hard. While Tufts agreed to implement changes to its sexual assault disciplinary system, it drew the line at the OCR's insistence that the school admit its guilt as a Title IX violator. Finding (at least temporarily) its backbone, the Tufts administration issued a statement saying that it "could not, in good faith, allow our community to believe that we are not in compliance with such an important law."[35]

The OCR responded to Tufts' defiance by threatening to cut all of its federal funding. That was an offer the university could not refuse. Tufts quickly capitulated and other schools got the obvious message: Comply or face massive retaliation. Based on the history of higher education in recent decades, such resistance seems highly unlikely.

KAFKA U.

Indeed, the new Title IX regimes have taken a decidedly Kafkaesque turn for individual professors who dare to question the new policies. Perhaps the most celebrated case was Northwestern University professor Laura Kipnis, who was actually brought up on charges of violating Title IX for writing a column criticizing Title IX.

Unlike the typical targets of campus speech police, Kipnis was an outspoken progressive feminist, but one who dissented from what she called "feminism hijacked by melodrama" and the ensuing "sexual panic" on campus. In an essay in the *Chronicle of Higher Education* titled "Sexual Paranoia Strikes Academe," Kipnis criticized new rules governing faculty-student dating that she said infantilized students. The new rules she wrote seem "designed for maximum stupefaction." Worse yet, she wrote, was the "climate of sanctimony about student vulnerability has grown impenetrable. No one dares question it lest you're labeled antifeminist, or worse, a sex criminal."[36]

The article drew immediate protests, with students calling Kipnis's essay "terrifying" and marching on the university president's office carrying mattresses (a popular prop in protests of sexual assault) demanding official condemnation of Kipnis's essay.[37] At first Kipnis was puzzled by the presence of the mattresses, since they were symbols of the sexual assault of students by other students, "and I'd been writing about the new consensual-relations codes governing professor-student dating. Also, I'd been writing as a feminist. And I hadn't sexually assaulted anyone. The whole thing seemed symbolically incoherent."[38]

She also assumed that since the protests centered on something she had written rather than any overt act on her part, "academic freedom would prevail." She was, therefore unprepared to be plunged into what she later described as "an underground world of secret tribunals and capricious, medieval rules," in which she "wasn't supposed to tell anyone about it."

Shortly after the protests began, Kipnis received a letter from Northwestern's Title IX coordinator informing her that two students had filed Title IX complaints charging her with "retaliation" for the article and subsequent tweets.* She was also told that the matter was serious enough for the university to hire outside investigators to in-

---

* "Please pause to note that a Title IX charge can now be brought against a professor over a tweet," Kipnis later wrote. "Also that my tweets were apparently being monitored." (Laura Kipnis, "My Title IX Inquisition," *Chronicle Review,* May 29, 2015)

vestigate her. "I stared at the email," she later wrote, "which was under-explanatory in the extreme. I was being charged with retaliation, it said, though it failed to explain how an essay that mentioned no one by name could be construed as retaliatory, or how a publication fell under the province of Title IX, which, as I understood it, dealt with sexual misconduct and gender discrimination."

But the Title IX machinery had been set in motion. Kipnis was subsequently told that she would not be allowed to have a lawyer accompany her during the investigations, although she was allowed a "support person" who would not be allowed to speak. Moreover, she was told, she wouldn't learn the specifics of the charges against her until she showed up for her interview with the out-of-town lawyers hired by the university. "Apparently the idea was that they'd tell me the charges, and then, while I was collecting my wits, interrogate me about them," wrote Kipnis. "The term 'kangaroo court' came to mind."[39]

Eventually, the investigators agreed to speak with her via a Skype session, during which Kipnis would learn the nature of the complaints against her. But she was told that she could not record the session, although she was allowed to take notes. "The reasons for these various interdictions were never explained," Kipnis later wrote, reflecting on these events.

As the inquisition proceeded, investigators told Kipnis that the students were willing to drop their complaints if she would agree to make a public apology. "I tried to stifle a laugh," Kipnis wrote. "I asked if that was all. No, they also wanted me to agree not to write about the case." In other words, self-immolation followed by silence. Kipnis refused.

Eventually, after a lengthy investigation, Kipnis was cleared of the charges in the complaint (although her academic "support person" was hit with a separate Title IX complaint for commenting on Kipnis's case).*

* "As a member of the Faculty Senate, whose bylaws include the protection of academic freedom—and believing the process he'd witnessed was a clear violation of academic freedom—he'd spoken in general terms about the situation at a senate meeting. Shortly thereafter, as the attorneys investigating my case informed me by phone, retaliation complaints were filed against him for speaking publicly

Despite her exoneration, Kipnis's case highlighted what she later described as the climate of fear that Title IX has created on campuses. There were simply too many subjects that could no longer be discussed openly on campus. "It's only when Title IX charges lead to lawsuits and the usual veil of secrecy is lifted that any of these assumptions become open for discussion—except that simply discussing one such lawsuit brought the sledgehammer of Title IX down on me, too," she wrote. But the chilling effect of the new "sanctimonious" campus culture is much wider.

> Most academics I know—this includes feminists, progressives, minorities, and those who identify as gay or queer—now live in fear of some classroom incident spiraling into professional disaster. After the essay appeared, I was deluged with emails from professors applauding what I'd written because they were too frightened to say such things publicly themselves. My inbox became a clearinghouse for reports about student accusations and sensitivities, and the collective terror of sparking them, especially when it comes to the dreaded subject of trigger warnings, since pretty much anything might be a "trigger" to someone, given the new climate of emotional peril on campuses.[40]

Title IX had provided would-be victims with a powerful weapon.

Anyone with a grudge, a political agenda, or a desire for attention can easily leverage the system. And there are a lot of grudges these days. The reality is that the more colleges

---

about the matter (even though the complaints against me had already been re-vealed in the graduate student's article), and he could no longer act as my support person. Another team of lawyers from the same firm has been appointed to con-duct a new investigation." (Laura Kipnis, "My Title IX Inquisition," *Chronicle Review,* May 29, 2015)

devote themselves to creating "safe spaces"—that new watchword—for students, the more dangerous those campuses become for professors. It's astounding how aggressive students' assertions of vulnerability have gotten in the past few years. Emotional discomfort is regarded as equivalent to material injury, and all injuries have to be remediated.*

Not surprisingly, even tenured faculty members have learned to keep their mouths shut as the Title IX bureaucracy grows in size, power, and intrusiveness.

* (Laura Kipnis, "My Title IX Inquisition," *Chronicle Review,* May 29, 2015)

PART VI

IS THIS
TIME
DIFFERENT?

CHAPTER 13

TIME FOR A BAILOUT?

EARLIER IN THIS BOOK, I asked if there was any reason to think that efforts to fix higher education will be any more successful this time around. Despite dozens of books, commissions, reports, and symposia, the higher education complex continues to feed itself—costs keep rising with little in the way of enhanced higher learning to show for it. Since *ProfScam* was first published twenty-eight years ago, colleges have bloated their administrations, universities have built Taj Mahals, and professors have become even more allergic to the actual teaching of undergraduates. More government aid has helped fuel higher tuitions, even as an increasing number of graduates find themselves unemployed or underemployed. Grades have inflated, degrees have been watered down, professors have churned out millions of unread and unreadable articles, and the liberal arts have been bludgeoned by indifference and ideology. Far from being places where students are encouraged to delve deeply into the life of the mind and expand their intellectual horizons, the university campus has become one of the most intellectually intolerant milieus in our culture—where one is less likely to encounter the Socratic method than a speech code, a trigger warning, or a safe place that insulates students from politically uncomfortable ideas.

Will this time be any different? Only an indifferent bettor ever wagers against the house more than once, but there are reasons to think that this time really might be different. Higher education has all of the outward signs of being a bubble and faces new and unprecedented challenges.

Other institutions that have appeared to be impervious to change have succumbed to the furious pace of technological and demographic change (just ask anyone in the media). The same tsunami may be about to hit the ivied walls of higher education. But change will not come easily. Both the political class and academia would prefer bailouts over reform, and the current crisis has generated more than its share of bad ideas that have political appeal but do little or nothing to fix the underlying problems. Most of those ideas involve politically attractive calls for more easy money and even "free" college educations.

OUR GREEDY COLLEGES

More than a quarter century ago, then secretary of education William Bennett promulgated what became known as the Bennett hypothesis.

In a 1987 op-ed piece provocatively headlined "Our Greedy Colleges," Bennett noted that colleges "are at it again." As they had done for years, they were planning to raise tuition three to four times faster than the rate of inflation. And as they did so, some of the luminaries of the academy blamed it on "continuing cutbacks of government support for student aid." This claim, Bennett wrote bluntly, "flies in the face of the facts." He noted that since 1980 federal spending outlays for student aid had risen 57 percent since 1980—even though inflation had risen only 26 percent.

"If anything," Bennett wrote, laying out his hypothesis, "*increases in financial aid in recent years have enabled colleges and universities blithely to raise their tuitions, confident that Federal loan subsidies would help cushion the increase* [emphasis added]."* Bennett notes that subsidies for students were greatly expanded in 1978. "In 1980," he noted, "college tuitions began rising year after year at a rate that exceeded inflation. Federal student aid policies do not cause college price inflation, but there is little doubt that they help make it possible."[1]

The last several decades have tested and generally confirmed his analysis. The tuition explosion of recent years has occurred despite what one observer called a "tsunami of public money" for higher education. By any measure, public support for colleges and universities has grown exponentially in recent decades. University of Colorado law professor Paul F. Campos notes that "public investment in higher education in America is vastly larger today, in inflation-adjusted dollars, than

---

*A recent report from the New York Fed seems to provide added support to Bennett's thesis. "We find that institutions more exposed to changes in the subsidized federal loan program increased their tuition disproportionately around these policy changes, with a sizable pass-through effect on tuition of about 65 percent. We also find that Pell Grant aid and the unsubsidized federal loan program have pass-through effects on tuition, although these are economically and statistically not as strong. The subsidized loan effect on tuition is most pronounced for expensive, private institutions that are somewhat, but not among the most, selective." (David O. Lucca, Taylor Nadauld, and Karen Shen, "Credit Supply and the Rise in College Tuition: Evidence from the Expansion in Federal Student Aid Programs," Federal Reserve Bank of New York Staff Report, July 2015, Number 733)

it was during the supposed golden age of public funding in the 1960s."*
While military spending is about 1.8 times what it was in 1960, taxpayer support for higher education is more than 10 times higher. "In
other words," Campos wrote, "far from being caused by funding cuts,
the astonishing rise in college tuition correlates closely with a huge increase in public subsidies for higher education. If over the past three
decades car prices had gone up as fast as tuition, the average new car
would cost more than $80,000."[2]

As Campos pointed out, state appropriations for higher education skyrocketed (in current dollars) from $11.1 billion in 1960 to
$48.2 billion in 1975—a fourfold increase. "By 1980, state funding for
higher education had increased a mind-boggling 390 percent in real
terms over the previous 20 years," he noted. Confirming both Bennett's and Howard Bowen's† theories, Campos noted: "This tsunami
of public money did not reduce tuition: quite the contrary."‡

But there is also a question of return on investment. If more money
is the answer, why hasn't higher education gotten better? In an academic study of collegiate spending, economists Robert E. Martin
and R. Carter Hill noted that given the cumulative investment among
research universities from 1987 to 2005 of more than a half trillion dollars, "there should be evidence of higher quality at these investment
levels." Instead, they wrote, most evidence suggests that the quality

---

*Campos noted that some of the increase has been driven by the increase in per-
centage of Americans who now go to college, which means that "total state appropriations per student are somewhat lower than they were at their peak in
1990." But, he writes, "it is disingenuous to call a large increase in public spending
a 'cut,' as some university administrators do, because a huge programmatic expansion features somewhat lower per capita subsidies."

†"Each institution raises all the money it can. Each institution spends all it raises."

‡"State appropriations reached a record inflation-adjusted high of $86.6 billion in
2009. They declined as a consequence of the Great Recession, but have since risen to
$81 billion. And these totals do not include the enormous expansion of the federal
Pell Grant program, which has grown, in today's dollars, to $34.3 billion per year
from $10.3 billion in 2000." (Paul Campos, "The Real Reason College Tuition
Costs So Much," New York Times, April 4, 2015)

of undergraduate education has declined in recent decades: "completion rates declined, grade inflation increased, students spend less time studying, adult numeracy/literacy rates declined, and critical thinking skills did not improve."[3]

Even so, the reaction to the current crisis is the familiar one: calls for increased taxpayer funding of colleges and universities and a massive federal infusion of subsidies into student loans. Easy money is being replaced by free money as the government gradually transforms loans into grants through a variety of programs that cap repayments and forgive debts. The result is a rolling, massive, and very expensive federal bailout. Most taxpayers likely are not aware of the extent of their obligations to pick up the tabs for student loans. But as Bennett would have predicted, the bailout will likely only worsen the current crisis, while saddling taxpayers with staggering new obligations.

The new initiatives will (1) shift billions of dollars of costs onto taxpayers, many of whom have not had the benefit of a college education themselves, (2) encourage more students to make poor educational choices, (3) inevitably drive higher education spending and tuition even higher, and (4) protect the higher education industry from having to reform itself.

THE STUDENT LOAN BAILOUT

The trajectory of the student loan crisis has been as predictable as the results of the subprime mortgage binge. Default and delinquency rates have been rising, especially among students who fail to get degrees. But even those statistics may mask the depth of the problem. Under federal law, students can delay payments for up to three years—under the so-called forbearance benefit—without technically being either delinquent or in default. On paper, the loan is still good, although as Jason Delisle noted, "it looks a lot like a default given that the borrower isn't making payments." But the loan balances in "forbearance" have risen from 12 percent of the total to 16 percent of the total outstanding student loan balance. That alarming number suggests, he writes, that there may be a hidden student debt bomb.[4]

That bomb is being passed to taxpayers.

Often bypassing Congress, President Obama has dramatically expanded efforts to subsidize college education and make student loans more affordable. Besides proposing to make community college "free," Obama expanded tax credits and Pell Grants, and presided over a massive reform of student loan programs. But perhaps his most dramatic initiative was his Pay as You Earn (PAYE) initiative, which let millions of students cap their loan payments at 10 percent of their income and opened the door to large-scale loan forgiveness. This is how it works. For eligible borrowers, monthly loan payments are capped at 10 percent of discretionary income, which is defined as income above 150 percent of the federal poverty level. After twenty years—if borrowers make regular payments—the loan is forgiven, and the taxpayers pick up the remainder of the tab. Inevitably, the current bailout involves picking winners and losers. The biggest winners (so far) from bailouts are graduates who go into government jobs or other forms of "public service." They can have their debts forgiven (i.e., transferred to the taxpayers) after just ten years. For the average student borrower, the administration estimates, the plans could mean they will have more than $41,000 of their debt forgiven.[5]*

---

*Economist Jeffrey Dorfman describes how this might work:

> In an extreme case, a person could pile up $100,000 in student loans going to an expensive school, graduate, and go to work for a nonprofit advocacy group with 501(c)(3) status in New York City. Imagine that our graduate stays single and is paid $40,000. She will pay only about $187 per month, which will not even cover the interest accruing on her loans.
>
> If she stays employed in public service for ten years, her loan balance will be forgiven at a point when she actually owes more than the original $100,000 balance because the payments were so low that the loan had negative amortization. In fact, over ten years, our imaginary student will have paid only slightly more than $22,000 to a government that gave her

Embedded in the plan are perverse incentives: the most frugal borrowers and the most successful graduates reap the smallest benefits. As an analysis in the *New York Times* conceded, Pay as You Earn "saves you money only if you borrowed big and earn little," especially for those in government or nonprofit jobs.[6] For students who (a) have lower debts, (b) have higher income in the private sector, the benefits are substantially less generous. "The result?" asked one skeptic. "We could have more government and nonprofit employees, but fewer of the private sector employees required to pay for all this."[7]

Critics questioned both the logic and the equity of the forgiveness programs. "Unless somebody can make a cogent argument why taxpayers should not only subsidize college students but subsidize more heavily those whose educations are not yielding an economic payback," wrote economist Jeffrey Dorfman, "this program makes no sense." In particular, it seemed perverse that the government was "providing larger subsidies to people pursuing careers that are in less demand in the marketplace." The incentives become even more perverse when one considers that government jobs often pay more than private sector jobs, "so why would borrowers working for the government be given more favorable terms?"

This question is worth considering. At the heart of the government's massive Public Service Loan Forgiveness program is the implied assumption that government jobs are inherently more valuable, and also somehow in need of an extra subsidy.* Writing in *Forbes*, Tom Lindsay asks the obvious question:

$100,000 to help pay for college. (Jeffrey Dorfman, "Here Comes the Student Loan Forgiveness," *Forbes*, June 19, 2014, www.forbes.com/sites /jeffreydorfman/2014/06/19/here-comes-the-student-loan-forgiveness)

*The privileging of government jobs becomes even more questionable when you consider these numbers from the Congressional Budget Office:

- Average benefits for federal workers whose education ended in a bachelor's degree were 46 percent higher than for similar workers in the private sector.

Why privilege these graduates over those who enter the private sector? If the official justification is that government and non-profit workers make a "superior" contribution to society, the Administration has yet to make the case for the "inferior contribution" of those in the private sector, whose wealth creation provides the surplus funds that the federal government chooses to redistribute.[8]

The program could have other consequences as well. While no one intends it, a forgiveness plan based on "public service" employment could turn into a form of job lock, freezing borrowers into nonprofit or government work, making student loans a form of indenture. For some graduates taking a job in a profit-making enterprise will not only cause their payments to spike, but could also cost them tens of thousands of dollars in loans that would otherwise be covered by the taxpayers.

Lindsay worried that the long-term effect of the strategy would be to "kill the goose, driving students away from the wealth-creating sector at the same time that its 'forgiveness tax' drains more wealth from our already debt-burdened Republic."

Needless to say, such programs do little to induce academia to reform itself, and that may be the point. Many of the reform plans on the table seem specifically designed to further inflate the bubble, while simultaneously relieving pressure on the higher education complex to engage in any sort of sustained introspection. This, of course, is exactly the way the complex wants it.

- Federal workers whose education culminated in a bachelor's degree averaged 15 percent higher total compensation than their private-sector counterparts.

Overall, the federal government paid 16 percent more in total compensation than it would have if average compensation had been comparable with that in the private sector, after accounting for certain observable characteristics of workers. (*Comparing the Compensation of Federal and Private-Sector Employees*, Congressional Budget Office, January 2012)

Indeed, free stuff, including artificially cheap student loans comes at a cost—a huge cost—to taxpayers. In early 2015, the Obama administration had to acknowledge that the student loan program had a nearly $22 billion shortfall in the previous year, reported *Politico*, "apparently the largest ever recorded for any government credit program."[9] That shortfall, which resulted from reduced debt payments to the government as a result of the "quasi-bailout" of student loans, was "larger than the annual budget for NASA, or the Interior Department and EPA combined" and would be "tacked onto the federal deficit," increasing it by nearly 5 percent.*

As large as that price tag on the bailout was, it may be just a down payment. Analyses by Barclays Capital have warned the bailout could lead to a deficit in the loan program of as much as $250 billion over the next decade.[10]

LETTING ACADEMIA OFF THE HOOK

But perhaps the greatest drawback to the current bailout is the effect it will have on higher education itself. In 1987, William Bennett noted that the problem with higher education is not that it is underfunded. Rather, said Bennett, "it is under-accountable and under-productive."

Despite having resisted reform for decades, including attempts to bring its underlying value into line with its price, the current crisis could be different because it targets academe's wallet rather than merely its conscience and thus is pushing institutions to be both more account-

---

* Reported *Politico*: "The main cause of the shortfall was President Barack Obama's recent efforts to provide relief for borrowers drowning in student debt, reforms that have already begun to reduce loan payments to the government. For more than two decades, budget analysts have recalculated the projected costs of about 120 credit programs every year, but they have never lowered their expectations of repayments this dramatically." (Michael Grunwald, "The College Loan Bombshell Hidden in the Budget," *Politico*, February 5, 2015)

able and more productive. Bailouts, on the other hand, could relieve the pressure on colleges and universities and free them to go about their business as usual, which would undoubtedly include a return to the law of more . . . more building, more expansion, and more tuition.

With the new flood of free money, colleges will have even less incentive than they have now to restrain their appetite for ever higher tuitions, and as a result, "it is natural to expect that the tuition hyperinflation under which this country is suffering will only rise further, and with it, student loan debt. And as student loan debt increases, so will the amount added to the national debt through loan forgiveness."[11]

But the worst consequence of all would be that the bailout would let the higher education complex off the hook.

CHAPTER 14

NETFLIX U.

IRONICALLY ENOUGH, ONE OF the most controversial challenges to the status quo in academia comes from within higher education itself. The new academic Trojan horses are known as massive open online courses, or MOOCs, an awful acronym, but one that reflects its geek roots. Inspired by a mass course at Stanford, MOOCs burst on the scene, trailing clouds of hype, in 2012. When they were embraced by Harvard, MIT, Berkeley, and a growing number of universities, techno-utopians seized on the new technology as the end of the university as we know it.

Futurist Nathan Harden saw the MOOCs as engines of creative destruction: "Big changes are coming," he wrote, "and old attitudes and business models are set to collapse as new ones rise. Few who will be affected by the changes ahead are aware of what's coming."

The live lecture will be replaced by streaming video. The administration of exams and exchange of coursework over the internet will become the norm. The push and pull of academic exchange will take place mainly in interactive online spaces, occupied by a new generation of tablet-toting, hyper-connected youth who already spend much of their lives online. Universities will extend their reach to students around the world, unbounded by geography or even by time zones. All of this will be on offer, too, at a fraction of the cost of a traditional college education.[1]

Heady stuff. But within a year, the backlash had set in, MOOCs hit a series of bumps, pilot programs stumbled, professors signed indignant letters, faculty members voted against participating, and the hype bubble was deflated. By 2015, one of the leading advocates was publicly wondering in the pages of the *New York Times* what had gone wrong. "Three years ago," he wrote, "technology was going to transform higher education. What happened?"[2]

What happened? I can't help but think of comedian Louis CK's response to complaints that it took too long for smartphones to download information: "Give it a second!" he said. "It's going to space! Can you give it a second to get back from space?" Well, exactly.

The last great pedagogical innovation was developed in the Greek agora more than two thousand years ago; the basic structure of the collegiate classroom hasn't changed in centuries; and almost no institution in the modern world has proven to be more impervious to reform than the modern university. And yet the MOOC enthusiasts are wondering why a few online computer and technology courses have not *transformed* higher education . . . in *three years?*

Give it time, will you?

Some of the reaction to the progress of the MOOCs has been, shall we say, overcaffeinated. It has not helped that some of the advocates made exaggerated claims for the new approaches. But this does not mean that the new technologies and approaches do not pose a major threat to the status quo; or that they will not in time help transform the academy, or at least parts of it.

We need to recognize that technology is easier to change than institutions. Even so, the free online courses strike academia at its point of maximum vulnerability. Universities can hardly complain that the MOOCs dehumanize and depersonalize education, since the modern university has already done all it can to minimize the interactions between elite faculty and undergraduates. The new online courses have exploded at a time when higher education has shown how little it cares about actual student learning. Obviously, they pose a direct challenge to academia's reliance on mass lectures, the absurdly anachronistic model where students sit in rows in a large hall while a professor talks at them. Unchanged in nearly a thousand years, the lecture seems oddly out of place in an age of tablets, apps, and digital media. Moreover, it is hard to imagine how the professoriate can successfully argue that the mass lecture is superior to a digital classroom that allows for interactive learning and feedback and that requires actual attention to the material and mastery of content. Needless to say, the mass lecture offers none of those features.

Far more ominously, the MOOCs could challenge the monopoly that colleges and universities have on credentialing, including the awarding of the coveted bachelor's degree. The genuine disruptive power of the new online alternatives is their ability to restore content to higher education and some meaning to the credentials that have become increasingly hollow. When universities no longer hold the keys to those credentials, their world will be rocked. Not surprisingly, then, some academics react to the rise of the MOOCs like members of an aboriginal tribe seeing an airplane for the first time: It may not mean the end of their way of life immediately, but it is certainly an omen that it is about to be profoundly shaken.

How big a threat do MOOCs pose? Let's imagine this possible future:

> Rather than showing up with a degree from the U of Some-where with a simple BA degree, a student arrives for her first interview with a degree or a bundle of certificates of mastery that includes courses with world-class scholars. She can show her prospective employer a stacked portfolio that includes a course in artificial intelligence from Stanford; courses in com-puter science from Cornell and Harvard; a course in Alexander the Great from Wellesley; a course in environmental law from Yale; and a course in globalization from Georgetown. Her degree also includes verified certificates from Princeton for a course in the paradoxes of war, a course from the Copenhagen Business School in social entrepreneurship, and the University of Penn-sylvania's Analyzing Global Trends for Business and Society.
>
> Moreover, she can demonstrate that in each of those courses she achieved actual mastery, in contrast to other graduates who may have gotten credit for C-level work in far less demanding classes.
>
> And our applicant shows up without a mountain of debt, since she was able to get her degree for a fraction of what her peers are paying.

That student could mark the beginning of the end for the business model that sustained higher education for decades.

NETFLIX U?

The modern mass online class famously traces its origins to a course taught by Stanford's Sebastian Thrun and Peter Norvig. When they offered Introduction to Artificial Intelligence—online for free—more than 160,000 students in 190 countries signed up. Relying on normal classrooms, it would take hundreds of years to reach so many students. Suddenly the mass online class became the Next Big Thing. Thrun himself launched Udacity, while his colleagues Daphne Koller and Andrew Ng launched a for-profit company called Coursera. Harvard and MIT supercharged the new movement by launching the non-profit edX, which was headed up by the charismatic Anant Agarwal.

The new firms were generously funded, raising tens of millions of dollars from venture capitalists. Perhaps because they did not fully recognize how radical the new online courses would prove to be, dozens of colleges and universities signed up as partners. Coursera's mission statement was ambitious: Its goal was "to take the best courses from the best instructors at the best universities and provide it to everyone around the world for free."

The number of courses quickly multiplied, and by mid-2015, Coursera had more than 12 million students and more than 117 partner institutions across the globe. Students, for example, could take a course in social psychology, offered by Wesleyan University; Enhance Your Career and Employability Skills from the University of London; Programming for Everybody (Python) from the University of Michigan; Fundamentals of Music Theory from the University of Edinburgh; Introduction to Finance from the University of Michigan; or Data Analysis and Statistical Inference from Duke University.[3]

At the same time, edX was offering nearly five hundred courses that students could take "at your pace, at home or in a café," offered by some of the top professors from the nation's most elite universities. The university was "open 24/7 and everyone is accepted."[4]

This is not only disruptive but breathtakingly radical, because the MOOCs are anti-elitist, but also profoundly meritocratic. There are no barriers to entry, no SAT or ACT scores, no legacy admissions preferences, no class or race bias, no affirmative action, no bloated lists of extracurricular activities—just the willingness to do the work and to achieve mastery. Equally radical, they will shift power from the institution to the student as academia is decentralized in a way familiar to so many other industries that have found themselves upended by consumer-driven on-demand models.

It will also raise questions across higher education: How can colleges continue to expect students to pay $40,000 to $60,000 a year for an educational experience that is inferior in so many ways to what students can find . . . for free? If history is any guide at all, Harden reminds us, whenever a "faster, cheaper way of sharing information emerges," it will sweep away what came before it.

HOW THEY WORK

There is a long history of attempts at distance learning, including the venerable correspondence course, but the MOOCs nevertheless represent something new: their size, their quality; their ability to be interactive; and the potential to shake up the process of credentialing. Many of the courses are excellent. "We're nearing the point," says one Harvard professor, "where it's a superior educational experience, as far as the lectures are concerned, to engage with them online."[5]

Coursera cofounder Daphne Koller explains how the new courses were different from what had come before. The courses start on a given day; students watch the videos on a weekly basis and do homework assignments. "And these would be real homework assignments for a real grade," she stressed, "with a real deadline."[6]

But the videos are not just standard videos. Periodically, the video pauses and students are asked to answer a question. The contrast with the mass lecture is significant. Koller explains: "[When] I ask that kind of a question in class, 80 percent of the students are still scribbling the last thing I said, 15 percent are zoned out on Facebook, and then there's the smarty pants in the front row who blurts out the answer before anyone else has had a chance to think about it."[7]

In the online courses, every student has to engage; and every student has to demonstrate mastery to pass. The courses use technology to evaluate student progress and provide grades. In courses that do not lend themselves to multiple choice grading, the MOOCs rely on "peer grading." But the real innovation in the MOOC is the ability to personalize instruction and to evaluate the effectiveness of both teaching and learning.

> Now, if two students in a class of 100 give the same wrong answer, you would never notice. But when 2,000 students give the same wrong answer, it's kind of hard to miss. So Andrew [Ng] and his students went in, looked at some of those assignments, understood the root cause of the misconception, and then they produced a targeted error message that would be provided to every student whose answer fell into that bucket, which means that students who made that same mistake would now get personalized feedback telling them how to fix their misconception much more effectively.[8]

The courses can also require mastery of the subject matter. While the traditional college courses offer credit to a student who might grasp only a fraction of the material, the online courses can set the bar higher. "Mastery is easy to achieve using a computer," Koller pointed out, "because a computer doesn't get tired of showing you the same video five times. And it doesn't ever get tired of grading the same work multiple times."

And once mastery is achieved? "At the end of the course, the students got a certificate. They could present that certificate to a prospective employer and get a better job, and we know many students who did. Some students took their certificate and presented this to an educational institution at which they were enrolled for actual college credit." And, unlike the bachelor's degree, which is increasingly untrustworthy as an indicator of what the student has achieved or mastered, the certificate from one of the elite online courses can be a reliable and specific indicator of what students have achieved and what they can do.

What does this mean for institutions of higher education? What happens when they lose their monopoly on credentialing? Until recently, that seemed highly unlikely.

Much of the prestige of higher education and society's forbearance when it comes to its foibles and failures rests on academia's monopoly on credentials. For all of its flaws, the BA is still regarded as an indispensable signal to employers and society, even if its actual meaning is largely opaque. But there is no reason that it should continue to be the exclusive gatekeeper.

STIGMAS AND SIGNALS

The most daunting barriers facing any alternative to the traditional BA were (1) the stigmas attached to online courses and (2) the reluctance by employers and others to accept alternative forms of signaling.

More specifically, the embrace of MOOCs by MIT and Harvard changed the game. If one understands anything about academia, it is the importance of "status anxiety" and the pressure to emulate the institutions at the pinnacle of prestige. Without the imprimatur of the elite institutions, it would have been a herculean task for online education to shake the stigma attached to it. Nathan Harden compares it to the transformation of online dating. "Fifteen years ago it was considered a poor substitute for the real thing, even creepy; now it's ubiquitous," he wrote. "Online education used to have a stigma, as if it were inherently less rigorous or less effective." The embrace of online courses by those elite institutions immediately gave the new technology credibility, noted Harden, while their announcement that they would offer certificates of mastery eliminates "one of the last remaining obstacles to the widespread adoption of low-cost online education."[9]

Author Kevin Carey agreed. "In a stroke," he wrote in the *Chronicle of Higher Education,* "the public perception of online higher education shifted from down-market for-profit colleges to the most famous universities in the world. It's hard to overstate how important that will be to acceptance of this burgeoning educational form."[10]

But will employers accept the new certificates? And will colleges begin to offer credits for the courses?

As Carey notes, the failure of MOOCs to dramatically disrupt higher education (so far) has little to do with the quality of the courses, which seem to be improving all the time. But certificates of mastery or verified certificates are still novelties, especially in contrast with the venerable BA, which is embedded in the employment policies of both the public and the private sectors. Even though the online courses provide students with "access to world class professors at an unbeatable price" they do not yet offer "official degrees, the kind that can get you a job."[11]

What would have to happen is that some colleges would begin to accept the MOOC credits; legislators would see the benefits of pressuring universities to accept them; and applicants would begin showing up with degrees that have rather more content than employers are used to seeing. The process of accreditation would be crucial.

GAME CHANGERS

In late 2012, the American Council on Education agreed to evaluate selected MOOC courses for actual college credit, a move that Coursera's cofounder, Andrew Ng, described as a game changer. In 2013, Coursera partnered with ten university systems to potentially offer credit for the online courses. It is hard to overstate the significance of such a move. As the American Enterprise Institute's Daniel K. Lautzenheiser notes, "if these partnerships hold up, they could go a long way in legitimizing MOOCs in the eyes of both potential students, who could transfer the credits to traditional institutions, and of employers, who could recognize MOOC credit as a valid signal of competency."[12]

But there are already signs of a shift within academia itself. In 2013, Georgia Tech launched an all-MOOC master's program in computer science, offering tuition that was significantly lower than the traditional course of study.[13] And in 2015, Arizona State University announced that it would allow students to take their entire freshman year of courses online—and offer credit for the courses for the edX MOOCs that could be applied toward an undergraduate degree at ASU or transferred to other universities that would recognize the credits. The move was hailed as a potential breakthrough for the MOOCs.[14] EdX CEO Agarwal said, "This is the first time any MOOC provider will offer a curriculum of courses that any learner can take for free or for a small fee as a verified student and then parlay that for credit if they pass the course. That automatic step of being able to convert a set of courses through university credit . . . has not been done before."[15]

How disruptive was the ASU announcement? Let's count the ways:

- The program would have no admission requirements: no SAT, no GPAs. Anyone anywhere in the world would be able to take the MOOCs for credit.

- Students would pay for the courses only if they passed. The program was therefore risk-free.

- If they passed the courses in the Global Freshman Academy, students would have to pay only $200 a credit. That alone is a game changer. The full cost for a freshman taking the online courses would be $5,160 (which includes a $45 per course verified student fee). Compare that with Arizona State's annual out-of-state tuition price tag of $24,503. Add in room and board and other on-campus expenses, and the cost rises to more than $39,600.

In one stroke, the ASU embrace of the online courses slashed the cost of a year of college by more than $34,000—*a cut of more than 85 percent.*

Perhaps even more consequential, was the announcement by MIT that it would begin incorporating MOOCs into its admissions program for master's degrees. Students who successfully complete the online courses and pass an online examination offered through the school's MOOC project, MITx, would be awarded a "micro-master's degree" from MIT. If they wished to continue, the successful completion of the MOOCs would "enhance" their chances of being accepted into the school's regular master's degree program. MIT will start with a pilot program in supply-chain management, but the implications for the future are clear. As the *Chronicle of Higher Education* noted: "MOOCs may soon become a prominent factor in admissions decisions at selective colleges."

But it gets better: Students who enter the full-fledged master's program at MIT would be able to complete their degree in a semester rather than a full year, slashing the cost of a master's degree from one of the nation's most prestigious university in half.[16]

THE BACKLASH

Given the threat the new model of higher education poses to the status quo, no one should be surprised that the status quo is hitting back hard.

Inevitably, there will be winners and losers. Resistance, therefore, was unavoidable. Higher education writer Steve Kolowich wrote that despite the early hype, the "political, regulatory, administrative, and faculty barriers to the kind of unfettered online education that MOOC promoters originally envisioned have proved quite high."[17]

But the most surprising thing about the backlash against the new digital learning is that anyone is surprised. One of the themes of this book has been the institutional resistance to any real reform on the part of the tenured professoriate and the entrenched bureaucracies. Many academics appear particularly offended by the appeals to the economic efficiency of the MOOC; for others, the mere suggestion that the MOOCs may be profitable causes them to break out in the intellectual equivalent of hives. At the heart of the blowback is the realization that the new courses—and the new forms of credentialing they will usher in—pose an existential challenge to the culture, finances, and structure of the modern university.

In April 2013, the philosophy department faculty of San Jose State University lashed out at the MOOCs, writing an open letter expressing their "fear that two classes of universities will be created: one, well-funded colleges and universities in which privileged students get their own real professor; the other, financially stressed private and public universities in which students watch a bunch of video-taped lectures and interact, if indeed any interaction is available on their home campuses, with a professor that this model of education has turned into a glorified teaching assistant."[18]

But the educational dystopia the philosophers describe is also a close approximation of what is already happening on many campuses, where students have been abandoned to an academic underclass. A more substantive critique came from the faculty at Amherst College, where 60 percent of the professoriate rejected a proposal to work with edX. "The MOOC format," the faculty statement declared, "is counter to the Amherst College Mission statement, which holds that 'Amherst College is committed to learning through close colloquy' and is a 'purposefully small residential community.' "[19]

But beneath their rhetoric about the liberal arts, the Amherst faculty gave away another very real concern about the economic impact of the courses. They worried that "once MOOC courses begin to be widely offered for transferrable credit, it is reasonable to suppose that MOOC courses will suck student tuition dollars away from so-called middle-tier and low-tier institutions." Thus the ascendancy of MOOCs could presage the end of the brick-and-mortar institutions.

This gets to the heart of the challenge posed by the MOOCs—it is ultimately all about the money. For nonelite institutions, the MOOCs could prove a threat to their very survival. "Why, after all, would some-one pay tens of thousands of dollars to attend Nowhere State University when he or she can attend an online version of MIT or Harvard practically for free?" asks Harden.

There are, however, some legitimate substantive concerns about the MOOCs. Early experience has shown a low completion rate for courses, while other scholars have raised questions about how well the courses would work in the humanities. In 2013, the University of Pennsylvania's Graduate School of Education released a study of a million users that concluded that only half of students who registered for a MOOC ever viewed a single lecture and only 4 percent of students completed the course.[20] The negative report made headlines, but needs to be seen in context: MOOCs are still a novelty and many of the so-called users are simply curious browsers.*

At Coursera, Koller and Ng have found that as many as 45 percent of the students who complete the first assignment will go on to complete the full course. They also found that when students pay a small fee ($50) for a verification feature that prevents cheating, completion rates rise to as high as 70 percent. A more recent study of 1.7 million participants of edX suggests that many students actually learn quite a bit from the MOOC, even if they do not complete work for the certificate. The survey found that 57 percent of participants said they intended to get the certificate, while 24 percent ultimately did.[21]

So what do these numbers tell us? Even if we accept the most conservative numbers—a mere 4 percent completion rate—the numbers

---

*But even accepting the abysmal completion rate, we are still talking about large numbers. Kevin Carey, for example, broke down the study's analysis of users of a course in mythology: "It's true that most of the people who had some contact with Mythology were not active users. It's also true that the remaining minority of active users constituted *25,000 people,* which is more than twice the total number of undergraduates enrolled at the University of Pennsylvania. And even though most of the 25,000 didn't finish, the 1,350 who did represent an order-of-magnitude increase in the number of people who learned Mythology from the same professor the previous year." ("Pay No Attention to Supposedly Low MOOC Completion Rates," EdCentral, December 12, 2013) are nevertheless impressive: That would translate into more than 600,000 certificates from Coursera alone.

The numbers also suggest that the online courses are attracting broad public interest, but that they are demanding. In other words, the MOOCs are not for everyone. Casual, unmotivated students quickly drop to the wayside when they realize that the courses are rigorous and demand attention and sustained effort. That means, of course, they may not be an attractive option to a large portion—perhaps a majority—of college students. MOOCs do not work particularly well with disengaged and unmotivated students, who are not likely to persist. But here is the rub. The status quo of higher education also does not work well for disengaged and unmotivated students. But it will still give them high grades and degrees, regardless of whether or not they have learned anything. The MOOCs will not.

The early experience suggests that completion rates will rise when the window-shopping phase ends and students become more invested in the courses. That will happen as the certificate's value becomes more tangible as both a transferable college credit and as an entry into the job market.

A COUNTERREFORMATION?

The other nagging problem for the MOOCs is how well they will work in nonscientific, nontechnical fields, including the humanities. What happens to class discussions? The back-and-forth of the Socratic method that has been such a staple of the liberal arts, but that has become so rare in the modern academy? Advocates insist that much of the discussion that used to take place in the classroom now takes place via a robust social media and message boards.

But how does the technology handle grading things like essays and term papers? Coursera founder Daphne Koller recalls that they originally tried to convince some of the humanities faculty that they could rely on multiple choice tests. "That didn't go over very well," she deadpanned.[22]

The alternative has been to rely on what is known as peer grading, which Koller calls a "surprisingly effective strategy." But it is obviously also a limited one and skepticism seems to be in order. One response to the rise of the MOOCs that is undoubtedly effective, however, is the so-called flipped class in which online learning is blended with classroom participation. They are called "flipped" because the lecture takes place at home, while what used to be considered homework takes place in the presence of faculty and peers. Koller's partner Andrew Ng says clearly, "We do not recommend selecting an online-only experience over a blended learning experience."[23]

But there are other problems as well. Despite all of the advantages that the MOOCs will bring to higher education, a great deal will be lost, including much of the collegiate experience. As even a MOOC enthusiast like Harden notes, students who learn remotely "won't get the social life, the long chats in the dining hall, the feeling of collegiality, . . . the concerts, the iron-sharpens-iron debates around the seminar table, the rare book library, or the famous guest lecturers (although some of those events are streamed online, too)."[24] But that merely creates an opportunity for the new universities to survive in the new digital world; they need to emphasize many of the qualities that are lacking in the online world, but do so in a financially rational way.

Another obvious objection is that the MOOCs are a logical extension—and even a further escalation—of the flight from teaching described both here and in *ProfScam*. But that is only partially the case. The mass online classes do not reverse the flight from teaching, but they do something that is perhaps more important: They *refocus attention on student learning* (which after all is the point). Inevitably, MOOCs will also force renewed attention to the lost and disdained art of teaching.

MOOCs could also lead to a sort of counterreformation, in which some institutions differentiate themselves by emphasizing what others do not. This might include affordable tuition, a nonsuffocating campus life, and actual teachers in actual classrooms.

How best to compete against the mass class? *With smaller classes.*

How to compete with online courses or star Harvard professors on videotape? *With courses of high quality taught by in-person professors.*

How to compete with new credentials that signal actual mastery? *By reinvigorating curricula, reversing grade inflation, and raising academic standards.*

Even the most enthusiastic techno-utopians have to recognize that neither college classes nor collegiate life will vanish in our lifetimes and elite liberal arts colleges could actually thrive in the new marketplace.

But the incentives for other second- and third-tier schools will also change. Right now, all of the incentives encourage institutions to offer inducements for professors to leave the classroom, but the new landscape of higher education may create a countervailing pressure to encourage real-life faculty members to teach students in person in real time.

The academy may even come to see that as an innovation.

CHAPTER 15

SMALLER, FEWER, LESS

WE KNOW THAT ANY proposals for change that do not reinforce the status quo will inevitably be rejected by the academic mandarins as "simplistic."

So let's keep this simple.

At the heart of the current crisis is the higher education complex's addiction to the "law of more": administrative bloat, edifice bloat, more spending, more students, and higher tuition. The corollary has been academia's "law of less." In return for all of this spending, academia has been giving less in return: lower teaching loads, a Swiss cheese curriculum, dumbed-down standards, and mediocre educations masked by inflated grades. The result is Generation Debt, saddled with expensive degrees of dubious value.

Academia's preferred solution would, of course, be more: more aid, more spending, more subsidies, more free college, and continuing bail-outs.

The right answer is to do the opposite. My alternative to the law of more is "smaller, fewer, and less." Admittedly, that may not be the most inspiring battle cry, but it directly addresses the current bubble.

COLLEGE FOR FEWER

"College for all" sounds appealing, but it is delusional. Too many students are already going to college, paying too much for degrees that they do not need. The reality is that not all good jobs require a bachelor's degree. Too many students have been misled or, worse, set up for failure by being pushed onto the college track, when alternatives might have been more appropriate. As a result, colleges find themselves inundated with students who are neither academically prepared nor especially interested in doing university-level work. On the flip side, millions of graduates find themselves saddled with student loan debt but stuck in jobs that do not require college degrees. Obviously, all of this has contributed to the declining value of the college degree. Encouraging even more students to attend college seems likely to further dilute the BA's significance.

What is the alternative?

First we have to recognize that not every student needs to or even should go to college. We ought to encourage the robust development of alternatives, including technical education and high quality certificates of achievement. This will require demystifying the bachelor's degree, which does not always signify what it purports to mean and should not be the sole indicator of academic competence.

A smaller pool of college students is not necessarily a bad thing. Once colleges and universities get over the need to constantly inflate their enrollment numbers, they can begin to impose higher admission standards. Only a small percentage of students in higher education should require remedial education. Higher admission standards would also have a trickle-down effect, by pushing secondary education to raise its graduation standards, something that is obviously long overdue.

SMALLER

The modern multiversity has sought to be all things to all people, endlessly multiplying programs, centers, majors, and degrees. It needs to be downsized, from its hubristic building programs to its bloated bureaucracies and noninstructional staff, and its distended academic ambitions. The easiest trims will be academic programs that have few or no students. But universities also need to recognize that not everything requires a four-year degree.

There is, after all, nothing sacred about four years. Why not three? Or two or one? As Charles Murray has noted, students who want to be software designers, accountants, hospital administrators, high school teachers, social workers, journalists, optometrists, or interior designers do not need to spend four years in college. Classes that would allow them to obtain "the academic basis for competence" would take one or perhaps two years. The rest is merely time-wasting, expensive filler.

Here is a radical idea: What would happen if a university announced that henceforth it would be offering a *three-year* bachelor's degree? At one stroke it would cut the cost of a college education. While such a shift would also cut the school's per-student revenue, it would also provide a distinctive way of competing for students, as well as put the institution on the cutting edge of reform.

This might also have the effect of forcing both institutions and students to focus more intently on the course of study and the quality of the instruction they receive.

The new digital courses could also upend the traditional four-year program. The CEO of edX, Anant Agarwal, argues that "we really have to reimagine education as we know it. We won't solve it just by tweaking one aspect of it. . . . we need to change everything on campus." This involves more than simply recognizing the obsolescence of the traditional classroom.

> Today, universities have a four-year program. I see a time in the future where rather than students coming in for four years to do a bachelor's degree, they'll come in having taken their first year of courses as MOOCs. Then they'll spend two years on campus, spend the final year getting a job and continuing to take MOOCs and becoming lifelong continuous learners.[1]

LESS

As we have seen, more generally means . . . more. Higher state and federal aid leads to increased spending and higher tuition; more student loans to more debt and, ironically, to yet higher tuition. Bowen's law has been confirmed repeatedly: "Each institution raises all the money it can. Each institution spends all it raises."

How about we stop inflating the bubble?

Too often, federal aid has been a magnet that has drawn faculty away from the classroom, while encouraging empire-building administrators to spend lavishly on expansion. None of this has made college more affordable or made the quality of that education notably better. This does not require massive immediate cuts, but it certainly would suggest that simply pumping billions of additional dollars into the higher education complex has proven to generate a poor return on investment. So if the law of more is played out, why not try a little less?

Rather than continuing to bail out student loans (which has the effect of removing market pressure on the higher education complex), why not begin to align loans to potential paybacks? Why not begin to treat student loans more like . . . loans? Rather than gifts in waiting? Might this lead to more prudent decision-making? And smarter borrowing choices?

Smaller, fewer, and less does not mean that students should continue to be shortchanged. A more tightly focused academia should reverse its abandonment of undergraduate education, taking responsibility not merely for the overall curriculum, but also for what happens in the classroom. This will mean different priorities and reward structures.

Professors may have to spend more time with students. Some may even have to work on Fridays.

OPEN, DEMOCRATIC, MERITOCRATIC, AND GLOBAL

The new university could also have a radically different admissions structure, one that relies less on SAT scores, extracurricular activities, and GPAs, and more on the willingness and ability to do the work. Arizona State University's decision to offer online credit for the full freshman year provides a model for how this might look: Anyone, anywhere in the world can sign up risk-free. Tuition is charged only upon successful completion of the MOOCs, and even then it is only a fraction of what has traditionally been charged. There are no limits on class sizes and no artificial barriers—no legacy admissions, no affirmative action, no elaborate admissions hoops. (Because the online courses require mastery for completion, this would also have the effect of raising admission standards by requiring students to demonstrate their ability to handle collegiate work.) Even if the completion rates for the courses is low in percentage terms, the actual number of students taking elite courses could rise significantly.

RESTORING THE AMERICAN MIND

If our colleges and universities are once again going to be places where students are encouraged to explore ideas, broaden their imaginations, and develop the quality and habit of critical thinking, they will also have to revitalize the liberal arts. This means more than merely classroom teaching, reading, and the curriculum (as desperately in need of reform as they all are).

Restoring the liberal arts requires a dose of actual liberalism (the small *l* variety) because liberal learning in the broadest sense is incompatible with the stifling and oppressive atmosphere of ideological hypersensitivity that has come to dominate so much of American higher education. The proliferation of speech codes, trigger warnings, and microaggressions would be merely amusing sideshows if they did not strike at the essence of what a college education is supposed to be: exposing the young to new and often troubling ideas. Someone who does not want to be offended or to have negative feelings "triggered" by others should be advised to turn off most media, avoid public transit, and consider an alternative to college. Academia cannot allow itself to be held hostage to the demands of the perpetually aggrieved if it expects to be a place where ideas flourish.

The academy should also push back against attempts to draw it into the labyrinth of adjudicating sexual interactions, something it is ill equipped and unsuited to handle either competently or fairly. The alternative is for universities to become islands of arbitrary and often unjust standards that defy logic and undermine due process rights.

REFORM AND ITS ENEMIES

Will any of this happen? Is any of it even possible?

Standing athwart any attempt to deflate the bubble are the hosts of academic administrators, bureaucrats, faculty members, and lavishly compensated university presidents. They have a powerful vested interest in fighting against any attempt to shrink their sinecures. Anyone who underestimates the encrusted inertia of the modern university has never attended a faculty meeting or debated a vice-president of academic affairs.

So what will have to happen?

Academia will, first of all, need a new sort of university president. The current breed is selected primarily for their ability to raise money and placate faculty members. In *ProfScam,* I noted that the search for the modern university president involves "an exhaustive, in-depth national hunt for candidates with genuine leadership skills, strong convictions, and a commitment to reform—and then eliminating them."[2] The reality is that despite their prestige and generous salaries, most presidents are impotent figureheads who must never challenge the core values of the higher education complex. The impotence of the president is often matched and enabled by the unwillingness of members of boards of trustees and regents to rock the boat. The result is that the elaborate organizational charts of universities are grossly misleading. No matter how many vice-presidents, provosts, and deans sprout up, the most important powers are tightly held by a professoriate armed with an enduring sense of entitlement and protected by tenure. Genuine reform will require a change in that settled reality: the abolition not merely of the antiquated institution of tenure but also systems of so-called shared governance that let the inmates quite literally run the asylum.

Somehow, most of the rest of the world manages to cope without anything like tenure, but academics insist they are somehow different. And so for a century or more we have had the sclerotic provision that creates a class of untouchable aristocrats who can't be fired no matter how awful their teaching has become or whether or not they ever do a stitch of research.

Faculty can vegetate on the payroll for decades regardless of their performance or the changing needs of the universities or the students who pay to attend them.

Admittedly, tenure may be protecting some dissident professors, but it has clearly not been able to stop the attacks on academic freedom. There is a reason for that: Tenure doesn't protect the freedom of most of the folks who teach on campuses these days. It provides no protections to academic staff or so-called contingent faculty or even assistant professors lusting after the gold ring of lifetime employment.

Tenure is nice for the privileged few who enjoy its protection, but it does nothing for everyone else on the outside, including students and the folks who pay the bills.

Ending or modifying tenure, however, will not be sufficient:

COLLEGES AND UNIVERSITIES will have to recognize that they will either change or become obsolete. This may mean that some of them will close their doors, a move that would require faculty members to find jobs that will require them to work in June, July, and August.

TRUSTEES will have to take more active roles, abandoning the model of passive governance so many of them have adopted in the last century. They could start by asking their school's administrators simple questions like "What would you think of the idea of offering a three-year bachelor's degree?" "Why aren't we offering credit for MOOCs?" "Why can't professors teach just one more class a year?" Be prepared for unhappiness.

ALUMNI can of course continue to be fans. But they need to get over the notion that the sports teams subsidize their alma mater. They do not. Instead, despite the bread and circuses they offer, they may actually be undermining both the quality of the education and integrity of the institutions they represent.

LEGISLATORS will have to begin asking for more accountability from public universities, including asking pointed questions about teaching loads, tuitions, graduation rates, and whether administrators are standing in the way of alternative credentials.

PARENTS will have to hold colleges to a higher standard by asking what exactly their children are getting in return for their tuition dollars.

FACULTY will have to get over their allergic reaction to undergraduate teaching. Changes in the reward structure that encourages them to crank out unread and unreadable research might help with this.

EMPLOYERS will have to begin looking past the traditional college degree to alternatives that actually signal knowledge, skills, and achievement.

SCHOLARS will have to reaffirm their commitment to genuine liberal learning, freedom of expression, and the diversity of ideas on campus. They need to push back hard against the notion that universities should "attempt to shield individuals from ideas and opinions they find unwelcome, disagreeable, or even deeply offensive."[3]

DONORS will have to examine their priorities. They need to ask tougher questions about the quality of the programs they are subsidizing and stop underwriting schools that despise their values and impose intellectual climates of stifling political correctness.

THE REST OF US will have to revisit the basic question: What is higher education for? And why have we been willing to put up with the status quo for so long?

NOTES

INTRODUCTION: SCENES FROM A GRADUATION

[1] Tom Wolfe, Foreword, *Declining by Degrees: Higher Education at Risk,* eds. Richard H. Hersh and John Merrow (New York: Palgrave Macmillan, 2005), xi.

[2] "Sweet Briar College Is Saved but Is Not in the Clear," *New York Times,* June 23, 2015.

[3] Michael McDonald, "Small U.S. Colleges Battle Death Spiral as Enrollment Drops," *Bloomberg Business,* April 14, 2014.

[4] Laura McKenna, "The Unfortunate Fate of Sweet Briar's Professors," *Atlantic,* March 10, 2015.

[5] Ibid.

CHAPTER 1. BURSTING THE COLLEGE BUBBLE

[1] "Chart of the Day: Cost of College Degree in U.S. Soars 12 Fold," *Bloomberg*, August 15, 2012.

[2] Kevin Carey, "How to Raise a University's Profile: Pricing and Packaging," *New York Times*, February 6, 2015.

[3] Benjamin Ginsberg, *The Fall of the Faculty: The Rise of the All-Administrative University and Why It Matters* (New York: Oxford University Press, 2011), 25.

[4] Roger Kimball, "the Rise of the Crybullies," *Wall Street Journal*, November 13, 2015.

[5] Peter Hassan, "UWM says 'politically correct' is no longer politically correct," Campusreform.org, October 21, 2015.

[6] Isaac Cohen, "Reflections on the Revolution," *Yale Daily News*, November 20, 2015.

[7] Andrew Martin and Andrew W. Lehren, "A Generation Hobbled by the Soaring Cost of College," *New York Times*, May 12, 2012.

[8] "New York Fed: Household Debt, Student Loan Delinquencies Climb," *Los Angeles Times*, February 17, 2015.

[9] Jeffrey J. Selingo, "Is College Worth the Cost? Many Recent Graduates Don't Think So," *Washington Post*, September 30, 2015.

[10] Jaison R. Abel, Richard Deitz, and Yaqin Su, "Are Recent College Graduates Finding Good Jobs?" Federal Reserve Bank of New York, *Current Issues in Economics and Finance* 20, no. 1 (2014); www.newyorkfed.org/research/current_issues/ci20-1.pdf.

[11] Richard Vedder and Christopher Denhart, "How the College Bubble Will Pop," *Wall Street Journal*, January 8, 2014.

[12] Abel, Deitz, and Su, "Are Recent College Graduates Finding Good Jobs?"

[13] Clifford Adelman, *The Toolbox Revisited: Paths to Degree Completion from High School Through College* (Washington, DC: US Department of Education, 2006).

[14] Jason Delisle, "The Hidden Student-Debt Bomb," *Wall Street Journal*, December 30, 2014.

[15] Cristian Deritis, "Student Lending's Failing Grade," *Moody's Analytics*, July 2011; image.exct.net/lib/fefb127575640d/m/2/Student+Lendings+Failing+Grade.pdf.

[16] Charles Murray, "Down with the Four-Year College Degree!" Cato Unbound, October 2008. See also Charles Murray, *Real Education: Four Simple Truths for Bringing America's Schools Back to Reality* (New York: Three Rivers Press, 2008).

[17] businessinsider.com/mark-cuban-sweet-briar-college-college-debt-bubble-crisis-2015-3#ixzz3UN6Mseq1.

[18] Sarah Lacy, "Peter Thiel: We're in a Bubble and It's Not the Internet. It's Higher Education," *Tech Crunch*, April 10, 2011; techcrunch.com/2011/04/10/peter-thiel-were-in-a-bubble-and-its-not-the-internet-its-higher-education.

[19] Jesse Colombo, "The College Bubble (incl. Education and Student Loan Bubble)"; www.thebubblebubble.com/college-bubble.

[20] Carey, "How to Raise a University's Profile."

21 Richard Arum and Josipa Roksa, *Academically Adrift: Limited Learning on College Campuses* (Chicago: University of Chicago Press, 2011).

22 Douglas Belkin, "Test Finds College Graduates Lack Skills for White-Collar Jobs," *Wall Street Journal*, January 16, 2015.

23 Alia Wong, "The Downfall of For-Profit Colleges," *Atlantic*, February 23, 2015.

24 Martin and Lehren, "A Generation Hobbled by the Soaring Cost of College."

CHAPTER 2. DÉJÀ VU: *PROFSCAM* TWENTY-EIGHT YEARS LATER

1 Charles J. Sykes, *ProfScam: Professors and the Demise of Higher Education* (Washington, DC: Regnery Gateway, 1988).

2 Ibid., 4.

3 Ibid., 82.

4 Ibid., 264.

5 Ibid., 24–25.

6 Charles Sykes, "Uncle Sam, Rock 'n' Roll, and Higher Education," The Cato Institute, Policy Analysis No. 136, July 25, 1990.

7 Sykes, *ProfScam*, 103.

8 Ibid., 43.

9 Joseph Berger, "Teach College Teachers to, Yes, Teach, Panel Says," *New York Times*, April 19, 1989. From the article: "Explaining why the group focused on teaching as a current issue, Mary Patterson McPherson, president of Bryn Mawr College, said that with the cost of tuition rising, educators felt that 'students are paying a great deal more and receiving less attention from the faculty.' She mentioned the controversy created by 'ProfScam: Professors and the Demise of Higher Education,' a book written by Charles J. Sykes and published last year by Regnery Gateway of Washington."

10 Bennett L. Rudolph, "Book Review: Professors and the Demise of Higher Education," *Grand Valley Review* 4, no. 2 (1989).

11 Stephen Joel Trachtenberg, "Academia Under Indictment," *AGB Reports*, Association of Governing Boards, January–February 1991.

12 Derek Bok, *Our Underachieving Colleges: A Candid Look at How Students Learn and Why They Should Be Learning More* (Princeton: Princeton University Press, 2006), 4.

13 Jeff Denneen and Tom Dretler, "The Financially Sustainable University," Bain & Company (with Sterling Partners), July 6, 2012.

14 Nathan Harden, "The End of the University as We Know It," *The American Interest* 8, no. 3 (December 11, 2012); www.the-american-interest.com/2012/12/11/the-end-of-the-university-as-we-know-it.

CHAPTER 3. THE (ESCALATING) FLIGHT FROM TEACHING

1 Charles J. Sykes, *ProfScam: Professors and the Demise of Higher Education* (Washington, DC: Regnery Gateway, 1988), 36.

2 Karen Herzog, "Educators Frustrated by Walker's Comments About Faculty Work," *Milwaukee Journal Sentinel*, January 29, 2015.

[3] Ibid.

[4] Charles Sykes, "Awkward: Walker Critic Isn't Teaching Any Classes," *Right Wisconsin,* February 2, 2015; rightwisconsin.com/perspectives/no-she-isnt-actually-teaching-any-classes-290421541.html.

[5] journalism.wisc.edu/sjmc_profile/jo-ellen-fair.

[6] Herzog, "Educators Frustrated by Walker's Comments About Faculty Work."

[7] Nathan Schacht, "Professors Critical of Gov. Walker Spend Little Time in Classroom," *Media Trackers,* February 6, 2015; mediatrackers.org/wisconsin/2015/02/06/professors-critical-gov-walker-spend-little-time-classroom.

[8] www.newstalk1130.com/onair/common-sense-central-37717/wait-how-many-uw-system-employees-13203494.

[9] Douglas Belkin and Mark Peters, "Wisconsin GOP Gov. Walker Takes Aim at College Outlays, Professors; Likely Presidential Candidate Proposes a $300 Million Cut to State's University System," *Wall Street Journal,* February 3, 2015. See also Charles Sykes, "UW Chancellor Makes Revealing Admission About Teaching," *Right Wisconsin,* February 4, 2015; rightwisconsin.com/perspectives/uw-chancellor-makes-revealing-admission-290832451.html.

[10] Andrew Hacker and Claudia Dreifus, *Higher Education? How Colleges Are Wasting Our Money and Failing Our Kids—and What We Can Do About It* (New York: St. Martin's Griffin, 2010), 13–14.

[11] Christopher Jencks and David Riesman, *The Academic Revolution* (Garden City, NY: Doubleday, 1968), 532.

[12] Clark Kerr, *The Uses of the University* (Cambridge, MA: Harvard University Press, 1963), 49.

[13] Michael Zimmerman, "I'm All for Government Aid for Colleges, but Not at the Expense of Scientific Research," *Chronicle of Higher Education,* September 9, 1987.

[14] "Competition for Federal Money Is Said to Have Damaging Effects on Scientists," *Chronicle of Higher Education,* February 27, 1987.

[15] "Teaching and Research: Research Ranked Highest Priority, Teaching Second," *U.: The National College Newspaper,* February 1989.

[16] Sykes, *ProfScam,* 54.

[17] James Steven Fairweather, "Beyond the Rhetoric: Trends in the Relative Value of Teaching and Research in Faculty Salaries," *Journal of Higher Education* 76, no. 4 (July–August 2005).

[18] Melissa Binder, Janie Chermak, Kate Krause, and Jennifer Thacher, "The Teaching Penalty in Higher Education: Evidence from a Public Research University," *Economics Letters* 117, no. 1 (October 2012), 41.

[19] Daniel S. Hamermesh, "10 Tips for Junior Faculty," *Inside Higher Ed,* May 25, 2011.

[20] Mark Bauerlein, "Professors on the Production Line, Students on Their Own," AEI Future of American Education Project Working Paper 2009-01 (Washington, DC: American Enterprise Institute, 2009).

[21] Gordon C. Winston, "The Decline in Undergraduate Teaching: Moral Failure or Market Pressures?" *Change* 26, no. 5 (September–October 1994), 12.

[22] Derek Bok, "Reclaiming the Public Trust," *Change* 24, no. 4 (July–August 1992), 16.

[23] Hacker and Dreifus, *Higher Education?*, 254.

[24] Sylvia Hurtado et al., *Undergraduate Teaching Faculty: The 2010–2011 HERI Faculty Survey,* Higher Education Research Institute, Graduate School of Education and Information Studies, UCLA, 2012.

[25] Ibid.

[26] John W. Curtis, "The Employment Status of Instructional Staff Members in Higher Education, Fall 2011," American Association of University Professors, Washington, DC, April 2014.

[27] Ibid.

[28] Douglas Belkin and Melissa Korn, "Colleges' Use of Adjuncts Comes Under Pressure," *Wall Street Journal,* February 16, 2015.

[29] David C. Levy, "Do College Professors Work Hard Enough?" *Washington Post,* March 23, 2012.

[30] Richard Arum and Josipa Roksa, *Academically Adrift: Limited Learning on College Campuses* (Chicago: University of Chicago Press, 2011), 8. See also Jeffrey F. Milmen, Joseph B. Berger, and Eric L. Dey, "Faculty Time Allocation: A Study of Change over Twenty Years," *Journal of Higher Education* 65 (1994); and William F. Massy and Robert Zemsky, "Faculty Discretionary Time: Departments and the Academic Ratchet," *Journal of Higher Education* 65 (1994).

[31] wisconsin.edu/reports-statistics/download/educational_statistics/ret-grad.pdf.

[32] "Getting What You Pay For?," a report by the American Council of Trustees and Alumni, April 2014; goacta.org/images/download/getting_what_you_pay_for.pdf.

[33] Sykes, *ProfScam,* 61.

[34] Bryan Solie, "Cunningham Should Retract Speech," *Daily Texan,* January 18, 1990.

[35] Naomi Schaefer Riley, *The Faculty Lounges: And Other Reasons Why You Won't Get the College Education You Paid For* (Chicago: Ivan R. Dee, 2011), 89.

[36] Jay Schalin, "Hardly an Academic Sweatshop: A Common-Sense Look at UNC Faculty Workloads Indicates That Professors Teach Less Than the System Claims," John William Pope Center for Education Policy, April 10, 2011; pope-center.org/commentaries/article.html?id=2504.

[37] Richard Vedder, Christopher Matgouranis, and Jonathan Robe, "Faculty Productivity and Costs at the University of Texas at Austin," policy paper from the Center for College Affordability and Productivity, May 2011.

[38] Ibid. See also Richard Vedder, "Time to Make Professors Teach," *Wall Street Journal,* June 8, 2011.

[39] Douglas Belkin and Mark Peters, "Wisconsin GOP Gov. Walker Takes Aim at College Outlays, Professors," *Wall Street Journal,* February 3, 2015.

CHAPTER 4. THE REALITY OF ACADEMIC RESEARCH

[1] Chester E. Finn, Jr., "Higher Education on Trial: An Indictment," *Current,* October 1984.

[2] John Hattie and H. W. Marsh, "The Relationship Between Research and Teaching: A Meta-Analysis," *Review of Educational Research* 66, no. 4 (Winter 1996).

[3] Paul Basken, "Cost Savings Appear Elusive in Push for Faculty Productivity," *Chronicle of Higher Education,* October 8, 2012.

[4] Charles J. Sykes, *ProfScam: Professors and the Demise of Higher Education* (Washington, DC: Regnery Gateway, 1988): 102.

[5] Ibid., 105.

[6] Ibid., 104.

[7] Russell Jacoby, "Stanley Fish Turned Careerism Into a Philosophy," *New Republic,* August 21, 2013.

[8] Mark Ware, "An Overview of Scientific and Scholarly Journal Publishing," International Association of Scientific, Technical and Medical Publishers, 2012; stm-assoc.org/2012_12_11_STM_Report_2012.pdf.

[9] Michael J. Mahoney, "Scientific Publication and Knowledge Politics," *Journal of Social Behavior and Personality* 2, no. 2 (1987).

[10] Rose Eveleth, "Academics Write Papers Arguing Over How Many People Read (and Cite) Their Papers," *Smithsonian Magazine,* March 25, 2014; smithsonianmag.com/smart-news/half-academic-studies-are-never-read-more-three-people-180950222/#UTZ65TIiaqrG6vLz.99.

[11] Aaron Gordon, "Killing Pigs and Weed Maps: The Mostly Unread World of Academic Papers," *Pacific Standard,* March 18, 2014; psmag.com/books-and-culture/killing-pigs-weed-maps-mostly-unread-world-academic-papers-76733.

[12] Eveleth, "Academics Write Papers Arguing Over How Many People Read (and Cite) Their Papers."

[13] Pietro Della Briotta Parolo et al., "Attention Decay in Science," arxiv.org/pdf/1503.01881v1.pdf.

[14] Mark Bauerlein, "Literary Research: Costs and Impact," Center for College Affordability and Productivity, November 2011; centerforcollegeaffordability.org/uploads/Literary_Research_Bauerlein.pdf.

[15] Mark Bauerlein, "The Research Bust," *Chronicle of Higher Education,* December 4, 2011.

CHAPTER 5. WHAT DO STUDENTS LEARN (AND DOES ANYBODY CARE)?

[1] "Getting What You Pay For?," a report by the American Council of Trustees and Alumni, April 2014; goacta.org/images/download/getting_what_you_pay_for.pdf. See *National Assessment of Adult Literacy: A First Look at the Literacy of America's Adults in the 21st Century* (Washington, DC: National Center for Education Statistics, NCES 2006-470, 2005).

[2] Douglas Belkin, "Test Finds College Graduates Lack Skills for White-Collar Jobs,"*Wall Street Journal,* January 16, 2015.

[3] For full results, see ets.org/s/research/30079/millennials.html. See also Todd Frankel, "U.S. Millennials Post 'Abysmal' Scores in Tech Skills Test, Lag Behind Foreign Peers," *Washington Post,* March 2, 2015.

[4] Derek Bok, *Our Underachieving Colleges: A Candid Look at How Students Learn and Why They Should Be Learning More* (Princeton: Princeton University Press, 2006), 8.

[5] ACTA, "Getting What You Pay For?"

[6] National Endowment for the Humanities, "50 Hours: A Core Curriculum for College Students," Washington, DC, October 1989.

[7] Richard Arum and Josipa Roksa, *Academically Adrift: Limited Learning on College Campuses* (Chicago: University of Chicago Press, 2011).

[8] Ibid., 15.

[9] Ibid.

[10] "It Takes More Than a Major: Employer Priorities for College Learning and Student Success. An Online Survey Among Employers Conducted On Behalf of the Association of American Colleges and Universities," Hart Research Associates, April 10, 2013.

[11] Derek Bok, *Higher Learning* (Cambridge, MA: Harvard University Press, 1986), 323–24.

[12] Arum and Roksa, *Academically Adrift,* 56.

[13] Charles J. Sykes, *ProfScam: Professors and the Demise of Higher Education* (Washington, DC: Regnery Gateway, 1988), 79.

[14] Charles Sykes, "Uncle Sam, Rock 'n' Roll, and Higher Education," The Cato Institute, Policy Analysis No. 136, July 25, 1990.

[15] Arum and Roksa, *Academically Adrift,* 3.

[16] Ibid.

[17] Philip Babcock and Mindy Marks, "Leisure College USA: The Decline in Student Study Time," Washington, DC: American Enterprise Institute, 2010.

[18] Ibid.

[19] Rebekah Nation (a pseudonym), *My Freshman Year: What a Professor Learned by Becoming a Student* (New York: Penguin Books, 2006), 113.

[20] Babcock and Marks, "Leisure College USA."

[21] Arum and Roksa, *Academically Adrift,* 71.

[22] Ibid., 4.

[23] Stuart Rojstaczer and Christopher Healy, "Where A Is Ordinary: The Evolution of American College and University Grading, 1940–2009," *Teachers College Record* 114, no. 7 (2012).

[24] gradeinflation.com.

[25] Travis Andersen, Nicholas Jacques, and Todd Feathers, "Harvard Professor Says Grade Inflation Rampant," *Boston Globe,* December 4, 2013.

[26] Ibid.

[27] ACTA, "Getting What You Pay For?"

[28] Murray Sperber, *Beer and Circus: How Big-Time College Sports Is Crippling Under-graduate Education* (New York: Henry Holt, 2000), 120.

[29] Sykes, *ProfScam*, 85.

CHAPTER 6. THE COLLEGE FOR ALL DELUSION

[1] David Freedlander, "Progressives: Big Ideas Will Win Us 2016," *Daily Beast*, December 10, 2014; thedailybeast.com/articles/2014/12/10/progressives-big-ideas-will-win-us-2016.html.

[2] Sahil Kapur "How a Ragtag Group of Lefties Mainlined Debt-Free College Into the Democratic Primary," *Bloomberg Politics*, May 8, 2015; bloomberg.com/politics/articles/2015-05-08/how-a-ragtag-group-of-lefties-mainlined-debt-free-college-into-the-democratic-primary.

[3] James Pethokoukis, "The Left's Terrible Big Idea for 2016? Free College for All," AEI Blog, December 11, 2014, aei.org/publication/lefts-terrible-big-idea-2016-free-college.

[4] Stephanie Riegg Cellini and Claudia Goldin, "Does Federal Student Aid Raise Tuition? New Evidence on For-Profit Colleges," Working Paper 17827, National Bureau of Economic Research, Cambridge, MA, February 2012; nber.org/papers/w17827. See also Andrew Biggs, "The Truth About College Aid: It's Corporate Welfare," *Atlantic*, May 21, 2012; theatlantic.com/business/archive/2012/05/the-truth-about-college-aid-its-corporate-welfare/257456.

[5] James Rosenbaum, *Beyond College for All: Career Paths for the Forgotten Half* (New York: Russell Sage Foundation, 2001), 57.

[6] ACT, *The Condition of College and Career Readiness 2014*, 2014; act.org/research/policymakers/cccr14/pdf/CCCR14-NationalReadinessRpt.pdf.

[7] Charles Murray, "Down with the Four-Year College Degree!" Cato Unbound, October 2008.

[8] Richard Arum and Josipa Roksa, *Academically Adrift: Limited Learning on College Campuses* (Chicago: University of Chicago Press, 2011), 55.

[9] Rosenbaum, *Beyond College for All*, 59–62.

[10] Ibid., 56.

[11] Ibid., 101.

[12] Ibid., 102.

[13] Ibid., 101.

[14] Andrew P. Kelly, "Big Payoff, Low Probability: Post-Secondary Education and Upward Mobility in America," prepared for the Thomas B. Fordham Institute's Education for Upward Mobility Conference, December 2, 2014.

[15] Martha Bailey and Susan Dynarski, "Inequality in Postsecondary Education," in *Whither Opportunity? Rising Inequality, Schools, and Children's Life Chances*, eds. Greg Duncan and Richard Murnane (New York: Russell Sage Foundation, 2011), 117–31.

[16] Jason DeParle, "For Poor, Leap to College Often Ends in a Hard Fall," *New York Times*, December 22, 2012.

[17] Kelly, "Big Payoff, Low Probability."

[18] Arum and Roksa, *Academically Adrift*, 68.

[19] Kelly, "Big Payoff, Low Probability."

[20] Richard Vedder, "Six Reasons Why Obama's Free Community College Is a Poor Investment," *Forbes*, January 11, 2015; forbes.com/sites/ccap/2015/01/11/six-reasons-why-obamas-free-community-college-is-a-poor-investment.

[21] Ibid.

[22] Murray, "Down with the Four-Year Degree."

[23] Charles Murray, *Real Education: Four Simple Truths for Bringing America's Schools Back to Reality* (New York: Three Rivers Press, 2008). This quote is from "Down with the Four-Year Degree."

CHAPTER 7. OUR BLOATED COLLEGES

[1] Andrew Martin and Andrew W. Lehren, "A Generation Hobbled by the Soaring Cost of College," *New York Times*, May 12, 2012.

[2] Debra Erdley, "Gee's Farewell from Ohio State Worth $6M; Now WVU Chief, He Says Role Not About the Money," *TribLive*, May 18, 2014; triblive.com/news/adminpage/6128172-74/university-gee-president#ixzz3V2mGwElv.

[3] Jordan Weissmann, "This State College President Earned $6 Million Last Year. Should You Be Mad?" *Slate*, May 20, 2014; slate.com/blogs/moneybox/2014/05/20/college_president_pay_is_it_too_high.html.

[4] John Hechinger, "Bureaucrats Paid $250,000 Feed Outcry Over College Costs," *Bloomberg*, November 14, 2012.

[5] Jon Marcus, "New Analysis Shows Problematic Boom in Higher Ed Administrators," New England Center for Investigative Reporting, February 6, 2014.

[6] Ibid.

[7] Frank Mussano and Robert V. Iosue, "Colleges Need a Business Productivity Audit," *Wall Street Journal*, December 28, 2014.

[8] Heather Mac Donald, "Less Academics, More Narcissism," *City Journal*, July 14, 2011.

[9] Andrew Hacker and Claudia Dreifus, *Higher Education? How Colleges Are Wasting Our Money and Failing Our Kids—and What We Can Do About It* (New York: St. Martin's Griffin, 2010), 29.

[10] Ibid., 33.

[11] Jeff Denneen and Tom Dretler, "The Financially Sustainable University," Bain & Company (with Sterling Partners), 2012.

[12] Susan Kinzie and Valerie Strauss, "$500,000 in Ladner Spending Itemized," *Washington Post*, September 22, 2005; washingtonpost.com//wp-dyn/content/article/2005/09/21/AR2005092102395.html.

[13] Susan Kinzie and Valerie Strauss, "Ladner's 3.75 Million Deal Severs Ties to American U," *Washington Post*, October 25, 2005; washingtonpost.com/archive/local/2005/10/25/ladners-375-million-deal-severs-ties-to-american-u/0eddc8d7-008c-4302-ba93-7b1d010db4e3.

[14] Clark Kerr, *The Uses of the University* (Cambridge, MA: Harvard University Press, 1963), 14.

[15] University of Minnesota, "About Centers and Institutes." centers.umn.edu.

[16] "Getting What You Pay For?," a report by the American Council of Trustees and Alumni, April 2014; goacta.org/images/download/getting_what_you_pay_for .pdf.

CHAPTER 8. ACADEMIA'S EDIFICE BLOAT

[1] Freddie DeBoer, "Boy, I Wonder Why College Is So Expensive," May 1, 2013; fred -diedeboer.kinja.com/boy-i-wonder-why-college-is-so-expensive-494258996.

[2] purdue.edu/newsroom/releases/2012/Q4/purdue-to-dedicate-france-a .-c%C3%B3rdova-rec-sports-center.html.

[3] Greg Winter, "Jacuzzi U.? A Battle of Perks to Lure Students," *New York Times,* October 5, 2003.

[4] Ibid.

[5] Howard R. Bowen, *The Costs of Higher Education: How Much Do Colleges and Universities Spend per Student and How Much Should They Spend?* (Washington, DC: Jossey-Bass, 1980).

[6] Frank Mussano and Robert V. Iosue, "Colleges Need a Business Productivity Audit," *Wall Street Journal,* December 28, 2014.

[7] Andrew Martin, "Building a Showcase Campus, Using an I.O.U.," *New York Times,* December 13, 2012.

[8] "The 13 Most Expensive College Stadium Renovations," July 24, 2014; stack.com /2014/07/24/most-expensive-college-football-stadium-renovations.

[9] "17 Insanely Expensive College Athletic Training Facilities," June 2, 2014; stack .com/2014/06/02/expensive-college-athletic-training-facilities.

[10] "University of Oregon Opens Incredible New Football Training Facility," August 2, 2013; stack.com/2013/08/02/university-of-oregon-football-facility.

[11] Matt M. Johnson, "Private Colleges Build Facilities to Attract Donations and Students," *Finance & Commerce,* September 28, 2011; finance-commerce.com /2011/09/private-colleges-build-facilities-to-attract-donations-and-students /#ixzz3aJ7aslYo.

[12] Winter, "Jacuzzi U.? A Battle of Perks to Lure Students."

[13] Andrew Martin, "Building a Showcase Campus, Using an I.O.U."

[14] Ibid.

[15] Jeff Denneen and Tom Dretler, "The Financially Sustainable University," Bain & Company (with Sterling Partners), 2012.

[16] Don Troop, "Moody's Issues Negative Outlook for Higher Education," *Chronicle of Higher Education,* July 14, 2014.

[17] Brian Burnsed, "Growth in Division I Athletics Expenses Outpaces Revenue Increases: And No Division II or Division III Institutions Generate More Revenue Than They Spend, According to a Recent Study," NCAA, August 20, 2014; ncaa .org/about/resources/media-center/news/growth-division-i-athletics-expenses -outpaces-revenue-increases. See also David L. Fulks, *Revenues & Expenses: 2004– 201,* NCAA Division I Intercollegiate Athletics Programs Report (Indianapolis,

IN: National Collegiate Athletic Association, 2012), 32, Table 3.9, 104, 105; ncaa
-publications.com/productdownloads/D12011REVEXP.pdf.

[18] Andrew Hacker and Claudia Dreifus, *Higher Education? How Colleges Are Wasting
Our Money and Failing Our Kids—and What We Can Do About It* (New York:
St. Martin's Griffin, 2010), 166.

[19] politifact.com/virginia/statements/2014/dec/22/jim-moran/moran-says-only-20
-colleges.

[20] Burnsed, "Growth in Division I Athletics Expenses Outpaces Revenue Increases."

[21] Steve Berkowitz, Jodi Upton, and Erik Brady, "Most NCAA Division I Athletic
Departments Take Subsidies," *USA Today,* July 1, 2013; usatoday.com/story/sports
/college/2013/05/07/ncaa-finances-subsidies/2142443.

[22] Brian Burnsed, "Growth in Division I Athletics Expenses Outpaces Revenue Increases."

[23] David Welch Suggs, Jr., "Myth: College Sports Are a Cash Cow," American
Council on Education; acenet.edu/news-room/Pages/Myth-College-Sports-Are
-a-Cash-Cow2.aspx.

[24] Berkowitz, Upton, and Brady, "Most NCAA Division I Athletic Departments
Take Subsidies."

[25] Ibid.

[26] Burnsed, "Growth in Division I Athletics Expenses Outpaces Revenue Increases."

[27] "Getting What You Pay For?," a report by the American Council of Trustees and
Alumni, April 2014; goacta.org/images/download/getting_what_you_pay_for.pdf.

[28] Donna M. Desrochers, *Academic Spending Versus Athletic Spending: Who Wins?*
(Washington, DC: American Institutes for Research, 2013), 2, 4, 10; deltacost
-project.org/sites/default/files/products/DeltaCostAIR_AthleticAcademic
_Spending_IssueBrief.pdf.

[29] Ibid.

[30] Ibid.

[31] ACTA, "Getting What You Pay For?"

CHAPTER 9. DOES THE EMPEROR HAVE ANY CLOTHES?

[1] Cyril Labbé. "Ike Antkare One of the Great Stars in the Scientific Firmament,"
International Society for Scientometrics and Informetrics Newsletter 6, no. 2 (2010):
48–52.

[2] nature.com/nature/journal/v434/n7036/full/nature03653.htm.

[3] Jonny Scott, "Postmodern Gravity Deconstructed, Slyly," *New York Times,* May 18,
1996.

[4] Editors of *Lingua Franca, The Sokal Hoax: The Sham That Shook the Academic World*
(Lincoln, NE: Bison Books, 2000), 1–2.

[5] One would have thought (wrongly) that the title might have been a tipoff. Alan
Sokal, "Transgressing the Boundaries: Toward a Transformative Hermeneutics
of Quantum Gravity," *Social Text,* Spring–Summer 1996.

[6] Alan Sokal, "Revelation: A Physicist Experiments with Cultural Studies," *Lingua Franca*, May–June 1996.

[7] Alan Sokal, "Transgressing the Boundaries: Toward a Transformative Hermeneutics of Quantum Gravity," *Social Text*, Spring–Summer 1996.

[8] Alan Sokal, *Beyond the Hoax: Science, Philosophy, and Culture* (New York: Oxford University Press, 2008), 26.

[9] Katha Pollitt, "Pomolotov Cocktail, and Selected Responses," *Nation*, June 10, 1996 (reprinted in *The Sokal Hoax*, 96–99).

[10] Declan Butler, "Investigating Journals: The Dark Side of Publishing," *Nature*, March 27, 2013.

[11] nature.com/news/2009/090615/full/news.2009.571.html.

[12] Ibid.

[13] John Bohannon, "Who's Afraid of Peer Review?" *Science* 342, no. 6154 (October 4, 2013): 60–65.

[14] Richard Van Noorden, "Publishers Withdraw More Than 120 Gibberish Papers," *Nature*, February 24, 2014; nature.com/news/publishers-withdraw-more-than-120-gibberish-papers-1.14763.

CHAPTER 10. A SCANDAL RECONSIDERED

[1] Kenneth L. Wainstein, A. Joseph Jay III, and Colleen Depman Kukowski, of the law firm Cadwalader, Wickersham & Taft LLP on behalf of the university: "Investigation of Irregular Classes in the Department of African and Afro-American Studies at the University of North Carolina at Chapel Hill," October 16, 2014. Referred to hereafter as the Wainstein report; 3qh929iorux3fdpl532k03kg.wpengine.netdna-cdn.com/wp-content/uploads/2014/10/UNC-FINAL-REPORT.pdf.

[2] Ibid., 21–23.

[3] Letter from provost John Etchemendy to faculty and teaching staff about the Stanford Honor Code, *Stanford Report*, March 24, 2015; news.stanford.edu/news/2015/march/provost-faculty-letter-032415.html.

[4] Amy Julia Harris and Ryan Mac, "Stanford Athletes Had Access to List of 'Easy' Classes: California Watch Report, *Stanford Daily*, March 9, 2011.

[5] Ibid.

[6] Richard Pérez-Peña, "Students Disciplined in Harvard Scandal," *New York Times*, February 1, 2013.

[7] Richard Pérez-Peña, "Harvard Students in Cheating Scandal Say Collaboration was Accepted," *New York Times*, August 31, 2012.

[8] Bradley Sacks, "Wainstein Report Reveals Extent of Academic Scandal at UNC," *Daily Tarheel*, October 22, 2014; see also Jack New, "Two Decades of 'Paper Classes,'" *Inside Higher Ed*, October 23, 2014.

[9] Wainstein report, 19.

[10] Ibid., 51.

[11] Michael McCann and Jon Wertheim, "Rashanda McCants, Devon Ramsay File Suit Against UNC, NCAA," *Sports Illustrated*, January 23, 2015; si.com/college-basketball/2015/01/06/rashanda-mccants-unc-paper-classes-lawsuit.

[12] *McCants v. UNC*, washingtonpost.com/news/grade-point/wp-content/uploads /sites/42/2015/01/UNC-Complaint-Filed-Copy-1-22-15.pdf.

[13] Ibid.

[14] Sara Ganim, "CNN Analysis: Some College Athletes Play Like Adults, Read Like 5th-Graders," CNN, January 8, 2014; cnn.com/2014/01/07/us/ncaa-athletes -reading-scores.

[15] "Opinion: UNC Should Use Wainstein's Report as a Springboard," *Daily Tarheel*, October 23, 2014.

[16] Ganim, "CNN Analysis: Some College Athletes Play Like Adults, Read Like 5th-Graders."

[17] Wainstein report, 14.

[18] Ibid., 17.

[19] Ibid., 1.

[20] Charles J. Sykes, *ProfScam: Professors and the Demise of Higher Education* (Washington, DC: Regnery Gateway, 1988), 95–97.

[21] Wainstein report, 3–4.

[22] Ibid., 54–55.

[23] Ibid., 56.

[24] Ibid., 60.

[25] Ibid., 58.

[26] Ibid., 51.

[27] Ibid., 18.

[28] Ibid., 78.

[29] Ibid., 81fn.

[30] Ibid., 44–45.

[31] Ibid., 24.

[32] Ibid., 20.

[33] Ibid., 92.

[34] Report of the Ad Hoc Committee on Athletics and the University, December 15, 1989 Faculty Council Meeting; 3qh929iorux3fdpl532k03kg.wpengine.netdna-cdn .com/wp-content/uploads/2014/04/Report-of-the-Ad-Hoc-Committee-on -Athletics-and-the-University-19891.pdf.

[35] Wainstein report, 20.

[36] Ibid., 66.

[37] Ibid., 21.

[38] Ibid., 5.

[39] Ibid., 2.

[40] Ibid., 92–93.

CHAPTER 11. GRIEVANCE U.

[1] Screenshot from wesleyan.edu/reslife/housing/program/open house.html, February 28, 2015. (Author's note: Some material has since been removed from site.) See also: Katherine Timpf, "Wesleyan Now Offering LGBTTQQFAGPBDSM Housing (Not a Typo)," National Review Online, February 25, 2015; nationalreview

.com/article/414398/weslyan-offering-lgbttqqfagpbdsm-housing-not-typo
-katherine-timpf.

[2] Screenshot from wesleyan.edu/reslife/housing/program/open house.html, February 28, 2015 (see previous note).

[3] Ibid.

[4] Bryan Stascavage, "Why Black Lives Matter Isn't What You Think, *Wesleyan Argus,* September 14, 2015

[5] An Open Letter to the Wesleyan Community from Students of Color, Posted at: wesleying.org/2015/09/25/an-open-letter-to-the-wesleyan-community-from -students-of-color/.

[6] Kate Zezima, "Everything Is Political These Days. Even Commencement Speeches," *Washington Post,* May 14, 2014.

[7] Richard Pérez-Peña and Tanzina Vega, "Brandeis Cancels Plans to Give Honorary Degree to Ayaan Hirsi Ali, a Critic of Islam," *New York Times,* April 8, 2014.

[8] Statement to the Purdue Community, November 11, 2015.

[9] "On Trigger Warnings," AAUP, August 2014. www.aaup.org/report/trigger -warnings.

[10] "Report of the Committee on Freedom of Expression," University of Chicago, January 2015. provost.uchicago.edu/FOECommitteeReport.pdf.

[11] Tyler Kingkade, "Obama Thinks Students Should Stop Stifling Debate On Campus," *Huffington Post,* September 15, 2015.

[12] Charles J. Sykes, *50 Rules Kids Won't Learn in School* (New York: St. Martin's Press, 2007), 73.

[13] Philip Wythe, "Trigger Warnings Needed in Classroom," *Daily Targum,* February 18, 2014; dailytargum.com/article/2014/02/trigger-warnings-needed-in-classroom.

[14] Todd Gitlin, "Please Be Disturbed: Triggering Can Be Good for You, Kids," *Tablet,* March 13, 2015; tabletmag.com/jewish-news-and-politics/189543/trigger -warnings-on-campus.

[15] Judith Shulevitz, "In College and Hiding from Scary Ideas," *New York Times,* March 21, 2015.

[16] Kaitlyn Schallhorn, "Feminist Students Feel 'Unsafe' Bringing Female, Conservative Speaker to Campus," *Campus Reform,* April 20, 2015; campusreform.org/ ?ID=6456.

[17] Shulevitz, "In College and Hiding from Scary Ideas."

[18] Kathleen Parker, "Fair Warning, Provoking a Thought Is Literature's Job," *Washington Post,* May 20, 2014.

[19] Peter Gray, "Declining Student Resilience: A Serious Problem for Colleges," *Psychology Today,* September 22, 2015.

[20] Eric Posner, "Universities Are Right—and Within Their Rights—to Crack Down on Speech and Behavior," *Slate,* February 12, 2015; slate.com/articles/news_and _politics/view_from_chicago/2015/02/university_speech_codes_students _are_children_who_must_be_protected.single.html.

[21] Gitlin, "Please Be Disturbed: Triggering Can Be Good for You, Kids."

[22] Walter Russell Mead, "The Wrong Time to Coddle," *American Interest*, March 23, 2015; the-american-interest.com/2015/03/23/the-wrong-time-to-coddle.

[23] Jennifer Medina, "Warning: The Literary Canon Could Make Students Squirm," *New York Times*, May 17, 2014.

[24] Miles Hilton, Lara Tang, and a third writer who wished to remain anonymous. "Reading Lit Hum's Rapes," *Bwog, Columbia Student News*, May 10, 2014; bwog.com/2014/05/10/reading-lit-hums-rapes/.

[25] Jessy Diamba, "A.S. Resolution Policy Aims to Protect Students from PTSD Triggers," *Daily Nexus*, March, 7, 2014; dailynexus.com/2014-03-07/a-s-resolution-policy-aims-to-protect-students-from-ptsd-triggers.

[26] Ibid.

[27] Edward Schlosser, "I'm a Liberal Professor, and My Liberal Students Terrify Me," *Vox*, June 3, 2015.

[28] ucop.edu/academic-personnel-programs/_files/seminars/Tool_Recognizing_Microaggressions.pdf.

[29] Cited in Jonathan V. Last, "The Campus Left Begins to Implode," *Weekly Standard*, March 26, 2015; weeklystandard.com/blogs/campus-left-begins-implode_899318.html?page=2. See also whitehotharlots.tumblr.com/post/114067452180/a-personal-account-of-how-call-out-culture-has?utm_source=newsletters&utm_medium=email&utm_campaign=JVL+03_25_15.

[30] Sam Hoff, "Students Defend Professor After Sit-In over Racial Climate," *Daily Bruin*, November 20, 2013.

[31] Josh Hedtke, "Tired of Racism Claims, UCLA Student Sets the Record Straight," *College Fix*, February 12, 2014; thecollegefix.com/post/16312.

[32] Heather Mac Donald, "The Microaggression Farce: The Latest Campus Fad, Which Sees Racism Everywhere, Will Create a New Generation of Permanent Victims," *City Journal*, Autumn 2014.

[33] Stephanie Kim, "Moore Hall Sit-In Addressing Discrimination Lacked Open, Tolerant Spirit," *Daily Bruin*, November 20, 2013.

[34] Ibid.

[35] The transcript was released by Marquette University. It is excerpted in Conor Friedersdorf, "Stripping a Professor of Tenure Over a Blog Post," *Atlantic*, February 9, 2015.

[36] Matt Lamb, "Student Told He Can't Openly Disagree with Gay Marriage in Class at Jesuit College," *College Fix*, November 17, 2014.

[37] John McAdams, "Marquette Philosophy Instructor: 'Gay Rights' Can't Be Discussed in Class Since Any Disagreement Would Offend Gay Students," *Marquette Warrior*, November 9, 2014; mu-warrior.blogspot.com/2014/11/marquette-philosophy-instructor-gay.html.

[38] John McAdams, "Marquette to Warrior Blogger: We're Going to Fire You," *Marquette Warrior*, February 4, 2015; mu-warrior.blogspot.com/2015/02/marquette-to-warrior-blogger-were-going.html.

[39] Ibid. www.marquette.edu/_emailtemplates/president-template/president-020515 .html.

[40] Interview with author, September 2015. See also Charles J. Sykes, "A case of Aca-demic Freedom," *Wisconsin Interest,* Fall 2015.

[41] Daniel Maguire on the McAdams Case at Marquette," The Academe Blog; aca-demeblog.org/2015/01/20/daniel-maguire-on-the-mcadams-case-at-mar quette/.

[42] McAdams, "Marquette to Warrior Blogger: We're Going to Fire You."

[43] Conor Friedersdorf, "Stripping a Professor of Tenure Over a Blog Post," op. cit.

[44] "After Gay Marriage Flap, Marquette Moves to Fire Tenured Prof," FIRE, February 5, 2015; thefire.org/gay-marriage-flap-marquette-moves-fire-tenured -prof.

[45] Statutes on Faculty Appointment, Promotion and Tenure, "Cause for Nonre-newal, Suspension, Termination Faculty Statutes," 306.03, Marquette Univer-sity; marquette.edu/provost/306.php.

[46] Ibid. 307.7 (2).

[47] Samantha Harris, "Speech Code of the Month: Marquette University," FIRE, March 9, 2015; thefire.org/speech-code-of-the-month-marquette-university.

[48] M. D. Kittle, "Marquette Professor Becomes Face of National Campus Free Speech Battle," *Wisconsin Reporter,* February 6, 2015.

[49] Ollie Gillman, "The Moment Yale Students Encircled and Shouted Down Pro-fessor Who Told Them to Just 'Look Away' if They Were Offended by Hallow-een Costumes," *Daily Mail,* November 7, 2015.

[50] Monica Wang, Joey Ye, and Victor Wang, "Students Protest Buckley Talk," *Yale Daily News,* November 9, 2015.

[51] Peter Berkowitz, "Yale Gives In to the Grievance Culture," RealClearPolitics .com, November 20, 2015.

[52] List of demands from Concerned Student 1950 group, *Columbia Daily Tribune,* October 23, 2015.

[53] Eugene Volokh, "Missouri Prof. Melissa Click apologizes for her role in trying to stop photographers at student protest," *Washington Post,* November 10, 2015.

[54] Laura Newberry, "Reporters Barred from Smith College Sit-in Held in Solidarity with University of Missouri Students Unless They Support Movement," UMassLive, November 19, 2015 www.masslive.com/news/index.ssf/2015/11/traditional _media_not_welcome.html.

[55] Katie Zavadski, "Amherst Students Protest 'Free Speech,' Demand 'Training' for Offenders," *Daily Beast,* November 13, 2015.

CHAPTER 12. RAPE U.

[1] snltranscripts.jt.org/93/93bdaterape.phtml.

[2] Robert Carle, "How Affirmative Consent Laws Criminalize Everyone," *Federal-ist,* March 30, 2015; thefederalist.com/2015/03/30/how-affirmative-consent-laws -criminalize-everyone.

[3] Jake New, "The 'Yes Means Yes' World," *Inside Higher Ed,* October 17, 2014; in
-sidehighered.com/news/2014/10/17/colleges-across-country-adopting
-affirmative-consent-sexual-assault-policies.

[4] Robert Carle, "How Affirmative Consent Laws Criminalize Everyone."

[5] FIRE Statement on California "Affirmative Consent" Bill, February 13, 2015; the
-fire.org/fire-statement-on-california-affirmative-consent-bill.

[6] Jed Rubenfeld, "Mishandling Rape," *New York Times,* November 15, 2014; nytimes
.com/2014/11/16/opinion/sunday/mishandling-rape.html?_r=1.

[7] David Bernstein, "YOU Are a Rapist; Yes YOU!" *Washington Post,* June 23, 2014;
washingtonpost.com/news/volokh-conspiracy/wp/2014/06/23/you-are-a
-rapist-yes-you.

[8] Robert Siegel, "Tom Wolfe Goes to College with 'Charlotte Simmons,'" NPR,
November 10, 2004; npr.org/templates/story/story.php?storyId=4163364.

[9] Emily Yoffe, "The College Rape Overcorrection," *Slate,* December 7, 2014; slate
.com/articles/double_x/doublex/2014/12/college_rape_campus_sexual
_assault_is_a_serious_problem_but_the_efforts.html.

[10] Janet Halley, "Trading the Megaphone for the Gavel in Title IX Enforcement,"
128 *Harvard Law Review Forum* 103, February 18, 2015; harvardlawreview.org/2015
/02/trading-the-megaphone-for-the-gavel-in-title-ix-enforcement-2.

[11] Sabrina Erdely, "A Rape on Campus: A Brutal Assault and Struggle for Justice at
UVA," Rollingstone.com, November 19, 2014. (The article has since been retracted and removed from the website.)

[12] "Statement from U-Va. President Teresa Sullivan on Sexual Assault Allegations,"
Washington Post, November 22, 2014; washingtonpost.com/local/education
/statement-from-u-va-president-teresa-sullivan-on-sexual-assault-allegations
/2014/11/22/342d40ec-728c-11e4-8808-afaa1e3a33ef_story.html.

[13] Sheila Coronel, Steve Coll, and Derek Kravitz, "Rolling Stone and UVA: The
Columbia University Graduate School of Journalism Report: An Anatomy of a
Journalistic Failure," *Rolling Stone,* April 5, 2015; rollingstone.com/culture
/features/a-rape-on-campus-what-went-wrong-20150405#ixzz3aP6qGO7a.

[14] "Full Text: Charlottesville Police Statement in U-Va. Sex Assault Case," *Washington Post,* March 23, 2015; washingtonpost.com/local/full-text-charlottesville
-police-statement-in-u-va-sex-assault-case/2015/03/23/ec4485bc-d193-11e4-8fce
-3941fc548f1c_story.html.

[15] Coronel, Coll, and Kravitz, "Rolling Stone and UVA: The Columbia University
Graduate School of Journalism Report."

[16] Ibid.

[17] Larry O'Dell, "Police Report on Virginia Gang-Rape Not the Final Word," *Sa-
lon,* March 24, 2015; salon.com/2015/03/24/police_report_on_virginia_gang
_rape_not_the_final_word.

[18] "Dear Colleague" letter from Russlynn Ali, assistant secretary for civil rights,
US Department of Education (April 4, 2011); 2.ed.gov/about/offices/list/ocr
/letters/colleague-201104.pdf perma.cc/WQ79-SGXC.

[19] Yoffe, "The College Rape Overcorrection."

[20] Christopher Krebs and Christine Lindquist, "Setting the Record Straight on '1 in 5,'" *Time*, December 15, 2014.

[21] Yoffe, "The College Rape Overcorrection." This analysis is based on the research of Callie Marie Rennison and Lynn A. Addington, "Violence Against College Women: A Review to Identify Limitations in Defining the Problem and Inform Future Research," tva.sagepub.com/content/15/3/159.abstract.

[22] Robin Wilson, "Presumed Guilty: College Men Accused of Rape Say the Scales Are Tipped Against Them," *Chronicle of Higher Education*, September 1, 2014; chronicle.com/article/Presumed-Guilty/148529/.

[23] Ibid.

[24] Yoffe, "The College Rape Overcorrection." Her account of Drew Sterrett's case is based on filings in his lawsuit against the University of Michigan: Drew Sterrett, Plaintiff, vs. Case No. 2014—Heather Cowan, Jay Wilgus, Stacy Vander Velde, Theodore Spencer, Susan Pritzel, Mikiko Senja, E. Royster Harper, Malinda Matney, Anthony Walesby and Laura Blake Jones, employees of the University of Michigan, sued in his or her personal and official capacities, jointly and severally; archive.freep.com/assets/freep/pdf/C422124157.pdf.

[25] Ibid.

[26] Teresa Watanabe, "More College Men Are Fighting Back Against Sexual Misconduct Cases," *Los Angeles Times*, June 7, 2014.

[27] George F. Will, "Colleges Become the Victims of Progressivism," *Washington Post*, June 6, 2014; washingtonpost.com/opinions/george-will-college-become-the-victims-of-progressivism/2014/06/06/e90e73b4-eb50-11e3-9f5c-9075d5508f0a_story.html.

[28] Joe Strupp, "Professors Slam George Will Campus Appearance After 'Hate Speech' Rape Column," *Media Matters*, October 17, 2014; mediamatters.org/blog/2014/10/17/professors-slam-george-will-campus-appearance-a/201212.

[29] Valerie Strauss, "Scripps College Uninvites George Will Because of Column on Sexual Assault," *Washington Post*, October 8, 2014.

[30] "Senators Blast George Will for Offensive Column on Sexual Assault," June 12, 2014; feinstein.senate.gov/public/index.cfm/press-releases?ID=7986216d-0993-4703-906c-2d275b41cd99.

[31] Joe Strupp, "The Chicago Tribune Turned Down George Will's 'Misguided and Insensitive' Rape Column," *Media Matters*, June 20, 2014.

[32] Derek Draplin, "George Will Explains How He Takes Campus Rape More Seriously Than Scripps College," *College Fix*, October 11, 2014; thecollegefix.com/post/19685.

[33] Halley, "Trading the Megaphone for the Gavel in Title IX Enforcement."

[34] "Rethink Harvard's Sexual Harassment Policy," *Boston Globe*, October 15, 2014; bostonglobe.com/opinion/2014/10/14/rethink-harvard-sexual-harassment-policy/HFDDiZN7nU2UwuUuWMnqbM/story.html.

[35] Marcella Bombardieri, "Tufts Accepts Finding It Violated Law in Sex Assaults," *Boston Globe*, May 9, 2014; bostonglobe.com/metro/2014/05/09/reversal-tufts

-accepts-finding-that-violated-title-sexual-assault-cases/AljGY7mlMlgZRXm
PIgsIxI/story.html.

36 Laura Kipnis, "Sexual Paranoia Strikes Academe," *Chronicle of Higher Education,* February 27, 2015.

37 Olivia Exstrum, "Students Carry Mattresses, Pillows to Protest Professor's Controversial Article," *Daily Northwestern,* March 10, 2015.

38 Laura Kipnis, "My Title IX Inquisition," *Chronicle of Higher Education,* May 29, 2015.

39 Ibid.

40 Ibid.

CHAPTER 13. TIME FOR A BAILOUT?

1 William Bennett, "Our Greedy Colleges," *New York Times,* February 18, 1987.

2 Paul Campos, "The Real Reason College Tuition Costs So Much," *New York Times,* April 4, 2015.

3 Robert E. Martin and R. Carter Hill, "Baumol and Bowen Cost Effects in Research Universities"; papers.ssrn.com/sol3/papers.cfm?abstract_id=2153122.

4 Jason Delisle, "The Hidden Student-Debt Bomb," *Wall Street Journal,* December 30, 2014.

5 Ibid.

6 Anna Bahr, "Obama's Move to Help Students Is Not as Forgiving as It Seems," *New York Times,* June 23, 2014.

7 Thomas Lindsay, "Forgive Us Our (Student Loan) Debts?" *Forbes,* December 13, 2014.

8 Ibid.

9 Michael Grunwald, "The College Loan Bombshell Hidden in the Budget," *Politico Magazine,* February 5, 2015; politico.com/magazine/story/2015/02/the-college-loan-bombshell-hidden-in-the-budget-114930.html#ixzz3aQf2w2SV.

10 Ibid.

11 Tom Lindsay, "Forgive Us Our (Student Loan) Debt," op. cit.

CHAPTER 14. NETFLIX U.

1 Nathan Harden, "The End of the University as We Know It," *American Interest* 8, no. 3 (December 11, 2012).

2 Kevin Carey, "Here's What Will Truly Change Higher Education—Online Degrees That Are Seen as Official," *New York Times,* March 5, 2015.

3 coursera.org.

4 edx.org.

5 Quoted in linkedin.com/pulse/what-moocs-good-giancarlo-colombo.

6 Daphne Koller, "What We're Learning from Online Education," Ted Talk, August 2012; ted.com/talks/daphne_koller_what_we_re_learning_from_online_education/transcript?language=en.

7 Ibid.

8 Ibid.

9 Harden, "The End of the University as We Know It."

[10] Kevin Carey, "Into the Future with MOOC's," *Chronicle of Higher Education,* September 3, 2012; chronicle.com/article/Into-the-Future-With-MOOCs/134080.

[11] Carey, "Here's What Will Truly Change Higher Education."

[12] Daniel K. Lautzenheiser, "Getting More Bang for Our College Bucks," American Enterprise Institute, September 9, 2013; aei.org/publication/getting-more-bang-for-our-college-bucks.

[13] Carl Straumsheim, "One Down, Many to Go," *Inside Higher Ed,* June 6, 2014; insidehighered.com/news/2014/06/06/one-semester-students-satisfied-unfinished-georgia-tech-online-degree-program.

[14] Tamar Lewin, "Promising Full College Credit, Arizona State University Offers Online Freshman Program," *New York Times,* April 22, 2015.

[15] John A. Byrne, "Arizona State, edX to Offer Entire Freshman Year of College Online," *Fortune,* April 22, 2015; fortune.com/2015/04/22/arizona-state-edx-moocs-online-education.

[16] Jeffrey R. Young, "MIT Master's Program to Use MOOCs as 'Admissions Test,'" *Chronicle of Higher Education,* October 7, 2015.

[17] Steve Kolowich, "The MOOC 'Revolution' May Not Be as Disruptive as Some Had Imagined," *Chronicle of Higher Education,* August 8, 2013.

[18] Steve Kolowich, "Why Professors at San Jose State Won't Use a Harvard Professor's MOOC," *Chronicle of Higher Education,* May 2, 2013; m.chronicle.com/article/Why-Professors-at-San-Jose/138941#sthash.dqtog6FI.dpuf.

[19] Steve Kolowich, "Why Some Colleges Are Saying No to MOOC Deals, at Least for Now," *Chronicle of Higher Education,* April 29, 2013.

[20] Tamar Lewin, "After Setbacks, Online Courses Are Rethought," *New York Times,* December 10, 2013.

[21] "Study on MOOCs Provides New Insights on an Evolving Space," *MIT News,* April 1, 2015; newsoffice.mit.edu/2015/mit-harvard-study-moocs-0401.

[22] Koller, "What We're Learning from Online Education."

[23] Geoffrey A. Fowler, "An Early Report Card on Massive Open Online Courses," *Wall Street Journal,* October 8, 2013.

[24] Harden, "The End of the University as We Know It."

CHAPTER 15. SMALLER, FEWER, LESS

[1] Helen Walters, ""We Need to Change Everything on Campus," Ideas.Ted.com, January 27, 2014; ideas.ted.com/we-need-to-change-everything-on-campus-anant-agarwal-of-edx-on-moocs-mit-and-new-models-of-higher-education.

[2] Charles J. Sykes, *ProfScam: Professors and the Demise of Higher Education* (Washington, DC: Regnery Gateway, 1988), 11.

[3] "Report of the Committee on Freedom of Expression," University of Chicago, January 2015. provost.uchicago.edu/FOECommitteeReport.pdf.

INDEX

Abbate, Cheryl, 178–79, 181–82
academic journals
    article citation of, 62
    Bohannon on bogus articles for, 125–26
    doctoral dissertation titles in, 60–61
    motivation to read, 61–62
    number of articles in, 61
    readership of, 62
    Social Text, hoax on, 121–24
academic research, 25, 32, 44–45, 58–59, 63–64
The Academic Revolution (Jencks and Riesman), 43
Academically Adrift (Arum and Roksa), 17, 51, 69–70,
    72
ACT. *See* American College Testing
ACTA. *See* American Council of Trustees and Alumni
Ad Hoc Committee on Athletics, UNC, 145
AFAM. *See* Department of African and American
    Studies
Agarwal, Anant, 231, 236, 246
Aguayo, Daniel, 120
Ali, Russlynn, 200
American Association of Collegiate Registrars and
    Admissions Officers, 18
American Association of University Professors, 49,
    158, 181
American College Testing (ACT), 83, 137, 231
American Council of Trustees and Alumni (ACTA),
    56, 72, 75, 115–16
    on endowments and tuition, 96–97
    required courses survey of, 69
    on underused programs, 102–3
    on university president salaries, 101
American Council on Education, 235
American Enterprise Institute, 86
American Institutes for Research, 66
    on administrative bloat, 98–99
American University, 101
Amherst College, Snowflake Rebellion at, 188
Anderson, Kent, 124
Antioch College, new policy on sexual assault,
    189–91
Antkare, Ike (fictitious character), 119–20
Arizona State University (ASU), 100
    MOOCs offer of credit from, 236, 247–48
Arnold, Mathew, 65
Arum, Richard, 17, 51, 69–70, 72–74
    on failure of colleges to teach, 88
Association of American Colleges and Universities,
    employer survey by, 70
ASU. *See* Arizona State University
Atlantic Magazine, 6
"Attention Decay in Science" study, 63
Auburn University, 24, 115, 145–46

BA. *See* bachelor degrees
Babcock, Philip, 72–73
bachelor degrees (BA)
    author on value of, 23
    five-year and six-year, 52
    Murray on, 14–15

Bailey, Martha J., 87
Bain & Company, 101, 112
    on college and university financial issues, 30–31
Banzhaf, John, on affirmative consent, 192
Bard College, cost of four-year education at, 10
Bauerlein, Mark, 46
    on research and publishing in humanities,
        63–64
Beall, Jeffrey, 126
    on predatory publishers, 124–25
Beginning Post-Secondary Students Survey, 88
Bennett, William, 220–21, 225
    on financial aid increases, 218–19
Bentham Science Publishing, 124
Berkman, David, on "rampant pandering," 78–79
Bernstein, David, on affirmative consent, 193
Bettison-Varga, Lori, 206
Beyond College for All (Rosenbaum), 84
Birgeneau, Robert J., 157
Blank, Rebecca, on bidding for professors and
    course loads, 42, 47
Blecher, Marc, on trigger warnings, 166
Bloom, Allan, 29
Bloomberg, 5, 98
Bohannon, John, on bogus articles for academic
    journals, 125–26
Bok, Derek, 29, 30
    on graduates, 68–69
    on student achievement, 70–71
    on teaching load, 47
Boston College, cost of four-year education at, 10
Bowen, Howard, 108, 220, 246
Bowen, William G., 157
Boyer, Ernest, 30
Bryn Mawr University, 45–46

California State University System, 99
Campos, Paul F., on financial aid increase, 219–20
Campus Sexual Assault Study, 201
Carey, Kevin, 16, 235, 239
Carle, Robert, on affirmative consent, 192
Cellini, Stephanie Riegg, 82
Center for College Affordability and Productivity
    study, 55–56
Charlottesville Police Department, report on UVA
    gang rape, 197–98
Christakis, Erika, 184–86
Christakis, Nicholas, 185–86
Chronicle of Higher Education, 101, 202, 210, 235, 237
Click, Melissa, 187
The Closing of the American Mind (Bloom), 29
Coleridge, Samuel Taylor, 107
college graduates, 68–69
    low wage and retail jobs of, 11
colleges, 71, 83–84, 88, 97, 244–45. See also
    universities
    amenities and administration spending in, 8
    Bain & Company on financial issues of, 30–31
    cost of degree in, 7
    cost of four-year education at various, 10
    degrees with no paychecks from, 12
    financial aid increases to, 218–21
    MOOCs critique by, 238

Moody's Investors Service on financial outlook
    of, 5
Snowflake Rebellion in, 8–9, 155
Collegiate Learning Assessment Plus test, 17, 66
Colombo, Jesse, 16
Columbia University, 77, 163, 167–68, 204
Committee on Freedom of Expression, on free
    speech, 158
community college
    Obama's proposal for, 88–89
    remedial classes in, 88
"contingent faculty"
    exploitation of, 50
    in higher education, 48–49
CoRec. See Frances A. Córdova Recreational Sports
    Center, Purdue
Corinthian Colleges, 18
Council for Aid to Education, 17
Coursera, 231–32, 235, 239–40
critical thinking, 4, 23, 70, 221, 248
Cross, Ray, 39
Crowder, Deborah, 139–44, 146–48
    fake classes of, 130–31
    network of enablers for, 134
    Nyang'oro ceded decision-making to, 137–38
Cuban, Mark, on education bubble, 15

Daniels, Mitch, on free speech, 158
Dartmouth College
    cost of four-year education at, 10
    "honest transcript" movement at, 77
Davis, Philip, 124
DeBoer, Freddie, CoRec at Purdue description by,
    105–6
Delisle, Jason, 13, 221–22
Delta Cost Project
    Academic Spending Versus Athletic Spending: Who
        Wins? by, 115–16
    Trends in College Spending: 2001–2011 by, 97
DeMuth, Christopher, 206
Denhart, Christopher, 11
Department of African and American Studies
    (AFAM), at UNC, 130, 137, 139, 145–46, 148
    Swahili 3 course in, 142–43
Department of Education, U. S., 98, 200
Derrida, Jacques, 121–22
Doe, John, 202–3
Dorfman, Jeffrey, on Pay as You Earn initiative,
    222–23
Dreifus, Claudia, 42–43, 47–48, 113
    on academic bloating, 100
Duke University, 231
    cheating scandal at, 132
    cost of four-year education at, 10
    grade inflation at, 76–77
Duncan, Greg J., 87
Dynarski, Susan M., 87

education bubble, 14, 112
    Colombo on, 16
    Cuban on, 15
    Thiel on, 15–16
Educational Testing Service (ETS), 66–67

edX, 231, 236, 239, 246
Erdely, Sabrina Rubin, 195, 197, 199
Etchemendy, John, 132
ETS. *See* Educational Testing Service

FAC. *See* Faculty Athletics Committee, UNC
faculty, 48–50, 58, 142–44
    independent journalism group analysis of
        teaching loads of, 40–41
    pressure to publish on, 60–64
    published and tenured, 24, 26
    research culture of, 25
    teaching loads of, 38–40
Faculty Athletics Committee, UNC (FAC), 145–46, 149
Fair, Jo Ellen, on teaching loads, 39–40
Fairweather, James, 46
FBS. *See* Football Bowl Subdivision
Federal Education Budget Project at New America
    Foundation, 13
Federal Reserve Bank of New York study, 11–12
    on financial aid increases, 219
Finn, Chester E., Jr., 57
FIRE. *See* Foundation for Individual Rights in
    Education
Fitzgerald, Susan, 5
Folt, Carol, 133
Football Bowl Subdivision (FBS), 113, 116
Forbes, 16
Fordham Institute, on remedial courses, 83, 89
Foundation for Individual Rights in Education
    (FIRE), 182–84
    on affirmative consent, 192–93
Frances A. Córdova Recreational Sports Center,
    Purdue (CoRec), 105–6
"free college for all," 81, 89
    ACT regarding, 83
    con job of, 84–86
    consequence of, 90
    problem with, 82–83
    unprepared students in, 83–84
"free money," 19–20
free speech, 155–56, 158, 166, 185–86, 188
Friedersdorf, Conor, 182

Gallup-Purdue Index, 11
Garshfield, Jason, 169
Gee, E. Gordon, 95–96, 107
Generation Debt, 10, 244
George Washington University, 16, 28, 192
Giovanni, Nikki, 141
Gitlin, Todd, 161, 165–66, 168
Goldin, Claudia, 82
Gordon, Aaron, 62
Green, Adam, 81

Hacker, Andrew, 42–43, 47–48, 113
    on academic bloating, 100
Hackett, Edward, on federal grants and research, 44
Halley, Janet, 194–95, 207–9
Hamermesh, Daniel S., 46
Harden, Nathan
    on MOOCs, 31–32, 228, 234, 239, 241
    on student empowerment, 32

Harris, Samantha, 184
Harvard University, 47, 59, 68, 138
    backlash on new sexual assault policies at, 207–9
    cheating scandal at, 132–33
    grade inflation at, 74
Hedtke, Josh, 175
HERI. *See* Higher Education Research Institute
high school counseling
    con job of, 84–85
    inflated and unrealistic expectations in, 85–86
high school students, unprepared for college work,
    83–84
higher education
    administrative bloating in, 96–101
    aims of, 65
    athletic edifice complex spending and subsidies
        in, 112–16
    Bowen thesis in spending of, 108
    college for fewer as alternative to, 244–45
    "contingent faculty" in, 48–49
    cost and value crisis in, 18–19
    debt levels in, 111–12
    downsize degree programs in, 245–46
    "ever bigger, ever more" model of, 10–11
    foreign TAs in, 26–28, 53
    fragility assumption in, 163–67
    grade inflation in, 74–77
    "honest transcript" movement in, 77
    instructional staff employment numbers in, 49–50
    intolerance in, 156–59
    law of less in, 243–44
    law of more in, 95, 112, 226, 243–44, 247
    lowering academic standards in, 17–18
    massive open online courses in, 31–32
    multiversity bloat in, 101–3
    Nassirian on crisis point in, 18
    paradox of, 23–24
    professoriate workweek in, 26
    ProfScam as indictment of, 21–22
    "profspeak" in, 25, 59
    reality of, complex, 19
    reality of students in, 20
    reform needs of, 250–51
    research examples in, 58–59
    restoring liberal arts in, 248
    reward system in, 43, 45
    skilled trade choice instead of, 90
    spread and growth of mass classes in, 53–54
    subjects taught in, 71–72
    Taj Mahal-ing of, 105–7, 109–11
    teaching versus research in, 44–45
    tenure abolition in, 249–50
    victimization culture in, 160–61
*Higher Education? How Colleges Are Wasting Our
    Money and Failing Our Kids—and What We Can
    Do About It* (Hacker and Dreifus), job interview
    story in, 42–43
Higher Education Research Institute (HERI)
    on abdication of teaching to TAs, 48
    on time spent teaching, 48
Hill, R. Carter, 108–9, 220–21
*The Hollow Men: Politics and Corruption in Higher
    Education* (Sykes), 29

"honest transcript" movement, 77
housing bubble, 7, 10, 13, 14, 16
humanities, 63–64, 240–41
    proficiency studies in, 66–68

The Idea of a University (Newman), 37
IEEE. *See* Institute of Electrical and Electronic
    Engineers
Indiana University, 62, 72
    "honest transcript" movement at, 77
Institute of Electrical and Electronic Engineers
    (IEEE), 127

Jacoby, Russell, 59
Jay, A. Joseph, III, 131
Jencks, Christopher, 43
John William Pope Center for Higher Education
    Policy study, 54–55
Journal of Higher Education, 46
junk courses, 4
    "Deadhead 101," 24–25
    Pocket Billiards or The Anthropology of Play, 24
    Recreation Interpretive Services, 24

Kalleberg, Arne, 149
Kelly, Andrew P.
    on lack of curriculum structure, 87–88
    on low-income students, 86–87
Kent State University, 72
Kenyon College, 100
Kerr, Clark, 43
    multiversity definition of, 101–2
    on undergraduate education, 44
Kezar, Adrianna, 50
Kim, Stephanie, 177
Kimball, Roger, 8
Kipnis, Laura, Title IX policies criticized by, 209–13
"knowledge factories," 43
Koller, Daphne, 231–33, 239–41
Kolowich, Steve, 237
Krohn, Maxwell, 120
Kukowski, Colleen Depman, 131

Labbé, Cyril, SCIgen computer program use of,
    120, 127
Lautzenheiser, Daniel K., on MOOCs partnerships,
    235–36
law of more, 95, 111–12, 226, 243–44, 247
Levy, David C., on teacher workload, 50–51
Lincoln, Abraham, 38
Lindsay, Tom, 223–24
Lovell, Mike, 182

Mac Donald, Heather, 100, 175–77
Maguire, Daniel, 181
Mansfield, Harvey, 74
Marks, Mindy, 72–73
Marquette University, 28
    limits of acceptable discourse conversation at,
        178–80
    McAdams blog controversy at, 180–84
Marshall, David, 169
Martin, James, 147

Martin, Lawrence B., on faculty production and
    publication, 58
Martin, Robert E., 108–9, 220–21
Massachusetts Institute of Technology (MIT), 120,
    227, 231, 237
massive open online courses (MOOCs), 227
    actual mastery in, 230, 233–34
    admissions structure difference with, 247–48
    ASU offer of credit for, 236, 247–48
    colleges and universities critique of, 238
    completion rate in, 239–40
    counterreformation in, 241–42
    course description of, 232–33
    economic impact of, 238–39
    evaluation of teaching and learning in, 233
    future threat example of, 230
    Harden on, 31–32, 228, 234, 239, 241
    humanities in, 240–41
    institutional resistance to, 237–38
    mass lectures versus, 229
    number of courses in, 231
    peer grading in, 241
    power shift from institution to student in, 231–32
    as rigorous and demanding, 240
    stigma of, 234–35
Massy, William F., 47
McAdams, John, 180–84
McCants, Rashad, 135, 140
McCants, Rashanda, 135
McNeely, Kathleen, 113
McPherson, Mary Patterson, 46
Mead, Walter Russell, 166
Michaels, Walter Benn, 50
microaggressions, 9, 33, 154, 170–73, 205, 248
    "Day of Action Statement" regarding, 176
    targeting grammar in, 174–78
MIT. *See* Massachusetts Institute of Technology
Modern Language Association, 63
Moeser, James, 145
MOOCs. *See* massive open online courses
Moody's Investors Service, 111–12
    on financial outlook of colleges, 5
    on student debt, 12–13
    on student loans, 13–14
Murray, Charles, 83, 245
    on bachelor degrees, 14–15
    on certification tests, 90–91
    on consequence of "college for all" movement, 90
*My Freshman Year: What a Professor Learned by
    Becoming a Student* (Nathan), 73

Nassirian, Barmak, on higher education crisis
    point, 18
Nathan, Rebekah, 73
National Assessment of Adult Literacy, 66
National Collegiate Athletic Association (NCAA),
    113–16, 135–36, 145
National Commission on Excellence in Education, 66
    millennials proficiency in literacy and
        mathematics study of, 67–68
National Crime Victimization Survey, 202
National Endowment for the Humanities survey, 69
National Survey of Student Engagement, 52

Nature, 124–25, 127
NCAA. *See* National Collegiate Athletic Association
New England Center for Investigative Reporting,
    on administrative bloat, 98–99
New School University, 51
New York Times, 18, 26, 28, 87, 109, 111–12, 121
    on Harvard cheating scandal, 132–33
New York University (NYU), 109
Newman, John Henry, 37, 156
Ng, Andrew, 231, 235, 239, 241
"nonaggression pact," 78
Northwestern University, 45
    Kipnis criticizing Title IX at, 209–13
Norvig, Peter, 230–31
Nyang'oro, Julius, 131, 137–39, 144, 146, 148
NYU. *See* New York University

Obama, Barack, 82, 88–89, 158, 199, 201, 225
    Pay as You Earn initiative of, 222–23
Oberlin College, 44, 162, 166–67
Ohio State University, 95–96, 107, 111
The Open Information Science Journal, 124
Our Underachieving Colleges (Bok), 29
Ovid and other titles, in crusade on triggering
    classics, 167–70

Parker, Kathleen, 163
Pell Grants, 83, 89, 219, 220, 222
Pethokoukis, James, 82
Platt, Matthew B., 133
Poliakoff, Michael, 56
Pollitt, Katha, 123–24
Posner, Eric, on bubble-wrapping students, 165
Prager, Dennis, 207
Problem Solving in Technology Rich Environments
    (PS-TRE), 67
ProfScam (Sykes), 26, 48, 61, 74, 78, 138, 217
    on academic science, 53
    on administrative bloat, 98
    "Five Ways of Teaching Badly" in, 52–53
    as indictment of higher education, 21–22
    on Lincoln story at UW, 37–38
    on multiversity, 102
    research examples from, 58–59
    on status of teaching in, 45–46
    Trachtenberg on, 28–30
    on university curriculum, 71
"profspeak," 25, 59
Progressive Change Campaign Committee, 81
PS-TRE. *See* Problem Solving in Technology Rich
    Environments
Public Service Loan Forgiveness program,
    government jobs privileging in, 223–24
Pullias Center for Higher Education, University of
    Southern California, 50
Purdue University
    CoRec at, 105–6
    number of administrative employees at, 98

Real Education (Murray), 90
Rensselaer Polytechnic Institute, 44
Riesman, David, 43
Riley, Naomi, 54

Rojstaczer, Stuart, on reasons for grade inflation,
    76–77
Roksa, Josipa, 17, 51, 69–70, 72–74
    on failure of colleges to teach, 88
Rolling Stone, 195–99
Rosenbaum, James, 84–86
Roth, Michael S., 156
Rubenfeld, Jed, on affirmative consent, 193
Rust, Val, as target of racial microaggression, 174–78

safe places, 8, 154–55, 162–63, 213, 218
Salovey, Peter, 186–87
Schmeidel, Stacey, 188
sexual assault, 33
    affirmative consent in, 191–93
    Antioch College new policy on, 189
    backlash on new, policies at Harvard, 207–9
    "Dear Colleague" letter for, 200–204
    farce becomes reality in, 194–95
    Kipnis criticizing Title IX on, 209–13
    Saturday Night Live skit on, 189–91
    UVA gang rape incident of, 195–99
    will backlash on critique of new policies in, 205–7
Shakespeare, William, 4, 66, 69
Shelley, Percy Bysshe, 105, 107
Shibley, Robert, 183, 204
Shulevitz, Judith, 161–62, 164
Smith College, 187–88
Snowflake Rebellion, 8–9, 155–56, 184–88
Sokal, Alan, *Social Text* journal hoax of, 121–24
Sommers, Christina Hoff, 162
Southern Methodist University, cost of four-year
    education at, 10
speech codes, 153, 163, 183, 218, 248
Sperber, Murray, 78
Stanford University
    cheating scandal at, 132
    inspired MOOCs, 227, 230–31
State of Wisconsin auditors, on teaching loads, 38
State University of New York, Stony Brook, 58
Stein, Herbert, 112
Sterrett, Drew, 203–4
Stribling, Jeremy, SCIgen computer program of,
    120–21, 127
student athletes, 138
    fake class enrollment of, 139
    SAT and ACT test scores of, 136–37
    tutors writing papers for, 140–41
student loans, 223–26
    align, to potential paybacks, 247
    delinquency and default rate on, 10, 13, 221
    Delisle on, 13, 221–22
    Moody's Investors Service on, 13–14
students, 4, 43–44, 83–84, 165, 231–32
    Arum and Roksa on learning of, 17, 69–70
    average wage of graduates, 11
    college-level work skills of, 71
    commencement speakers protest by, 156–57
    debt burden of, 7, 10–13
    gaps between high-and low-income, 86–87
    Harden on empowerment of, 32
    higher education reality of, 20
    mortgage debt compared to debt of, 10

students (*continued*)
    studying time spent by, 72–73
    writing decline of, 73–74
Suárez-Orozco, Marcelo, 177
Sullivan, Teresa, 196–97
Sweet Briar College, Virginia, 15
    amenities at, 5–6
Sykes, Charles J., 21–22, 26, 28–30, 37–38

TAs. *See* teaching assistants
teaching, 44–46, 48, 52–53, 88, 233
    flight of professoriate from, 38
    workloads in, 38–41, 42, 47, 50–51
teaching assistants (TAs), 4
    abdication of teaching to, 48–49
    foreign, in higher education, 26–28, 53
"The Teaching Penalty in Higher Education:
    Evidence from a Public Research University"
    study, 46
Texas A & M, 109
Thiel, Peter, on education bubble, 15–16
Thrun, Sebastian, 230–31
Title IX, 162, 164, 207–13
Title VII, 164
Trachtenberg, Stephen Joel
    on *The Hollow Men: Politics and Corruption in
    Higher Education*, 29
    on *ProfScam*, 28–30
trigger warnings, 33, 154, 160–62, 166–70, 205,
    212, 218

Udacity, 231
universities, 3, 71, 77, 101
    Bain & Company on financial issues of, 30–31
    cost of four-year education at, 10
    flight of professoriate from teaching at, 38
    as intellectually intolerant, 218
    MOOCs critique by, 238
    student rebellion of 1960s in, 43–44
University of California, 43, 48, 100
    microaggression training at, 171–73
University of California, Berkley, 110, 227
University of Cincinnati, 110, 114
University of Colorado, Boulder, 72, 110
    study of grades at, 75
University of Connecticut, number of
    administrators at, 99–100
University of Georgia, 64
University of Illinois, Chicago, 50
    BA classes at, 24
University of Massachusetts, 72
    John Doe incident at, 202–3
University of Michigan, 87, 96, 110, 231
    Sterrett incident at, 203–4
University of Minnesota, 100
    as multiversity, 102–3
University of Missouri, Snowflake Rebellion at,
    9, 187
University of Nebraska, 103
    fudging of numbers at, 54
University of North Carolina, Chapel Hill, 76
    academic advisors and faculty knowledge of fake
    classes at, 142–44

    fake class scandal at, 129–31, 133–34, 137–49
    fudging numbers at, 55
    "honest transcript" movement at, 77
    McCants lawsuit against, 135–36
    study of athletes at, 136
University of North Carolina, Greensboro,
    24, 97
    fudging of numbers at, 54–55
University of Oklahoma, 110
University of Oregon, 110
University of Southern California, 50, 111
University of Texas, 52
    Center for College Affordability and Productivity
    study of, 55–56
    mass classes at, 53–54
University of Vermont, 64, 103
University of Virginia (UVA), 96–97
    gang rape incident at, 195–99
University of Washington, 110
University of Wisconsin, Madison (UW), 27, 37, 52,
    75, 153
    flight of professoriate from teaching at, 38
    independent journalism group analysis of
    teaching loads at, 40–41
    media analysis of course loads at, 41
University of Wisconsin, Milwaukee, 28
The Uses of the University (Kerr), 102
UVA. *See* University of Virginia
UW. *See* University of Wisconsin, Madison

Vassar College, 72
Vedder, Richard, 11
    on " free" community college, 89
Volokh, Eugene, 173

Wainstein, Kenneth L., UNC investigative report
    by, 131, 137–44, 146–47
Walker, Scott, 39
Wall Street Journal, 13, 26, 42
Washington Post, 26, 51, 197, 205–6
Washington University, 72
Watson, Kenjus, 176
Wesleyan University, 231
    cost of four-year education at, 10
    safe places at, 154–55
    Snowflake Rebellion at, 155–56
"Where A Is Ordinary: The Evolution of American
    College and University Grading, 1940–2009"
    study, 75
Will, George, critique of new sexual assault
    policies, 205–7
Williams College, 48, 100
Willingham, Mary, 136
Winston, Gordon, on undergraduate teaching, 46–47
Wolfe, Tom, 4, 187, 194
Wythe, Philip, on trigger warnings, 160–61

Yale University, 9, 138, 193
    Snowflake Rebellion at, 184–87
Yoffe, Emily, 194, 200–204

Zemsky, Robert, 47
Zimmerman, Michael, 44